PHILOSOPHY AND HISTORY OF BUDDHISM SERIES

Volume one

Rimé
Buddhism without prejudice

Rimé
Buddhism Without Prejudice

THE NINETEENTH CENTURY NON-SECTARIAN
MOVEMENT AND ITS TIBETAN CONTEXT

Peter Oldmeadow

EU RP (for authorities only)
eucomply OÜ
Pärnu mnt 139b-14
11317 Tallinn, Estonia
hello@eucompliancepartner.com +3375690241

Shogam Publications
Carlton North, Victoria, 3054
www.shogam.org

Copyright © Peter Oldmeadow
First Edition 2012

All rights reserved. No part of this book may be reproduced without prior written permission from the publisher.

National Library of Australia Cataloguing-in-Publication data:

Oldmeadow, Peter.
Rimé: Buddhism without prejudice / Peter Oldmeadow
ISBN 9780980502220 (pbk.)
Includes index.
Buddhism—Doctrines.
Buddhist philosophy.
Buddhism —Tibet —Doctrines.
294.3372

Cover design by Mila Nikko © IDEE
Cover photograph by Traleg Kyabgon Rinpoche

To my parents
Russell and Diana Oldmeadow

Contents

Preface	xi
Note on names and transliteration	*xi*
Acknowledgements	*xii*
Introduction	1
Section 1: The Schools and their Relations	7
The period in which the Schools arose	*7*
The Schools and politics in Tibet	*10*
Monastic organisation	*12*
Monasticism and intellectual study	*13*
Schools and lineages	*18*
Loss of lineages	*20*
Section 2: Some Antecedents of the Rimé Movement	23
The Buddha and the idea of skilful means	*23*
The Third Karmapa, Rangjung Dorje (1284–1339)	*29*
Mahāmudrā and Dzogchen	*34*
Karma Chagme (1613–1678)	*38*
Jigme Lingpa (1729–1798) and the heritage of Longchenpa (1308–1364)	*40*
Shabkar Tsogdruk Rangdröl (1781–1851)	*43*
Fourth Panchen Lama, Lobsang Chökyi Gyaltsen (1570–1662) and Khöntönpa (1561–1637)	*44*

Section 3: East Tibet and the Rimé Movement	47
East Tibetan Context	47
Upheaval in nineteenth century Kham	52
Bon in East Tibet	54
Termas (gter ma) and tertöns (gter ston)	57
Jamgön Kongtrul Lodrö Thaye (1813–1899)	60
The life of Jamgön Kongtrul	60
The Five Treasuries of Jamgön Kongtrul	64
Jamgön Kongtrul and shentong	66
Jamgön Kongtrul and Chokgyur Lingpa	70
The three-year retreat and the eight practice lineages	71
Jamyang Khyentse Wangpo (1820–1892)	77
Jamyang Khyentse's inspiration of Rimé	77
Background and early life of Jamyang Khyentse	78
Jamyang Khyentse and the Longchen Nyingthig	80
Jamyang Khyentse and the terma tradition	81
Chokgyur Dechen Lingpa (1829–1870)	84
Chokgyur Lingpa, the Great Treasure Revealer	84
Life and principal termas of Chokgyur Lingpa	84
Chokgyur Lingpa and Rimé	89
Dza Patrul Rinpoche, Orgyen Jikme Chökyi Wangpo (1808–1887)	90
Mipham Rinpoche, Jamgön Mipham Gyatso (1846–1912)	94
Mipham the philosopher	94
Life of Mipham	95
Mipham's philosophical position	97
Mipham, Kongtrul and logic—a short anecdote	98
Mipham's other interests	99
Section 4: The Heritage of the Rimé Movement	100
Khenpo Shenga, Shenpen Chökyi Nangwa (1871–1927)	100
Jamyang Khyentse Chökyi Lodrö (1893–1959)	102
Dilgo Khyentse Tashi Peljor, Rabsel Dawa (1910–1991)	104
Tulku Urgyen Rinpoche (1920–1996)	107

Kalu Rinpoche, Karma Drubgyu Tenzin,
    Rangjung Kunkhyab (1905–1989)   *109*
Dezhung Rinpoche, Kunga Tenpay Nyima (1906–1987)   *112*
Tenzin Gyatso, His Holiness the Fourteenth
    Dalai Lama (b. 1935)   *118*

Conclusion   126
Notes   131
Recommended Reading   159
Bibliography   160
Table of Tibetan Names   170
Index   177

Preface

THIS BOOK HAS ITS origins in two series of talks on the nineteenth century Rimé (non-sectarian) movement in Tibet given in 2009–2010 at Yeshe Nyima in Sydney and at the Buddhist Summer School held at the Maitripa Centre at Healesville, not far from Melbourne in Victoria, Australia. Both series of talks were at the invitation of Traleg Kyabgon Rinpoche and were held under the auspices of Kagyu E-Vam Buddhist Institute and Yeshe Nyima, of which Traleg Rinpoche is the director.

The book covers the same material as the talks and, like the talks, is divided into four sections. I have tried to retain some of the flavour of the talks. However, as well as making corrections and clarifying points that were not adequately explained in the talks, I have added some new material and have provided an academic apparatus including endnotes and bibliography for those who would like to delve more deeply into the topics covered in the book.

Note on Names and Transliteration

Tibetan names have been given in phonetic transcription in a form commonly used in English publications and in the media. Thus, for example, I use Jamyang Khyentse Rinpoche in place of the more academic Wylie transliteration (Jam dbyangs mkhyen brtse'i rin po che). Full Wylie transliteration is given at the back of the book for the names of all the important Tibetan figures discussed. When Tibetan words are included in italics within parentheses in the body of the text I have followed the Wylie system of transliteration, for example, 'treasure revealer' or *tertön* (*gter ston*). I have included the romanised Sanskrit in parentheses for terms that have become part of the accepted technical vocabulary of serious study of Buddhism in the West. These include words like 'emptiness' (*śūnyatā*), 'birth-and-death' (*saṃsāra*) and 'Buddha-nature' (*tathāgatagarbha*).

Where a term or name is primarily known in its Tibetan form, I have used that. Thus, for example, I have used Dzogchen (*rdzogs chen*) rather than the Sanskrit Mahāsandhi, and *rigpa* (*rig pa*) ('pure awareness') rather than the Sanskrit *vidyā*. Where I have used both Sanskrit and Tibetan together, I have used an S. and T. to differentiate them. Thus, for example, 'calm state' (S. *śamatha*, T. *zhi gnas*).

Acknowledgements

Firstly, and most particularly, I would like to thank Traleg Kyabgon Rinpoche for inviting me to participate over many years in the Buddhist Summer Schools and at the Kagyu E-Vam Institute and Yeshe Nyima in Melbourne and Sydney, by presenting talks and seminars which draw on my academic training in a way that may be useful to Buddhist practitioners and to those interested in Buddhism. I must also thank Rinpoche for inviting me to prepare the talks which are the basis for this book for publication through Shogam Publications. I have long believed that the inclusive, non-partisan approach adopted by Rinpoche in the Buddhist Summer Schools and in the seminars he organises, is a contemporary expression of the Rimé spirit. Furthermore, as is appropriate to our contemporary circumstances, Rinpoche embraces the Dharma in its multiple Tibetan and tantric forms and also in its various expressions in the Zen and Theravada traditions. Rinpoche also encourages a fruitful dialogue between Buddhism and other traditions and disciplines in our society.

The process of preparing this book for publication has been greatly facilitated by the excellent work of the transcribers, whom I warmly thank. I am grateful also to Richard Stanley for useful suggestions and for making corrections on draft material. Most importantly, the help and advice offered by my wife, Wendy Oldmeadow, has been invaluable. She has acted as editor, proofreader, constructive critic and helper in myriad ways, and to her I give my heartfelt thanks. Of course, responsibility for any remaining errors or omissions in this book is entirely my own.

It is my sincere hope that this book will be of benefit to Dharma practitioners and to those with an interest in Buddhist religion and culture.

Peter Oldmeadow
November 2011

Introduction

THE TERM 'rimé' (*ris med*) is an ordinary word in the Tibetan language, meaning 'unbiased'. It was adopted by Jamgön Kongtrul in the nineteenth century to identify a non-sectarian approach to Buddhism in Tibet—The Rimé approach. Literally, *ris* means 'part' or 'side', and *med* means 'without'; thus Rimé means 'impartial' or 'unbiased'. Rimé has sometimes been translated as 'eclectic', but that could imply throwing different things together and mixing them up, which is not correct. Rather, the Rimé approach is to recognise the value of the different traditions and to benefit from them, as opposed to combining or mixing them in a syncretic way.

Non-sectarianism has a long history in Tibetan Buddhism and has also been widely valued in Buddhism generally. Sectarianism also has a long history in Buddhism, and in the Tibetan context it has often been fuelled by rivalry between the schools of Buddhism which had its roots in essentially unrelated issues of political power and patronage. In this book I try to place a particularly focused expression of Tibetan non-sectarianism (which is now generally known as 'the Rimé movement') within the broader context of the relationship between the Tibetan Buddhist schools. I also present these developments in terms of the history of both sectarianism and non-sectarianism in Tibet. This, I hope, will provide a lens through which we might better view Tibetan Buddhism and Tibetan history, and may provide a helpful perspective on the present day configuration of Tibetan Buddhism.

For the principal figures discussed in this book, non-sectarianism is a Buddhist principle not only in the more passive sense of the value of tolerance and acceptance of difference, but also in a more active sense in relation to the discernment of truth or truths found in Buddhist teachings. For these Rimé figures, non-sectarianism flows from the conviction that contradictions and incompatibilities between different presentations of the Buddha's teachings and different approaches to practice are only apparent, and that these difficulties dissolve when the right perspective is adopted. In the Rimé approach, different views and styles of practice, and even different lifestyles, are understood as skilful adaptations to meet the needs of different mentalities, and individuals at different stages of their spiritual development. However, this should not be understood as a kind of relativism. Rather, according to the leading advocates of the Rimé approach, it is only from the highest perspective, the perspective of Buddhahood, that the true intention or true significance of all the Buddha's teachings can be realised.

The nineteenth century Rimé movement reaffirmed the different paths and lineages present in Tibet as valid and effective ways to enlightenment. Centred in Kham in East Tibet, it played an important role in reviving marginalised traditions and saving some that were on the point of extinction. The central figures in the movement opposed the solidification of teaching lineages and schools, as well as political rivalries between them, and encouraged study and practice of all lineages in an unbiased fashion. By encouraging an inclusive approach to Buddhist thought, by gathering and promoting a wide range of practices, and by invigorating and ensuring the health of important Buddhist lineages, the Rimé movement played a major role in shaping present day Tibetan Buddhism. By approaching Buddhism without prejudice, the nineteenth century Rimé movement has profoundly contributed to the survival of Tibetan Buddhism through the difficult circumstances that it has faced in the past sixty years, when its very existence has been at stake.

Some writers have been reluctant to use the expression 'Rimé movement', arguing that what took place in nineteenth century Kham should not be artificially separated from a wider cultural renaissance that took place in East Tibet during the eighteenth and nineteenth centuries.[1] I am aware of the danger of reification and throughout this work I contextualise the movement in the broader Tibetan context and in the particular circumstances in East Tibet. The Rimé movement has no 'essence' and should be understood in terms of the causes and conditions which constitute it. The label 'Rimé movement' is a convenient way to identify a cluster of attitudes, people and events that shifted practice and had an enduring influence. These people influenced each other, shared common ideals and ideas, wrote together and explicitly set out to preserve and promote an inclusive practice of Buddhism. They recognised at the time that what they were doing had antecedents and was of vital importance for the present and for the future. They may not have thought of themselves as a 'movement' but that does not mean this is not a useful label for us to use, since a 'movement' is often only recognised as such retrospectively when its full significance is grasped.

Three figures were at the heart of the movement: Jamyang Khyentse Wangpo (1820–1892), Jamgön Kongtrul Lodrö Thaye (1813–1899) and Chokgyur Dechen Lingpa (1829–1870). Jamyang Khyentse Wangpo was in many ways the inspiration for the movement. He came from a background in both the Sakya and Nyingma traditions, but was in fact the holder of all of the major lineages. The Rimé movement sometimes refers to eight major practice traditions; Jamyang Khyentse was the holder of them all and could teach any of the traditions of Tibet in their own distinctive style and manner. Jamyang Khyentse remained a kind of ultimate authority in the movement; whenever any doubt or question emerged, he was the final arbiter. It was Jamyang Khyentse who inspired Jamgön Kongtrul to let go of his own personal residue of partiality toward a particular tradition.

Jamgön Kongtrul's background was mainly in the Karma Kagyü tradition. He was born into a Bon background and it is through him that the non-Buddhist tradition of Bon comes more directly into the picture within the Rimé movement. He also had strong connections to the Nyingma tradition. Jamgön Kongtrul was the most prolific writer and scholar of this main group of three and was the first to use the term *rimé* systematically for the non-sectarian approach to Buddhism. He wrote largely at the behest of Jamyang Khyentse, filling large volumes covering all aspects of theory and practice. He also compiled a comprehensive collection of treasure teachings, the *terma* (*gter ma*) traditions, for the first time. He was also a sage, a meditator and a teacher, but if we are to identify his role in this particular group, he is certainly the main scholar and writer of the three.

The third figure, Chokgyur Lingpa, was quintessentially a visionary. He was a *tertön* (*gter ston*), a discoverer of concealed treasures (*gter ma*), which are teachings understood to have been concealed in an earlier period either physically or in the mindstream of great teachers. Semi-literate, with very little education, he found his vocation, so to speak, through Jamgön Kongtrul and Jamyang Khyentse. There had been some doubts about his status as a visionary and *tertön* and it was only after he met Jamgön Kongtrul, who sent him off with a letter of introduction to see the Great Lama, Jamyang Khyentse, that he was duly recognised as a *tertön* and his public career as a visionary, we might say, began.[2]

From this point on, Jamyang Khyentse, Jamgön Kongtrul and Chokgyur Lingpa worked very closely together. In fact they were teachers to each other, each regarding the other two as their gurus, operating in a kind of mutual guru/

disciple relationship. They even discovered *termas* together where all three of them were involved in the revelation of particular teachings. They are the three main figures of the Rimé movement, the absolute heart of the movement.

There are others to consider as well, including Patrul Rinpoche (1871–1927), Mipham Rinpoche (1846–1912) and Khenpo Shenga (1871–1927). Patrul Rinpoche was very close to the main group and is perhaps best known to us as the author of *The Words of My Perfect Teacher*, the renowned introduction to the *ngöndro* (*sngon 'gro*), the preliminary practices, of the *Longchen Nyingthig* (*Heart Essence of Great Expanse*) tradition of Dzogchen. Patrul Rinpoche was a very popular teacher—he took the teachings to the ordinary people in East Tibet, particularly popularising Śāntideva's *Bodhicaryāvatāra* (*The Introduction to the Life of a Bodhisattva*), and promulgating the practice and invocation of the Bodhisattva of Compassion, Avalokiteśvara (*spyan ras gzigs* pronounced 'Chenrezig'), through the six syllable mantra *oṃ maṇi padme huṃ*.

Mipham Rinpoche could be described as the principal philosopher of the Rimé movement. Mipham developed a logical and epistemological defence of practice-oriented approaches, with special attention to the philosophy of Dzogchen. He developed a scholastic presentation in the language of Buddhist philosophical discourse, an academic orientation that had been largely absent up until then.

Khenpo Shenga was another philosopher associated with the movement. His approach was to present Buddhism by going back to the principal original Indian texts and providing glosses and commentaries on them while bypassing the disputes that had divided the Buddhist schools in Tibet for hundreds of years.

It is probably fair to say that modern Tibetan Buddhism, particularly outside the Gelug school, is largely a product of the Rimé movement.[3] The legacy of the Rimé movement has been carried by the various Khyentse reincarnations. Perhaps best known to us is Dilgo Khyentse Rinpoche (1910–1991), who carried the heart of the Rimé movement in the second half of the twentieth century. Before Dilgo Khyentse came Jamyang Khyentse Chökyi Lodrö (1893–1959), and it was probably he above all who embodied Rimé in Tibet at this earlier stage. Khyentse Chökyi Lodrö's death in Sikkim in 1959 came at a tragic time which saw the widespread destruction of Buddhism in Tibet and the flight of tens of thousands of people from that country. Almost seamlessly, Dilgo Khyentse took up the mantle of Rimé, holding together much of Tibetan Buddhism in the diaspora in India, Nepal and Bhutan, and then in the West. From the time of the diaspora,

His Holiness the Fourteenth Dalai Lama has been central in maintaining the unity of the Tibetan people. His Holiness consciously and deliberately teaches in the non-sectarian Rimé manner, drawing on the different Tibetan traditions.

In the case of both Khyentse and Kongtrul there have been multiple *tulkus* (reincarnations or emanations) (*sprul sku*), not a single *tulku*.[4] There are various Kongtruls including Jamgön Kongtrul, Shechen Kongtrul and Dzigar Kongtrul, but all are understood to carry on the activity of the Kongtrul lineage. Kalu Rinpoche (1905–1989) is another important figure. Although Kalu Rinpoche did not go by the title of Kongtrul, he was recognised and understood to be an activity emanation of Jamgön Kongtrul Rinpoche. Kalu Rinpoche played a very important part in the preservation of Tibetan Buddhist tradition and its introduction to the West. It was Kalu Rinpoche, for instance, who was the first to lead a three-year retreat for Westerners.[5] The lineages of Chokgyur Lingpa have also continued through a line of *tulkus* and through his descendants, most notably in recent times through his great-grandson, Tulku Urgyen (1920–1996), who established various monasteries and retreat centres in Nepal, including the Ka-Nying monastery which was inaugurated in 1976 in Kathmandu.

Most of the Tibetan lamas we see in the West have been influenced by the Rimé movement. The Sixteenth Karmapa requires special mention, as he was very closely connected in various ways to the movement, as was his predecessor the Fifteenth Karmapa in Tibet. Another (less well-known) figure is Dezhung Rinpoche (1906–1987), a Sakya Lama, and a quintessential Rimé teacher. It was Dezhung Rinpoche who went to the United States of America in 1960 and taught in universities there. It is through him that the Rimé movement became known and studied academically.

What follows is an exploration of the Rimé movement. First we will set the context by discussing the different schools of Tibetan Buddhism and the relationship between them. We will then look at some of the precursors to the Rimé movement and some of the figures who inspired it. The main section is an exploration of the movement itself and those involved. Finally, we will examine how the movement shaped contemporary Tibetan Buddhism and look at its enduring influence today.

Section 1

The Schools and their Relations

IN PRESENT DAY TIBETAN BUDDHISM there are four major schools or orders: the Nyingma, Sakya, Kagyü and Gelug. These are sometimes called 'sects', but we shall leave aside that term due to its current negative implications in the West.[1] To better understand the context in which the Rimé movement arose it is helpful to categorise the schools in four different ways: in terms of the period in which they arose, their involvement in political power, their monastic orientation and the place of intellectual study within them.

The Period in which the Schools Arose: the Old (*rnying ma*) and New (*gsar ma*) Schools

The first obvious division is that which separates the Old school and the New schools. This is basically a distinction between the Nyingma school and the others. In Tibet the name Nyingma actually means 'old ones'. Initially it did not refer to the name of the school, but to those who practised the old ways dating back as early as the eighth century C.E. The Sarma (*gsar ma*), 'new ones', were following the new lineages which began to be introduced in the eleventh century.

Buddhism was officially established in Tibet in the eighth century with the founding of Samye Monastery and the first ordination of Tibetans as monks. Prior to this Buddhism had been coming into Tibet in various ways, but it was at this point that it became officially established—this was the beginning of monastic Buddhism and its enshrinement as the official religion of the state through King Trisong Detsen (ruled 754–797). The three main figures at this time were King Trisong Detsen, the Abbot Śāntarakṣita (who arrived in Tibet from north-eastern India ca. 767 at the invitation of the king), and the tantric figure

Padmasambhava (also known as Guru Rinpoche or 'the Precious Guru').[2] These three together founded Samye Monastery and presided over the establishment of Buddhism in Tibet. At the time, Tibet controlled most of central Asia and indeed a significant part of what is presently China, and southwards into Nepal and northern India. Tibet was a huge and powerful empire which took on Buddhism as a state religion, a unifying religion, as opposed to a series of local religions. Buddhism was seen as a necessary and suitable doctrine for such a vast empire, one that was capable of embracing all its different facets and diversity.

Śāntarakṣita and Padmasambhava may be understood as representing the two main forms of Buddhist practice that were introduced to Tibet at this stage. The monk Śāntarakṣita embodied the ideal of a monastic who primarily followed the path of the Mahāyāna sūtras. The sūtras lay out the path of virtue (generosity, ethical conduct, patience and so on) which combined with philosophical investigation and meditative discipline lead gradually to liberation from suffering and to full awakening (Buddhahood) for the benefit of all. Padmasambhava was not a monastic. He followed the path of tantra which is known as Vajrayāna (the Adamantine Path) or as Mantrayāna (the Mantra Path). The Vajrayāna has the same aim (Buddhahood) as the Sūtra Path but uses radically different methods that aim at a rapid transformation of deluded emotions and views into enlightened awareness. The methods of tantra include yogic practices, mantras and visualisations to transform energy and integrate body, speech and mind into the enlightened state.

Samye Monastery was opened ca. 779, but by the middle of the ninth century Buddhism in Tibet had entered a dark period, a period in which the monastic basis of Buddhism was suppressed and virtually disappeared.[3] For approximately one hundred and fifty years the monasteries were closed and there was a good deal of civil disorder; the empire broke up and the centralised authority broke down, and as a result several different kingdoms and factions arose in Tibet. In the late tenth century things had begun to turn around due to the reintroduction of the monastic rule (*vinaya*) to Central Tibet from distant north-eastern Tibet (Amdo) where it had been preserved.[4] The kings of Western Tibet played a major role in reintroducing monastic Buddhism. They were gravely concerned over the forms Buddhism had been taking in the interim—the types of practices that were evolving and misunderstandings which had arisen. The kings felt that Buddhism in Tibet had become corrupted and they wanted to reintroduce a form of Buddhism that was acceptable to the royal court. This marked the beginning of the second diffusion of Buddhism throughout Tibet, and was the origin of the New schools.

A great figure of this era was Atiśa (982–1054), who was invited from north-eastern India to help re-establish monastic Buddhism. Atiśa's disciple Dromtön (1008–1064) established the Kadam school, the monastic order based on the graduated path, where a thorough study and practice of sūtra-based Buddhism is undertaken prior to optional tantric practice which, if practised, must be co-ordinated with sūtra-based teaching and monastic vows. The Kadam tradition of Atiśa and Dromtön was revivified by Tsongkhapa (1357–1419) in the fifteenth century in what was known as the 'New Kadam' tradition and was institutionalised as the Gelug school.[5]

The eleventh century also saw the founding of the Sakya school based on a blend of sūtra teachings and the tantric practices of the Indian tantric master Virūpa which were bought back to Tibet by Drokmi (993–1077). The Sakya school was founded by Drokmi's disciple Könchok Gyalpo (1034–1102), a member of the powerful Khön family in southern Tibet, a family with which the Sakya tradition has remained closely associated. Also late in the same century Marpa (1012–1096) travelled to India and brought back texts and practice traditions which he then transmitted. His most famous disciple was the yogi Milarepa (1040–1123) and, in turn, Milarepa's most famous disciple was Gampopa (1079–1153), who established the monastic Kagyü tradition out of which many Kagyü sub-schools arose. These are called the Dagpo Kagyü after the area from which Gampopa originally came and where he later established his monastery.[6] Dagpo Kagyü includes the Karma Kagyü (also known as Karma Kamtsang Kagyü) which is the biggest of the Kagyü schools, the Drikung Kagyü and Drukpa Kagyü among its fourteen different sub-schools.[7] Since the main Dagpo Kagyü practice lineages were originally introduced into Tibet by Marpa, these traditions are embraced by the term Marpa Kagyü. However, Marpa Kagyü also includes lineages tracing back to Marpa which were not transmitted by Gampopa, such as that of Milarepa's yogi disciple Rechungpa (1084–1161).

With this new influx came new tantric texts and practices brought into Tibet in the eleventh century, largely from north-eastern India. The new tantras were significantly different to those which had been brought over earlier from the north-west of India—from present day Kashmir and northern Pakistan. Since the followers of the New schools were using newly translated tantras and sūtras these schools are also sometimes called the New Translation schools.[8] Naturally there were people who were quite happy with the old texts and practices they were following, and they were referred to as the 'old·ones' (*rnying ma*). They did not really constitute a school but were the 'old ones' in the sense that they adhered to the old ways—their old tantras and translations.

With the development of new styles of Buddhism and with the emergent distinction between the old and new traditions we see the old tradition responding with a need for a more palpable identity, and this is where the founding figure of Padmasambhava comes into the picture. The 'old ones' rallied around the figure of Padmasambhava and identified him explicitly as founder of their school. Of course, Padmasambhava had not founded a particular school but he had brought tantric Buddhism to Tibet in the early period and was thus regarded as a principal source of their practice traditions and teachings.[9] The followers of the 'old ones' were also facing polemical criticism as, according to the new schools, some of their tantrism and doctrines were of doubtful authenticity. By the mid-eleventh century some Nyingmas were feeling the pressure to defend their practices and their doctrines.

We can therefore see the division between the Old and New schools as an important one. These issues, and others not yet discussed, surrounding the authenticity of the old traditions were addressed many centuries later by the Rimé movement which affirmed the complete validity of both the Old and New traditions.

The Schools and Politics in Tibet

A second way of thinking about the four schools is in terms of their respective political involvement. The Gelug, Sakya and Kagyü traditions were all involved in political power at various stages in Tibet. The Nyingmas were only very marginally involved, largely because they were not really an organised school. There was no head of the Nyingma school until the diaspora from Tibet following the flight of the Fourteenth Dalai Lama in 1959. His Holiness, while attempting to organise the sixty to seventy thousand Tibetans who went to India and Nepal, suggested that the Nyingmas needed a head and spokesperson, in line with the other schools. The Nyingmas unanimously decided on Dudjom Rinpoche (1904–1987) as they regarded him both as a master of immense learning and realisation and as "the acknowledged representative of Guru Padmasambhava himself."[10] After Dudjom Rinpoche, Dilgo Khyentse Rinpoche became head of the Nyingmas. So, throughout the many centuries of its existence in Tibet, there had been no head of the Nyingma school. Nor were they organised monastically like the other schools. They were not centralised, so their involvement in politics was very minimal. The other schools were quite different.

Many people are familiar with the Gelug role in Tibetan politics. Since the time of the Fifth Dalai Lama (1617–1682) up until 1959 the Gelugs were the dominant group both numerically and also politically. By the seventeenth century, the position of the Dalai Lama had become the most influential one in the Gelug monastic system although the Dalai Lama was not strictly speaking the head, which was a position accorded the abbot of Ganden monastery, the oldest Gelug monastery.[11] From the time of the Fifth Dalai Lama, the Dalai Lamas were also temporal heads of the Tibetan government. It was under the Dalai Lamas and the Gelugs that Tibet was united more completely than it had been since the time of the empire in the ninth century. The Gelugs were the driving force behind what we might call the unification of the Tibetan state from the seventeenth century until recent times.

The Sakyas had been in control of Tibet in the thirteenth century. Like the Gelugs after them, the Sakyas came to political power with the backing of the Mongols. There were close relations between the Tibetans and the Mongols, who were led by the various Khans. The Mongols were very powerful from the time of Genghis Khan in the thirteenth century until the eighteenth century. At its height the Mongol empire reached from China in the East to present day Poland and Turkey in the West. The Mongols were tremendously powerful, and with their backing the Sakya Khön family and the monastic organisation associated with them became the dominant group in Tibet. It should be noted that the way Buddhist schools became powerful and effective was through alliances with important Tibetan families and foreign powers such as the various Mongol groups. In turn, it was through political connections, and through the part that religious figures like Sakya Paṇḍita Kunga Gyaltsen (1182–1251) played in them, that the Mongols were converted to Buddhism. The Khans entered into a 'patron/priest' relationship, where the Tibetans acted as priests and religious advisors to the Mongols, and the Mongols provided the patronage and political muscle. Of course, tribute was paid to the Mongols in part measure through taxes on the Tibetans.

By the middle of the fourteenth century, partly due to rivalry amongst the

Mongol clans and partly because of family rivalries in Tibet, the Sakyas were seriously challenged by various Kagyü groups associated with secular rulers. The Phagmodru Kagyü and the Drikung Kagyü were involved, and there was a period when political power in Tibet was linked with various Kagyü schools, including the Karma Kagyü. Nevertheless, in this period effective control was never fully established, and it is with the rise of the Gelugs and through their relationship with the Mongols that a longer-term stability was established. The title of Dalai Lama was actually given to the Third Dalai Lama by the Mongol leader Altan Khan—'Dalai' is a Mongolian word, meaning 'ocean', understood as referring to an ocean of merit or knowledge.[12] Conveniently, the Fourth Dalai Lama was born as a great-grandson of Altan Khan, which helped tighten up the relationship. The Fifth Dalai Lama (1617–1682), often referred to as the 'Great Fifth', was able in 1642 to unify Tibet with Mongol backing and take political control. This was maintained by the Dalai Lamas and their regents in Tibet until 1959, with the Gelugs remaining the dominant group throughout this period of three centuries.

Rimé is not a political movement, but political considerations do enter into its background and are significant, partly due to the fact that East Tibet (Kham and Amdo) was always somewhat independent. It is primarily in Kham that the Rimé movement arose. Part of the context for the movement is a reassertion of the independence of East Tibet from both the political dominance and also the doctrinal orthodoxy of Central Tibet. We will explore the relationship between politics and doctrinal orthodoxy within the framework of monasticism and intellectual study further on in this Section.

Monastic Organisation

Another way to categorise the schools is in terms of monastic organisation. Looked at in this way we find that the Gelug and Sakya were the most monastically organised. It must be remembered that the Gelugs had come out of the Kadam tradition, which is explicitly monastic, and Tsongkhapa had established the movement which gave birth to the Gelug School as a reform movement with a strong monastic ethos. Likewise the Sakyas always had a very strong monastic base. In contrast, the founding of the Kagyü tradition is much less rooted in monastic institutions, and so too the Nyingma. We have mentioned the umbrella term

Marpa Kagyü. Marpa was a layman, his chief disciple Milarepa a yogi—neither of them monks. Gampopa, Milarepa's chief disciple, was a monk. In these three leading Kagyü figures we see a range from layperson, to yogi, to monk, and this has remained somewhat typical of Kagyü tradition—it embraces these different life situations. Gampopa, the monk, gave the Kagyü tradition a monastic basis, bringing together the Kadam sūtra tradition of Atiśa and the tantric tradition of Milarepa in a monastic framework. However, within the Kagyü there was a far greater retention of a mix of practitioners than in the case of the Sakya and Gelug traditions.

Turning to the Nyingma in the early period, the period when the monasteries were closed (ca. 840–1000 C.E.), we find that the old tradition survived through lay practice. This resulted in a different kind of religious community (*saṅgha*) called the 'white *saṅgha*' (distinguished from the monastic or 'red *saṅgha*') where people follow some kind of vow; they were not monks or nuns, yet they were still practising within a community of committed practitioners. The great Nyingma monasteries like Shechen and Dzogchen monastery, and others, were built during or after the seventeenth century. (Kathok monastery had been built in the twelfth century but it had fallen into disrepair and was only rebuilt in the seventeenth century.) Up until the time of Gelug ascendancy the Nyingmas had not been monastically organised and it had been very much a lay tradition practised in households, small hermitages and retreat centres.

Monasticism and Intellectual Study

The most monastically organised schools, the Gelug and the Sakya, placed a great deal of emphasis on intellectual study. In modern times we are aware of the strong academic curriculum of the Gelugs, but in former times the Sakyas also emphasised epistemology (theories of knowledge) and logic and were famous for great philosophers, such as Sakya Paṇḍita. There is an obvious and marked contrast between the schools with rigorous traditions of intellectual study (Gelug and Sakya) and the Kagyü and Nyingma, where tantric practice in particular and meditation practice in general, were seen as the supreme value and study itself was seen as preparation for practice.[13]

In the Gelug and Sakya traditions we find an emphasis on academic study in a monastic environment and this is conducive to centralisation and a more conservative approach. The scholarly approach tends to be very structured and gradualist; the spiritual path is presented as a series of well-defined steps built on a very strong foundation of intellectual studies. In Tibet this approach emphasised the Indian side of the tradition, and leaned toward ideas of orthodoxy and correct thinking (as related to the Indian sourced texts and the great scholars (*paṇḍita*) of India). This tended to create a somewhat restricted view of what could be called authentic Dharma (Buddhist doctrine and practice). Authentic Dharma tended to be regarded as what was Indian or at least could be shown to be based on Indian texts.

The emphasis on Indian origin and the criteria of doctrinal orthodoxy placed textual study, interpretation of texts (hermeneutics), critical evaluation and philosophical studies in a pre-eminent position. On the philosophical front we find a dominance of Madhyamaka ('Middle Way') philosophical interpretation, to the extent that Madhyamaka was considered the touchstone for interpreting the whole path, including the tantric path. The whole path should be understood within the framework of Indian philosophy, one might say. The division between scholastic and non-scholastic approaches in Tibet is an important one for us to appreciate because in the scholastic traditions we get various critiques of the non-scholastic traditions, Dzogchen being particularly targeted. Dzogchen ('Great Perfection' or 'Great Completion') is a tradition primarily transmitted through the relatively non-scholastic Nyingma school. Similarly targeted was Mahāmudrā, as taught by Gampopa, which was transmitted through the Kagyü school (also practice-orientated and non-scholastic). The philosophy of Dzogchen and Mahāmudrā will be discussed in Section 2, but here we need to take account of some criticisms of Dzogchen and Kagyü Mahāmudrā.

The criticisms of Dzogchen were basically that it was a Tibetan creation, heavily indebted to Chinese Buddhism and not being of Indian origin, therefore most likely inferior and inauthentic. The critics of Dzogchen associated it with what they termed Hva Shang Mahāyāna, or basically Chinese Ch'an or Chinese Zen Buddhism, which they labelled a form of quietism. In the critics' characterisations of these traditions, all the practitioner had to do was stop the mind, and instantaneously enlightenment would follow. Naturally this made the whole academic enterprise redundant and tended towards debunking the *raison d'être* of monastic and scholarly endeavour. The recalling of Ch'an or Zen Buddhism harked back to the earlier famous debate that had taken place in Tibet in the eighth century between representatives of Indian and Chinese forms of Buddhism.

According to official Tibetan history (written much later and from a monastic perspective), the Indians had been conclusive victors in this debate, affirming the path to be a gradual, structured one, and censuring the way of Chinese Zen or Ch'an. Dzogchen was grouped together with this quietism, and heavily criticised as a shutting off of the mind without any particular syllabus of intellectual study or preparation. According to some critics, including Sakya Paṇḍita, the great scholar of the Sakya school, Mahāmudrā as taught and understood in Kagyü tradition was no better—more or less the same thing under a different name.[14] So there was a kind of tension between the mainstream academic traditions and the Mahāmudrā and Dzogchen traditions of the Kagyü and Nyingma schools respectively.

One must remember there had never been a Mahāyāna Buddhist canon in India; there was no fixed body of Mahāyāna Buddhist texts—this came later in Tibet. When the Buddhist canon was assembled by Butön (1290–1364) in the fourteenth century, the Nyingma tantras (the old tantras) were excluded because they were thought to be of doubtful authenticity. Part of the official justification for their exclusion was that they supposedly lacked Indian origins. Because Sanskrit texts were unavailable, the old tantras were presumed to be miscellaneous inventions of unknown people. There was the implication that they were made up by Tibetans, they were not really of a verifiable standard, and certainly not authentic enough to be included in the canon.

It was on the basis of Butön's canon that Tsongkhapa was able to carry out his great and influential work. For Tsongkhapa, who virtually defined Gelug doctrine, the touchstone of orthodoxy was 'Indian-ness', the Indian texts, and in particular the Madhyamaka philosophy. Tsongkhapa was positioning Madhyamaka, and a particular school within it, the Prāsaṅgika Madhyamaka, as the pinnacle of philosophy. In synopsis, the greatest exponent and interpreter of Madhyamika, the one who understood it perfectly, was held to be Candrakīrti, the great seventh century Indian scholar. Tsongkhapa, in turn, was seen by the Gelug followers to have understood Candrakīrti properly. Thus the dominant scholastic and intellectual position became the Prāsaṅgika Madhyamaka of Candrakīrti as interpreted by Tsongkhapa. It was not as though Tsongkhapa was focused on politics, or anything of that sort, but he was the founder of the Ganden Monastery which was the founding monastery of the Gelug tradition that soon became dominant politically and numerically. Later, many monasteries were turned into Gelug monasteries, and thereby progressively the Madhyamaka doctrine gained ascendancy over the others, leaving the other doctrines somewhat stigmatised. This was the situation from the time of the Fifth Dalai Lama onwards. The geographical centre for it all was Lhasa in Central Tibet, in the three great Gelug monasteries, Ganden, Sera and Drepung. From this period on we can categorise schools in terms of power and size into Gelug, the dominant school, and the rest.

For our discussion of the Rimé movement this particular categorisation is pertinent, as the Rimé movement is predominantly non-Gelug. Quite specifically it is a movement concerned with the reassertion of non-Gelug traditions, and the formation of a new kind of synthesis—a synthesis in the sense of a bringing together, not a mixing up, of traditions, including the Kadam tradition that constitutes the basis of the Gelug school.[15] The Rimé movement is basically very inclusive, allowing for many different practices and approaches, recognising them as valid and making them available in their own terms.

There is no set doctrinal position in the Rimé movement. There are certain tendencies, but one need not be an adherent of Prāsaṅgika Madhyamaka for instance. A part of what the movement achieved was a rehabilitation of practice lineages, and openness to a greater variety of philosophical positions than those associated with the orthodoxy established in Central Tibet by the Gelug organisations.

There is no disrespect or anti-Gelug sentiment in the argument being presented here. In the world of 'realpolitik' it is quite probable that Tibet would not have been unified in the way it was without the Gelug organisation. With political power and organisation there has to be, and inevitably there is, an application of force in various ways. The Fifth Dalai Lama, for example, was a great figure in most people's eyes, and himself completely non-sectarian (perhaps apart from a few doubts he may have had about the Kagyü, as they were politically troublesome at the time).[16] He was also well disposed to the Nyingma and a practitioner of Dzogchen, but in spite of all this, in the political situation at the time, he applied political power and sanctioned the closing down of monasteries. In fact an entire school, the Jonang school, was closed down under him, its printing blocks placed under seal and its libraries closed.[17] The libraries remained closed until the Rimé movement some centuries later. (A lama closely associated with Jamyang Khyentse and Jamgön Kongtrul, Losel Tenkyong, secured the agreement which allowed Jonang works to be reprinted and their libraries re-opened.)[18] Nevertheless, under the Fifth Dalai Lama, a whole school had in fact been closed down, and beyond that, entire monasteries forcibly converted into Gelug monasteries. Quite a few Kagyü monasteries were included in this enforced conversion. It is worth noting that prior to the ascendancy of the Fifth Dalai Lama some Gelug monasteries had been forcibly converted to Kagyü.

Closure of monasteries was often partly justified by doctrinal argument. In the case of the Jonang, the justification for closing the school was found in their adherence to the doctrine of 'other-emptiness', which contrasted to the interpretation of 'self-emptiness' of Tsongkhapa—or the *shentong* (*gzhan stong*) versus *rangtong* (*rang stong*) argument, as it is known in Tibetan. The distinction between *shentong* and *rangtong* concerns the nature of 'emptiness' (*śūnyatā*) and how it is understood in relation to ultimate reality.[19]

The 'other-emptiness' or *shentong* position put forward by the Jonang was that a proper understanding of emptiness was not a complete negation. Emptiness to them was more akin to the negation of error—but once the error is negated, and one sees what is empty, then something is left—something remains, that is, ultimate reality. Ultimate reality is empty of other, empty of duality for example, or empty of delusion, but it is not empty of itself. 'Other-emptiness' means emptiness of everything that is not itself; it is empty of all else. Ultimate reality is here asserted in a positive fashion. In contrast, the position of Tsongkhapa, called 'self-emptiness' or *rangtong*, refers to an emptiness that is itself empty, so there is nothing at all that survives negation. In Tsongkhapa's intellectual presentation, emptiness is understood in terms of what is called technically a 'non-affirming negation', which is to state that reality is itself empty. Not a trace of anything is not empty. Even ultimate reality is empty, empty of itself, so it cannot be said to be existent or real. This was Tsongkhapa's position of self-emptiness.

The other-emptiness of the Jonang was strongly asserted by the writer Dölpopa Sherab Gyalsten (1292–1361), the greatest figure of the Jonang school. Tsongkhapa took particular exception to Dölpopa's presentation, seeing it as an example of a flawed understanding of emptiness.[20] Other critics who came after Tsongkhapa, suggested the other-emptiness doctrine was an eternalistic doctrine, essentially the same as the doctrine of the 'heretics' (*tīrthaka*), in that it strongly implied a truly existent ultimate, equivalent to the Hindu *Ātman* or *Brahman*. Any suggestion of eternalism was, of course, anathema to Tsongkhapa's followers, and consequently the influential Dölpopa and the Jonang school became their target.

One of the most powerful figures in Jonang history was Tāranātha (1575–1634). In 1615 he established a very impressive and influential monastery in

Tsang, near Shigatse in southern Tibet, teaching other-emptiness.[21] Tāranātha was a great defender of Dölpopa, but in addition, probably to the disadvantage of the Jonang school, he was also very influential amongst the Mongols and was courted by them. Tāranātha may in turn have courted the Mongols, among whom he opened a significant number of Jonang monasteries. Tāranātha died in Mongolia at around the time the Fifth Dalai Lama took control, and the Dalai Lama appears to have seized the opportunity of neutralising a potentially powerful rival group with strong Mongol connections, basically by closing them down and pronouncing them unorthodox. Thus, in the hard world of realpolitik the Fifth Dalai Lama closed down the Jonang monasteries. Schools that upheld other-emptiness became doctrinally suspect, and somewhat politically suspect as well, due to Tāranātha's connections with opposing factions in Tibet, and in particular with rivals in Tsang in southern Tibet. Gareth Sparham puts it well:

> The Glorious Fifth and his advisors wanted to take no chances with another power center developing in gTsang, particularly when it was associated with a scholarly and religious figure much loved by many Mongolians. To declare the views of the sect antithetical to those of Tsong kha pa, and by extension to the Dalai Lamas who had inherited his spiritual mantle, was a draconian measure no doubt, but it was a sure way to prevent their further spread amongst the Mongolians which might sway them from unwavering and single-pointed support.[22]

In the end, various monasteries were converted, particularly those of the Jonang and the troublesome Kagyüs who had an alliance with the princes of Shigatse in Tsang.[23] Overall a kind of doctrinal orthodoxy was turned to serve a political purpose. Part of what the Rimé movement accomplished was a resuscitation of these ostracised doctrines and a bestowal on them of a respectability that had been denied.

Schools and Lineages

It is important to recognise that Schools are not lineages. Schools are a matter of monastic and institutional organisation, whereas a lineage is a line of transmissions of teachings and transmissions of practice over generations. Lineage also involves a guru/disciple relationship and the actual transmission that goes with that. Certain lineages have tended to be associated with particular schools and indeed one way a lineage survives or prospers is to have a strong basis within a school. For example, in the Lamdre (*lam 'bras*) ('Path and Result') teachings there is a whole body of teachings that tend to be associated with the Sakya school. Lamdre teaching is based on *Hevajra Tantra* and various sūtra teachings and was mainly promulgated through the Sakya tradition. Lamdre is not identical to Sakya and is not intrinsically a Sakya teaching but it has had sustained institutional backing from the Sakya school. Likewise we tend to associate the Six Yogas of Naropa with the Kagyü school, because they were promulgated through Tilopa, Naropa, Marpa, and Milarepa, and became central practices of the various Kagyü traditions. The four primary and eight sub-schools of Kagyü all pass on the Six Yogas of Naropa and the Mahāmudrā traditions that came through Naropa and through Maitrīpa. Even so, there is nothing intrinsically Kagyü about the Six Yogas, it is simply that the lineages we associate them with, institutionally, have belonged to the Kagyü school.

In relation to Dzogchen, we tend to think of the Nyingma school. Dzogchen teachings are traced back to the Indian Garab Dorje (Prahevajra in Sanskrit), and then through various figures like Padmasambhava and, more particularly, the Indian master Vimalamitra and the Tibetan translator Vairocana (who is said to be one of the first Tibetans ordained as a monk by Śāntarakṣita). These figures are associated with the Old tradition, and were the main transmitters of the tradition, and thus it is the Nyingmas who incorporated Dzogchen traditions into their own particular presentation of the path. In the Nyingma tradition of paths or vehicles (*yāna*), there is a nine vehicle scheme. The first three vehicles relate to sūtra. The next three are the outer (or lower) tantras, and the three vehicles at the zenith of this system are the inner (or higher) tantras, Mahāyoga, Anuyoga, and Dzogchen (or Atiyoga).[24] Thus, in the Nyingma school Dzogchen is the highest presentation of the Buddhist teachings, and for this reason we tend to associate Dzogchen with Nyingma, but there is no intrinsic necessity to do so. For one thing, Dzogchen teachings are also found in the Bon tradition, which does not accept the Nyingma nine vehicle arrangement. In addition, Dzogchen practice and doctrine can also be understood as a complete tradition in itself; there is no intrinsic need to place it within another framework at all. However, because its fullest preservation and presentation has been predominantly through the Nyingma, it is usually associated with that tradition.

Bearing in mind this distinction between lineages and schools it is interesting to reflect on the various sources of the different traditions within the schools. Let us take the Kagyü tradition of Gampopa as an example. Gampopa was not only drawing on what he received from Milarepa (which were basically tantric traditions coming from Naropa and Tilopa and the Mahāmudrā teachings from Maitrīpa and others), he was also drawing on his former training as a Kadam monk and his schooling in the traditions of Atiśa. In forming the monastic basis of the Dagpo Kagyü and all the schools within it such as Karma Kagyü, Drikung Kagyü and Drukpa Kagyü, Gampopa brought together the sūtra traditions of Atiśa with the tantric traditions of Milarepa. These two, sūtra and tantra, coming through different lineages, were brought together and presented in a harmonious relationship, in a way that presents no contradiction.

The other Tibetan Buddhist schools also brought together sūtra and tantra. We can see in the case of the Sakya tradition, for example, that their distinctive teaching is associated with the Lamdre ('Path and Result') tradition. This tradition and the presentation of the Sakya school as a whole combines tantric traditions of the great Indian tantric master (*mahāsiddha*) Virūpa with sūtra teachings and the fundamental teachings of a graduated path as taught in the monastic universities of northern India at the time Drokmi studied there in the eleventh century. We also find that, despite being one of the 'new' schools, Sakya from the beginning included lineages and practices from the old period, such as those associated with the meditation deity Vajrakīlaya. Thus we see that despite the misgivings of some (including its foremost scholar Sakya Paṇḍita) about Dzogchen and the old ways, some old traditions were extensively practised within the Sakya school. Later, especially due to the influence of lamas in the Khyentse lineage who belonged to the Sakya school, Dzogchen became widely accepted among the Sakyas. Similar stories can to be told of all the schools and thus we can see that any notion of any single 'pure' school is unsustainable.

Loss of Lineages

One consequence of the connection between lineages and schools is that when a lineage lacks major institutional backing it can easily become marginalised, or lost. Along with the preservation of doctrinal diversity and freedom, a goal of the nineteenth century Rimé teachers was to revive traditions in danger of weak-

The Schools and their Relations

ening or dying out. A good example is Shangpa Kagyü. In the enumeration of the 'eight practice lineages' (see Section 3) by Jamgön Kongtrul and others we find Shangpa Kagyü listed separately from Marpa Kagyü, that is to say, there are traditions coming from Marpa, and also separate Kagyü traditions coming under the title of Shangpa Kagyü. In fact these Shangpa Kagyü lineages go back to two Indian women, Niguma and Sukhasiddhi. Through these two realised women we have a separate series of Six Yogas and a separate Mahāmudrā tradition quite independent from the yogas and Mahāmudrā coming down through Naropa. Niguma was either the consort or the sister of Naropa. The variant of the tradition she would go on to transmit was received by her in pure vision from Vajradhara (the Ultimate, personified)—it was not derived from what she received from Naropa personally. These practices were passed on to a Tibetan, Khyungpo Naljor, in the eleventh century, who studied with many important figures in India, and are primarily the legacy of the two women, Niguma and Sukhasiddhi. Khyungpo Naljor returned to Tibet in the eleventh century and established his seat in West Tibet at Zhangzhong in the Shang valley from which the name 'Shangpa' ('relating to Shang') is derived.[25]

During the twelfth and thirteenth centuries a number of Shangpa institutions were founded, each one an independent entity, and thus the Shangpa never became an institutionalised school or monastic tradition. In fact, the full Shangpa tradition was passed on exclusively on a one-to-one basis for seven generations; from that point on it was more widely taught. Political circumstances were not to shine fortune on the Shangpa Kagyü, for they ended up being adopted by and aligned with the Jonang tradition which, as we have seen, was to be closed down. Tāranātha was a major lineage holder of the Shangpa Kagyü, and with the closing of the Jonang school in the seventeenth century, the fortunes of the Shangpa tradition somewhat waned. Despite the fact that Shangpa never ceased to exist, it remains an example of how an important practice lineage lacking institutional support can weaken severely.

During the nineteenth century, Jamyang Khyentse and Jamgön Kongtrul, amongst their other endeavours, specifically sought out practices and lineages in danger of dying out. They were tireless, with a seemingly endless appetite for a new practice, never missing an opportunity to receive a new teaching or transmission. They seemed to have found time to actually practise many of these in addition to preserving them. Their efforts in the preservation and revivification of the Shangpa Kagyü serve as a good example. In particular, Jamgön Kongtrul made Shangpa practice (the yogas and Mahāmudrā of Niguma and Sukhasiddhi) a central part of his own practice. He established a retreat centre where fifteen months of the three-year non-sectarian program were devoted to Shangpa Kagyü practices, testimony to the emphasis he placed on this particular tradition which had been on the brink of extinction.

Section 2
Some Antecedents of the Rimé Movement

SO FAR WE HAVE focused on the different ways of understanding the development of the four main schools of present day Tibetan Buddhism and have glimpsed the various ways this impacted on the development of the Rimé movement. We will now turn to the antecedents of the Rimé movement.

The Buddha and the Idea of Skilful Means

As we have seen, it was in the Rimé movement that the idea of a non-partisan approach became explicit. (The Rimé movement derives its name from this common meaning of 'unbiased' or 'not taking sides'.) However, there are many antecedents to this approach in Buddhism. In fact, the approach has been absolutely integral to Buddhist self-understanding right from the beginning, most obviously with Śākyamuni Buddha himself.

For the Buddha, the Dharma is a way of reaching realisation. According to the Pāli canon, after the Buddha achieved awakening he hesitated to teach, realising the difficulty of conveying a realisation so profound. Persuaded by the gods to teach for the 'benefit of gods and men' he reflected on how and to whom he might communicate his experience. Thus began a long period of teaching in which he taught in many ways to a variety of audiences, always recognising the capacity of the audience to understand, and the vast gap between what could be expressed and the goal to be realised. The Buddha taught differently when he was teaching to farmers to when teaching scholarly people, and so on.[1] Herein lies the germ of the idea, more explicitly developed in Mahāyāna Buddhism, that the Buddha was able to utilise skilful means (*upāya* or *upāyakausalyatā*) adapted to his audience when teaching. Entailed in this idea is the understanding that one and the same formulation of the Dharma will not be suitable for all people.

Furthermore, for the Buddha, the Dharma is not something to be clung to nor is it of ultimate value in itself. Its value lies in its ability to lead aspirants to realisation. Various metaphors and similes express this idea. For instance there is the famous raft simile, where the Buddha likens the Dharma to a raft. A raft is for crossing a river, and once we get across the river there is no need to keep carrying the raft around on our backs, for then it becomes an impediment.[2] In other words we should not be overly attached to the doctrine or the formulation per se, the purpose of which is get across the 'river' or 'ocean' of birth, death and suffering (saṃsāra). The Buddha also likens the teachings to medicine, and therefore crucial to healing an illness—the illness of ignorance, or the problem of suffering.[3]

From a related perspective, the Dharma is understood to present that which is necessary and to dispense with what is superfluous to the task. This is made clear when the Buddha says that what he knows is like a forest, but what he teaches is like a handful of leaves.[4] In other words, out of the vastness of his knowledge, he teaches precisely what is useful to people in any given moment and situation.

These ideas run right through the Buddha's approach and through Buddhism itself: the Dharma is essentially what is conducive to the end of suffering, and the realisation of truth. These are the criteria by which it is to be judged. The Buddha did not want people to believe or take on trust what he said simply because he was saying it, but rather he wanted each person to go away and test it for themselves, and to conclude for themselves whether it really did ameliorate suffering, and loosen the grip of the conflicting emotions, the *kleśas*. So as a touchstone for the Dharma we find the idea that the Dharma is that which serves the purpose of realisation.

The idea of skilful means and the idea of different formulations of the Dharma to suit different mentalities become more explicit in the Mahāyāna.[5] In the Mahāyāna these ideas become linked to the idea of a hierarchy of teachings or truths, each suitable to different people. The hierarchy of teaching or truths may also be understood as applicable to a single individual at different stages on the path to awakening (*bodhi*). This is obvious in the distinction made in the Mahāyāna between Hīnayāna ('lesser vehicle') and Mahāyāna ('great vehicle').[6] In this framework the Hīnayāna is understood to include the basic teachings of Buddhism on suffering, the moral law of cause and effect (*karma*), impermanence, non-self, the path and so on, and is not superseded by the Mahāyāna. Rather, the Hīnayāna is understood as the most suitable vehicle or path for certain people and as a foundational presentation of Buddhist truths necessary as a basis for all people before proceeding to more subtle perspectives. The Mahāyāna does not negate the Hīnayāna nor does it deny its efficacy. The Mahāyāna is regarded as 'great' (*mahā*) because it embraces a greater motivation (working for the liberation of all as opposed to the focus on individual liberation characteristic of the Hīnayāna), has a higher goal (complete Buddhahood rather than the end of suffering), and offers a deeper understanding of reality. This deeper understanding is through an apprehension of 'emptiness' (*śūnyatā*) which is held to be more profound than the understanding of impermanence or non-self in the Hīnayāna. In philosophical terms 'emptiness' does not negate the teaching of impermanence or non-self as presented in the Hīnayāna, but rather it brings out a deeper understanding and makes explicit (*nīta*) what is implicit (*neya*) in the 'lower' teaching.

The Mahāyāna is also regarded as 'great' because it offers a vast array of 'skilful means' through which it opens the path to a greater range of people and lifestyles—for example, to lay people engaged with the world. In certain sūtras of the Mahāyāna the whole life of the Buddha comes to be understood in terms of 'skilful means'—Śākyamuni Buddha, actually awakened long ago, deliberately takes birth and lives his life in a palace, followed by renunciation, spiritual practice, realisation and teaching as skilful means to show beings the path to Buddhahood and the life of an awakened person.[7]

Of course, this topic could be elaborated upon endlessly in terms of Mahāyāna Buddhist textual interpretation (hermeneutics) and philosophy, but enough has been said to allow us to return to the Tibetan context.

The observation was made earlier that Tibetan scholastic traditions showed strong tendencies to refer back to Indian sources for legitimisation—the Indian tantras for instance, but also to Indian philosophical texts. Tibetan scholars were often critical of the old tantras and the practice of Dzogchen, and doctrinal positions associated with them. This meant, inevitably, that the Old school, or the 'old ones', (hardly even a school as such at this point), felt the need to justify themselves and their position. We get a presentation to this effect as early as the eleventh century, when Mahāpaṇḍita ('great scholar') Rongzom Chökyi Zangpo (1012–1088), a member of the Old school, felt the need to defend Dzogchen. He chose to present Dzogchen very much in line with earlier Buddhist tradition, in that he did not deny the validity of other positions and philosophical perspectives, but rather presented 'higher' positions (such as Dzogchen) as a clarification of what is to be found in 'lower' positions. Rongzom states:

> In the treatises of the Buddhist teachings, one can make distinctions of higher and lower views, where the higher ones clarify points in the lower ones. Other than that, they do not improve on the lower ones or go against them.[8]

Rongzom says that different systems are suited to different intellects or understandings.[9] If the highest position is presented to someone unable to understand it, it is rendered useless. The message, just as the Buddha taught, needs to be geared to the audience.

Interestingly, the very early presentation of Buddhist teachings known as Abhidharma, is an attempt to refine and condense all the different presentations given by the Buddha to particular audiences into a lucid, abstract philosophy. The origin of Abhidharma lies in the wish to present the Buddha's teachings without reference to time and place. But the point remains: for a teaching to be effective it has to be effective for the person who hears it. The point of the 'higher' teachings is to clarify material in the 'lower' teachings, and in this sense they are not contradictory teachings at all.

A large part of the Buddhist approach to hermeneutics (interpretation of canonical texts) is devoted to bringing texts into harmonious relationship. From the viewpoint of Buddhist hermeneutics, the teachings of the Buddha cannot be contradictory and therefore the challenge is how to place them in correct relationship with each other so that apparent contradictions are resolved. Texts that appear on the surface to be contradictory are approached with the attitude that they can be reconciled. The claim is that out of a seemingly contradictory disarray, a perfectly valid Buddhism can be discerned, and for one who has this discernment the contradictions disappear.

The hermeneutic process of interpretation often involves establishing a hierarchy of teachings or views. A problem may arise with such a hierarchy in that from the 'lower' perspective, the 'higher' perspective may not be comprehensible and may appear incompatible with the 'lower' viewpoint. What is non-contradictory from a 'higher' perspective may not appear to be so from the 'lower' one. Implicit in this interpretive process is the principle that the 'higher' teachings are more encompassing, and enable a panoramic view that one cannot have from the ground, so to speak. Rongzom, who is of the Old school, and concerned principally to defend Dzogchen, argues that from the 'higher' perspective (such as Dzogchen), one sees that all of the teachings are indeed "of one taste."[10]

The type of presentation and defence of the higher teachings mounted by Rongzom in the eleventh century has been repeated through to the present day. Let us consider for a moment a teaching on Dzogchen given by His Holiness the Fourteenth Dalai Lama in 1984. Drawing on Jamyang Khyentse Chökyi Lodrö, one of the early twentieth century Khyentse teachers who was considered to be an activity emanation of the great Rimé figure Jamyang Khyentse Wangpo, His Holiness says:

> As is said in an oral transmission by the great lama Jamyang Khyentse Chökyi Lodrö, when the Great Nyingmapa adept Longchen Rabjam gives a presentation of the ground, path and fruit, he does so mainly from the perspective of the enlightened state of a Buddha, whereas the Sakyapa presentation is mainly from the perspective of the spiritual experience of a yogi on the path, and the Gelukpa presentation is mainly from the perspective of how phenomena appear to ordinary sentient beings. His statement appears to be worthy of considerable reflection; through it many misunderstandings can be removed.[11]

His Holiness was speaking at the time in terms of schools rather than specific teachings, but the point is the same: it is necessary to take into account the perspectives from which a teaching is given. We should remember that as a Gelug monk His Holiness principally belongs to the tradition of Tsongkhapa, but as protector of the Tibetan people, and as a protector of the Dharma more broadly, (and also as a practitioner of Dzogchen), he adopts a perspective which encompasses all schools and paths.

We see from the quote that, according to His Holiness, the Nyingma Dzogchen perspective is principally the perspective of a Buddha, ('the enlightened state'), and the Gelugpa position of Tsongkhapa is predominantly presented from the viewpoint of ordinary consciousness. This does not mean Tsongkhapa's presentation is a deluded one—nothing of the sort—but merely that Tsongkhapa is presenting from our everyday viewpoint, the view of ego, and how things appear to us. The presentation of the view from Buddhahood, which is the view of Dzogchen, differs from the presentation from the point of view of dualistic consciousness (that of ordinary sentient beings). According to the Dalai Lama, the Sakya presentation is different again—it is more akin to the perspective of somebody advanced on the path ('a yogi'). This means that each of the views is perfect from its own perspective and appropriate to a particular individual or understanding. Each one must be understood from its own perspective.

One could perhaps put it another way although His Holiness does not explicitly do so. The position of Tsongkhapa is like the sūtra position; it is perfect from that point of view. The point of view of Sakya, at least as presented in this quotation, is from the perspective of tantra. Both Gelugpa and Sakya positions are from the point of view of the path, albeit at different stages on the path. The point of view of Dzogchen, however, is not in essence from the path at all but from the point of view of the result, which is Buddhahood.

So, from Rongzom in the eleventh century to His Holiness the Dalai Lama in the twentieth and twenty-first centuries we have essentially the same response to the critique of the Dzogchen traditions. Others have defended the Mahāmudrā of Gampopa in a similar fashion. It should be noted that followers of Dzogchen and Kagyü Mahāmudrā rarely suggest the inadequacy of path methods, or suggest that other traditions are wrong. Furthermore they concede that the criticisms made against them may serve a positive function. If we take Sakya Paṇḍita's criticisms of Dzogchen and Kagyü Mahāmudrā (referred to in Section 1) as an example, we find that Jamgön Kongtrul did not suggest Sakya Paṇḍita was wrong to have made them, but that, in fact, it was necessary for him to have done so to avoid the likelihood of people being misled by the apparent contradictions in the higher teachings. Jamgön Kongtrul points out that in the context in which Sakya Paṇḍita made the criticisms, it was correct to criticise.[12] Jamgön Kongtrul was not suggesting Sakya Paṇḍita was suffering from a limited point of view, but rather that he was presenting in a particular way from another perspective. Actually, Jamgön Kongtrul was regarded as the reincarnation of Sakya Paṇḍita, and so it is even less likely he would be suggesting his previous reincarnation was a fool!

In regard to the connections of the Rimé movement to schools, the closeness of the Kagyü and Nyingma traditions is significant for a variety of reasons. Firstly, both of them are basically practice traditions, and both of them contend that the correct view is realised in practice, not in intellectual endeavour or presentation, that is to say, the definitive meaning is only realised in practice. In the Mahāmudrā traditions of the Kagyü and in Dzogchen, there is the idea that these are practice lineages of definitive meaning.[13] According to Tsele Natsok Rangdröl (b. 1608), a master of both Dzogchen and Mahāmudrā and a forerunner to the Rimé movement, the distinctive feature of these practice lineages is that the view and meditation are not separate: the recognition of the unfabricated basic state is both the view and the meditation.[14] When certain writers of Rimé (or Rimé orientation) refer to the practice lineages of definitive meaning, they often barely perceive a need to separate Kagyü Mahāmudrā and Dzogchen.

In keeping with a greater emphasis on practice and less emphasis given to doctrine, there are strong yogic traditions in both the Nyingma and Kagyü, and strong traditions of lay practice. As we have seen, the monasteries were closed down in the ninth century, and practice only survived in Central Tibet through lay practice. Later, in the Kagyü tradition emphasis was on meditation practice whether pursued in a monastic context or as a yogi or as a layperson. The coming together of the Kagyü and Nyingma was perhaps inevitable given this emphasis on meditation and this approach to practice. The convergence of the traditions and the possibility of integrating both became evident with the Second Karmapa, Karma Pakshi (1203–1283), and entirely explicit with the Third Karmapa, Rangjung Dorje (1284–1339).

Having explored these antecedents, we will now turn to the Third Karmapa and other figures who may be regarded as forerunners of the Rimé movement.

The Third Karmapa, Rangjung Dorje (1284–1339)

Rangjung Dorje was born in 1284 into a Nyingma family of practitioners in Central Tibet, where he became a monk in the Karma Kagyü tradition. Recognised as the Third Karmapa, and hence the head of the Karma Kagyü school, he was trained in the Six Yogas of Naropa, Mahāmudrā and other principal practices of the tradition, of which he became the principal lineage holder.

As well as attaining realisation through practice of Mahāmudrā, the Third Karmapa also practised Dzogchen. The foremost Nyingma figure of the time was Longchenpa (1308–1364) and he and the Third Karmapa shared a principal guru, Kumārarāja (1266–1343). Indeed, Longchenpa and the Third Karmapa knew each other and gave each other teachings. The Third Karmapa experienced a profound vision of Vimalamitra (one of the main founding figures of Dzogchen in Tibet) and received the entire Dzogchen teachings directly from Vimalamitra in this manner. This was recognised as a *terma* (treasure) teaching, and so Rangjung Dorje was recognised as a *tertön* (treasure revealer), having received a revealed teaching (understood to have been previously given by Vimalamitra) through visionary means. This Dzogchen *terma* has been passed down through the Karmapas and the Karma Kagyü tradition in what is known as the *Karma Nyingthig* (*The Heart Essence of the Karmapas*). In Dudjom Rinpoche's work, *The Nyingma School of Tibetan Buddhism: Its Fundamentals and History*, we can see that the Third Karmapa is regarded as a major lineage holder of Dzogchen and as a "fountain-head of the teaching."[15]

In one of his very famous prayers, called *Aspirations for Mahāmudrā of Definitive Meaning*, the Third Karmapa teaches the unity of Mahāmudrā, Dzogchen and Madhyamaka (the philosophical presentation of 'emptiness' based on the sūtra teachings). He says:

> Free from mental fabrication it is Mahāmudrā,
> Free from extremes it is Great Madhyamaka ('Middle Way'),
> And everything included here, it is also called Dzogchen ('Great Completion' or 'Great Perfection').
> May I attain the confidence that, in understanding one, I realise the meaning of all.[16]

The second line of this prayer refers to the aspect of Madhyamaka philosophy that teaches avoidance of the extremes of 'eternalism' on one side, and 'nihilism' on the other. One must find the 'middle' which avoids these extremes. In one sense it could be said all Buddhist philosophy teaches this fundamental position. In debate for instance, a standard approach is to attack an opponent and to expose them as either a nihilist or an eternalist. Recalling Tsongkhapa's criticism of 'other-emptiness' (*gzhan stong*), we see a classic example of an accusation of eternalism, the positing of an eternal absolute, which is non-Buddhist. Those who criticise 'self-emptiness' (*rang stong*), on the other hand, say it strays into nihilism. They hold that if there is nothing but emptiness the whole thing falls apart: there has to be something in order for 'being empty' to make sense.

In the first and third lines of the prayer the Third Karmapa also says, "Free from mental fabrication it is Mahāmudrā ... And everything included here, it is also called Dzogchen." Also in the prayer, he says: "May I attain the confidence that, in understanding one, I realise the meaning of all." Thus he is saying these three (Madhyamaka, Mahāmudrā and Dzogchen) all point to one realisation.[17]

The Third Karmapa also wrote a very famous commentary on Nāgārjuna's poem, or hymn, the *Dharmadhātustotra* (*In Praise of the Dharmadhātu*). This poem is an extremely interesting text, accepted by all Tibetan traditions as an authentic work of Nāgārjuna, the great teacher on emptiness. In this text, unlike in his other famous works, Nāgārjuna presents emptiness both positively and negatively; he does not present it strictly in terms of negation, as is the case with Candrakīrti and Tsongkhapa. In his commentary the Third Karmapa gives great credence to the *Dharmadhātustotra*, explaining how the Ultimate (that is, emptiness) can be approached both positively and negatively. Because of this position the Third Karmapa has often been identified as a supporter of *shentong*, the 'other-emptiness' view. Karl Brunnhölzl, in his book, *In Praise of Dharmadhātu*, argues that this is a heavy-handed interpretation and that it is unnecessary to apply simplistic labels like this.[18] He makes the point that the Third Karmapa, in his commentary on Nāgārjuna's text, deliberately presents from different points of view, and this is largely a pedagogic device, a way of teaching skilfully.[19] Brunnhölzl argues that the thrust of this commentary by the Third Karmapa is that the realisation of emptiness is about letting go of views. Getting stuck on 'is not' (which is easy to do if we take the *rangtong* view) is still to hang on to 'is not'; and if we get stuck on 'is' (which one might do if following the *shentong* view) we still hold on to 'is'. The Third Karmapa is actually taking us through both viewpoints in order to get us to let go of all views. Thus, if the therapeutic of *rangtong* goes too far, and we become attached, we should complement it with *shentong*. Realisation is letting go of views, not taking a particular view. To quote Brunnhölzl:

> The Karmapa's explanations in this commentary are often somewhat tantalizing, since he constantly plays with the terms "self empty" and "other empty", shifting their perspectives and setting up paradoxes. Being a pedagogic approach in itself, this can only be understood as cutting through any attempt to adhere to either the one or the other as something to hold on to, in order to realise what a mind free from all reference points would be like.[20]

In this context, when the Third Karmapa says, "free from extremes it is Great Madhyamaka" the use of the adjective 'Great' with 'Madhyamaka' is significant.

It indicates a broader understanding of Madhyamaka than the interpretations of Nāgārjuna by Candrakīrti and his followers (and later, after the Third Karmapa, by Tsongkhapa).[21]

The use of the term 'Great Madhyamaka' has to do with the way the Buddhist teachings are presented. In Mahāyāna Buddhist hermeneutics, where textual integration is a primary objective, Buddhist sūtras are usually taught as belonging to one of three 'turnings of the wheel of Dharma' (*dharmacakrapravartana*). Three different ways of presenting the teachings of the Buddha are acknowledged. These are understood to correspond to three different periods in which the Buddha taught and to three different approaches to the fundamental truths of Buddhism. According to Mahāyāna Buddhism the 'first turning' is common to all Buddhism; the second and third 'turnings' are specifically Mahāyāna.

The 'first turning' includes the core Buddhist teachings on suffering, causes of suffering, nirvāṇa, the path, impermanence, and so on. These teachings were systematised in what is known as Abhidharma. The 'second turning' centres on the *Prajñāpāramitā Sūtras*, where *śūnyatā* or 'emptiness' is taught, basically in terms of negation. Philosophically we associate this with the great philosopher Nāgārjuna, who revealed the depths of these texts more systematically through the philosophical system of Madhyamaka. In the 'third turning' emptiness (*śūnyatā*) is presented both positively and negatively with particular attention given to mind (*citta*) and its nature. This was elaborated in the philosophical system of Yogācara, in particular by Asaṅga (fourth century C.E.) and his half-brother Vasubandhu. The mind is understood negatively as 'empty'—it is not a thing and it has no colour, shape, form and so on—and yet it not a mere nothing since it is also characterised by what is known technically as 'luminosity' or 'clarity' (*prabhasvara*), which relates to the mind's awareness or knowing (*jñāna*) capacity. According to Yogācara, these two, emptiness and clarity, are inseparable, and a complete understanding of the significance of *śūnyatā* must include both. The teachings on Buddha-nature (*tathāgatagarbha*) also belong to the 'third turning' and here too we find the idea that Buddhahood, and reality, cannot be understood only in negative terms (for example, the end of suffering) but must also be understood in terms of the positive qualities of enlightened mind.

In the Tibetan context the question arose—and this is to put it in a very abridged fashion, as hundreds of years of debate went into this—as to which teachings were indeed higher and definitive (*nīta*), those of the second or third 'turning'. Most contentious was the status of the presentation of emptiness in the two 'turnings'. Was the presentation of *śūnyatā* in the second or the presentation in the third 'turning' higher and definitive? There was also a lot of discussion and argument over different presentations of the teachings by different philosophers operating *within* the same framework of the second or third 'turning'. To take one example, within the Madhyamaka framework of the 'second turning', is the presentation of Buddhapālita (470–550 C.E.) (later identified as Prāsaṅgika Madhyamaka), or the presentation of Bhāvaviveka (ca. 500–578 C.E.) (later identified as Svātantrika Madhyamaka), higher?

The basic conclusion of the *rangtong* 'self-emptiness' position, put by Tsongkhapa, which became the dominant position in Tibet, was essentially that the 'second turning' was the definitive teaching. The 'third turning' teachings needed to be seen and interpreted in line with this understanding. The Madhyamaka is understood in the *rangtong* position as 'self-emptiness' as taught by Candrakīrti and Tsongkhapa. However, when people such as the Third Karmapa, and later the Rimé teachers, refer to Madhyamaka, they usually understand the ultimate intention of both the second and third turnings to be identical. Their view of Madhyamaka combines both the Madhyamaka and the Yogācāra position. Actually, this had been a common view in Tibet, because when Śāntarakṣita brought Buddhism to Tibet, he had already combined Yogācāra and Madhyamaka in a subtle way. So the Third Karmapa's phrase "Free from extremes it is Great Madhyamaka," refers to both second and third turning teachings, and points to the ultimate intention of the Mahāyāna sūtras and the philosophies of Nāgārjuna and Asaṅga being the same. Furthermore, as his *Aspirations for Mahāmudrā* makes clear, the intention of Madhyamaka is no different to Mahāmudrā or Dzogchen. 'Intention' (*abhisamaya*) is a technical term in Buddhist philosophy, referring to a kind of final understanding. So that we do not mistakenly believe that Mahāmudrā, Dzogchen and Madhyamaka have different intentions, the Third Karmapa's aspirational prayer is as follows: "May I attain the confidence that, in understanding one, I realise the meaning of all."

The Third Karmapa is tremendously important, particularly from the Karma Kagyü perspective. In many ways he brought together Mahāmudrā and Dzogchen, and although it has not always been explicitly acknowledged this way, the presentation of Mahāmudrā in the Karma Kagyü tradition has taken on some of the flavour of Dzogchen. We will now turn to this subject.

Mahāmudrā and Dzogchen

The term 'Mahāmudrā' refers to both practice and realisation—it is both a practice tradition, and an ultimate realisation. Literally *Mudrā* means seal, and *Mahā* means great. The *mudrā* or seal, or the stamp, refers to emptiness; everything is stamped with emptiness, and in understanding emptiness one understands everything. That is Mahāmudrā. It is pointing to the realisation of the ultimate nature of everything. In terms of practice, the focus is towards understanding the ultimate nature of the mind; to understand that is to understand the ultimate nature of everything. Mahāmudrā is found in all the New schools, but finds a particularly full expression in the Kagyü tradition.

One way of classifying Mahāmudrā in the Kagyü tradition is to identify Sūtra Mahāmudrā, Tantra (or Mantra) Mahāmudrā and Essence Mahāmudrā.[22] This particular division is not seen in the other New schools of Sakya and Gelugpa. Indeed the Sakya tradition does not accept the idea of Essence Mahāmudrā or Sūtra Mahāmudrā at all. According to them, Mahāmudrā is tantra. The Gelug school recognises Sūtra and Tantra traditions of Mahāmudrā.[23]

The Kagyü idea of Sūtra Mahāmudrā is based on the idea of Buddha-nature and the ultimate nature of mind, coming from the Buddha-nature teachings of Buddha's third turning. It is a realisation of emptiness through the sūtras, through the practice of the perfections, and involves a progression through the paths (*mārga*) and bodhisattva levels (*bhūmi*). Unlike the usual sūtra approach there is more direct investigation of the nature of mind and our inherent Buddha-nature and in this approach the instructions are consistent with the tantra approach.[24] Approaching emptiness in this way, more conceptually and without the complex empowerments and initiations associated with the tantric path, is what characterises Sūtra Mahāmudrā. Realisation of Mahāmudrā is reached in this way.[25]

Tantra Mahāmudrā, also known as Mantra (or Secret Mantra) Mahāmudrā, is based on tantra. Practice of tantra in this context is made up of the generation stage and the completion stage. In the completion stage, when visualisation is dissolved and a very subtle mind arises, realisation of the ultimate nature of mind, which is Mahāmudrā, may occur. The sūtra approach relies on a more conceptual mind, and the tantra approach relies on a very subtle mind that can only be accessed through tantra. The Mahāmudrā of Milarepa, for example, is mainly

Tantra Mahāmudrā. Milarepa emphasised realisation of Mahāmudrā through the completion stage practice of *tummo* (*gtum mo*) or 'inner fire' (*caṇḍāli*). This is one of the 'Six Yogas' of Naropa.[26]

Essence Mahāmudrā is different again, being even more direct—a pointing at the nature of mind leading to direct realisation. This requires a qualified student for whom there have been 'pointing out' instructions (*ngo sprod*) and transmission by a realised guru. It is essential to have the lama or guru to point out the essential nature of mind.[27] To use a technical term, this approach does not involve 'fabrication'. In 'non-fabrication' (*ma bcos* or *spros bral*) we are not using ideas or concepts at all. This is in contrast to the use of ideas and concepts in the sūtra approach, where we are (at least initially) fabricating a particular state of mind. Even tantric practices, though subtle, are still based on transformation (*pariṇāma*), and consequentially involve fabrication of some kind. Essence Mahāmudrā is a non-fabricated direct recognition of the nature of mind.

Ultimately, Mahāmudrā involves progression through the 'Four Yogas' which culminate in a state of 'non-meditation' where there is no distinction between meditating and not meditating, so there is no fabrication at all.[28] Essence Mahāmudrā is the quintessence of all Mahāmudrā and is very close, if not identical, to the heart of Dzogchen. However, Mahāmudrā and Dzogchen do have their own distinct methods and approach.[29]

Turning to Dzogchen, the term itself means 'great perfection' or 'great completion', and refers to the perfection of Buddhahood. Dzogchen holds that the perfection of Buddhahood is our primordial nature or state, our fundamental nature. This primordial nature is pure from the beginning, unsullied, and applicable to every individual. The technical term is *kadag* (*ka dag*). In Tibetan *dag* means pure, and *ka* is the first letter of the alphabet, and so refers to beginning. In fact this state, or this nature, is present even in the ordinary deluded states of mind or awareness. It is always present, even in our confused condition; we do not have to get rid of our ordinary state of mind, nor do we need to fabricate a different state of mind. Non-fabrication at this level ties in with being 'spontaneously present'—*lhündrub* (*lhun grub*) in Tibetan.

This brings us to another technical term, *rigpa* (*rig pa*). The nature of mind is *rigpa*, or pure awareness—being always there, even in deluded states. What is required is recognition of this nature. We do not have to produce it or get rid of anything for it to be there, we 'simply' have to recognise that it is there. If we have this recognition, if we actually realise *rigpa*, then delusion unravels naturally by itself or 'self-liberates'.

A fourth Tibetan technical term, *rangdröl* (*rang grol*), needs explanation at this point: *rang* meaning 'self' and *dröl* meaning 'liberation'—'self-liberation'. Thoughts and confusion unravel by themselves upon the recognition of our original state. We need do nothing; with recognition, they self-liberate.[30] As the Dzogchen texts say, thoughts and delusions are like painting on water: if we paint on water it just dissolves. But to experience this self-liberation one needs to recognise the primordial state, which is pure from the beginning and has the nature of *rigpa*.[31]

We have introduced four key terms in relation to Dzogchen: primordial purity (*ka dag*), spontaneous presence (*lhun grub*), pure awareness (*rig pa*) and self-liberation (*rang grol*). Another key aspect of Dzogchen is the role of the guru in pointing out, or introducing the practitioner to a direct experience of the natural state. This is essential in Dzogchen—it is not something we can awaken to by ourselves. To quote His Holiness the Fourteenth Dalai Lama on Dzogchen:

> Throughout beginningless time, there has always been present, within us all, a pure awareness—that in-dwelling rigpa which in Atiyoga is evoked in all its nakedness, and which constitutes the practice. In other words, in Dzogchen the whole path is based on this rigpa: first you are introduced to it directly, then you put it into practice.[32]

In these teachings on Dzogchen, His Holiness is referring to the 'three words' (or 'statements') of Garab Dorje, the founder and first human teacher of Dzogchen. According to tradition, when Garab Dorje died (or passed from the presence of mortals), it is said that a casket fell to Mañjuśrīmitra, his disciple, with three statements contained within it. These three statements are an encapsulation of the essence of Garab Dorje's teaching. The first of these statements was 'recognition' (recognition of the nature of mind). The second was 'certainty', or as it is sometimes translated, 'deciding on one point'—that is the training, becoming certain about this state. The third point is 'confidence', or in other words, stability.

In these teachings His Holiness is following the commentary of Patrul Rinpoche, one of the great Rimé masters. His Holiness points out that these three statements (recognition, certainty and confidence) correspond to the view, the path, and the result. The view is the recognition, the path is the gaining of certainty and the result is being confident of the ultimate state in all situations. Dzogchen in its purest form is effortless: it does not require fabrication. Practice is remaining completely aware, continually awake in *rigpa*. The result is confidence, a 'knowing' in every situation.

We can see how, in essence, Mahāmudrā and Dzogchen can be seen as the same. Various teachers from a very early period have said this. For example, Karma Pakshi, the Second Karmapa, writing in the thirteenth century, directly stated that Dzogchen and Mahāmudrā differ in name only.[33] And, as we have seen, Tsele Natsok Rangdröl, a master of both Dzogchen and Mahāmudrā declared that the distinctive characteristic of both is that the view and meditation are not separate: the recognition of the unfabricated basic state is both the view and the meditation.

Both Dzogchen and Mahāmudrā have a strong tantric dimension. Both Mahāmudrā and Dzogchen developed in a tantric milieu and although they are in a sense 'beyond' or independent of tantra they draw freely on tantric practice and terminology. In the Kagyü tradition we have the classification, 'Tantra Mahāmudrā', which indicates that tantric practice can lead directly to the realisation of the nature of mind; in the Nyingma tradition there is a close association between Dzogchen and the inner tantras of Mahāyoga and Anuyoga, especially the latter.[34]

The more conceptual and less direct approach found in Sūtra Mahāmudrā also has its counterpart in Dzogchen. For example, Dzogchen has its own preliminary practices (not to be confused with tantric *ngöndro*, the tantric preliminaries) which include sūtra-like meditations to facilitate the realisation that the mind does not arise from anywhere, reside anywhere or go anywhere.[35] Dzogchen also includes practices to stabilise and calm the mind using techniques analogous to sūtra tranquillity *śamatha* (T. *zhi gnas*) meditation and exercises to develop understanding of the unchanging or immovable nature of mind, analogous to sūtra *vipaśyanā* (T. *lhag mthong*) practices.[36]

More generally, the attitude in both Kagyü Mahāmudrā and Dzogchen seems to be not to reject any technique or method but rather consider whether it is useful to the practitioner as a skilful means (*upāya*) to develop the capacity to enter into non-fabricated meditation (or 'non-meditation') without being limited or trapped by the method. This seems to be the intention behind certain statements found in Dzogchen and Mahāmudrā texts which appear to denigrate the methods of sūtra, the Buddhist treatises (*śāstra*) and tantra. An oft-quoted verse from Saraha, the Indian *mahāsiddha* (realised practitioner of tantra and Mahāmudrā), expresses this attitude of independence:

> It is empty of any mandala.
> Empty of devotees who make burned offerings,
> Detached from any mantras, mudras and visualization of deities.
> It cannot be realised through tantras and shastras.
> This indestructible awareness, which is our own
>   natural state of being, is perfect in its natural state.[37]

Both Mahāmudrā and Dzogchen stress realisation of the nature of mind. Gampopa states its critical importance:

> Without the insight into the nature of mind, one will not attain the awakening of Buddhahood. As for me, I value the realization of the nature of mind as better than excellent meditation.[38]

Karma Chagme (1613–1678)

Karma Chagme was a very important Karma Kagyü teacher who made the relation of Mahāmudrā and Dzogchen even more explicit than those who preceded him. Karma Chagme was born in East Tibet and became a monk early in the seventeenth century at the time of the Tenth Karmapa, Chöying Dorje (1604–1674). As we have seen, this was a period of considerable political upheaval during which the Gelugs emerged ascendant. The Karma Kagyü were embroiled in these troubles and as a result the Tenth Karmapa was forced to spend long periods in exile and the strength of the Karma Kagyü School in Central Tibet was greatly diminished.[39] During this time Karma Chagme played a very important role in propagating and protecting the teachings. For many he was inseparable from the Karmapa, especially as both are regarded as emanations of Avalokiteśvara. Karma Chagme strongly promoted Avalokiteśvara practice and was a tremendous force for stability for the Karma Kagyü tradition in this turbulent time.

    Karma Chagme undertook many retreats, one of which went for thirteen years. In this retreat he is understood to have come to full realisation of Mahāmudrā, of Dzogchen, and of various forms of Avalokiteśvara practice. As Karma Chagme was very famous and highly realised he did sometimes interrupt his retreat to teach through a hole in the wall in his retreat house. It was during this time he met and enthroned a young *tertön*, a visionary discoverer of concealed texts, called Mingyur Dorje (1645–1667).[40]

When he was seven years old Mingyur Dorje had a vision of Karma Chagme and longed to meet him although Karma Chagme was in retreat. Finally, at about eleven years of age he met Karma Chagme who became his main (or 'root') guru. Karma Chagme recognised Mingyur Dorje as a *tertön* and gave him teachings that completely opened his mind, allowing him to produce vast amounts of treasure texts. Mingyur Dorje only lived until twenty-three years of age. It is said that some *tertöns* are like an extremely bright flame, blazing with amazing intensity and beauty for a brief period, and then they are gone. Mingyur Dorje was certainly one of these. Karma Chagme, who belonged to the Karma Kagyü tradition, became the chief holder of Mingyur Dorje's *termas* which were thereafter promulgated within branches of both the Nyingma and Kagyü schools.

There is a branch of Nyingma called the Palyül tradition which had its seat at Palyül monastery (which was established in East Tibet in 1655). Karma Chagme and Mingyur Dorje were the principal gurus of the founder and first throne holder of Palyül, Kunzang Sherab (1636–1699). The main lineages that the Palyül maintain are the *termas* of Mingyur Dorje, known as *Namchö* ('Sky Dharma' or 'Sky Teachings'), and the teachings of Karma Chagme. Thus through the Palyül tradition we have a branch of the Nyingma school that practises both Mahāmudrā and the Karma Kagyü traditions that came through Karma Chagme, in addition to the *terma* traditions of Mingyur Dorje and other Nyingma traditions. Through Karma Chagme these *termas*, and additional Nyingma practices, were introduced into Karma Kagyü tradition, and we end up with a branch of the Karma Kagyü, known as Nedo Kagyü, doing essentially the same practices as a branch of the Nyingma.[41]

In a work published in English translation as *A Spacious Path to Freedom: Practical Instructions on the Union of Mahāmudrā and Atiyoga*, Karma Chagme makes it quite explicit that he is continuing what the Second Karmapa, Karma Pakshi, and the Third Karmapa, Rangjung Dorje, set out to do in bringing Mahāmudrā and Dzogchen together. Karma Chagme states that, in terms of lineage, if one belongs to the Karma Kagyü lineage, Dzogchen is included and should not be seen as separate.[42] This is principally due to the influence of the Second Karmapa

Karma Pakshi, the Third Karmapa Rangjung Dorje and Karma Chagme himself. Karma Chagme, in another of his works, *Mountain Dharma* (*ris chos*), which was taught during Karma Chagme's thirteen-year retreat, includes instructions for the practice of both Mahāmudrā and Dzogchen.[43] Karma Chagme also expressed the quintessential points of Mahāmudrā and Dzogchen in a short work published in English translation as *The Quintessence of the Union of Mahamudra and Dzokchen*[44] and as *The Union of Mahamudra and Dzogchen*.[45]

Jigme Lingpa (1729-1798) and the Heritage of Longchenpa (1308-1364)

Jigme Lingpa (1729–1798) belonged to the Nyingma tradition. Many say he is the direct inspiration for the Rimé movement although he never used that term and was primarily focused on preserving and propagating Nyingma teachings and practices at a time they were under pressure in Central Tibet where he lived. Nonetheless he had a major impact in East Tibet and on the development of the Rimé movement.

Jigme Lingpa came from a poor background, and was an ordinary monk, not a recognised incarnation. He gave up his monastic robes and adopted the lifestyle of a simple yogi after his first three-year retreat which he began in 1756 at the age of twenty-seven.[46] Jigme Lingpa is celebrated as the discoverer and propagator of the *Longchen Nyingthig* Dzogchen teachings and practices. These teachings became widely disseminated in East Tibet and were central to the practice of several of the key figures associated with the Rimé movement. Jamyang Khyentse Wangpo, even though he belonged to the Sakya tradition, is regarded as a reincarnation of Jigme Lingpa. In turn, Jamyang Khyentse Wangpo is understood to have many reincarnations through to the present day who are regarded as emanations of Jigme Lingpa's mind, speech and activity. These reincarnations are key lineage holders of the *Longchen Nyingthig*, and great non-sectarian teachers.

Jigme Lingpa revived and developed the legacy of the great Nyingmas who lived during the time of Longchenpa (1308-1364) and the Third Karmapa. Longchenpa had brought together the Nyingma Dzogchen teachings and presented them in harmonious relation to sūtra and tantra teachings, including those belonging to the traditions of the New schools. Longchenpa's approach brings to mind the way Gampopa unified sūtra and tantra teachings in the Kagyü traditions and integrated elements of Milarepa's oral instructions and Mahāmudrā teachings with them. Longchenpa was bringing together not only the old orally transmitted traditions of the Nyingma, the *kama* (*bka' ma*) traditions from India, but also the concealed treasure traditions, the *terma* (*gter ma*) traditions, that are understood to go back to Padmasambhava and his close disciples.

According to Nyingma understanding, Padmasambhava perceived during his lifetime that the time was not right for the transmission of the bulk of these teachings, and so concealed them for later discovery and dissemination. This is similar to the understanding in the Mahāyāna tradition in India according to which the *Prajñāpāramitā Sūtras* were concealed during the time of the Buddha for later dissemination after the basic teachings of Buddhism were established. Despite disagreement about the authenticity of these Mahāyāna scriptures and others that started appearing around 100 B.C.E., and their non-acceptance by non-Mahayanists, by 400 C.E. the majority of Buddhists in India had accepted them as authentic. Analogously, in Tibet from the eleventh and twelfth centuries onwards texts claiming to date from the Imperial period and attributed mainly to Padmasambhava were becoming prominent. These were said to have been concealed by Padmasambhava or his Tibetan consort Yeshe Tsogyal either physically or as teachings 'concealed' in the mindstreams of Padmasambhava's twenty-five closest disciples.[47] It is believed by the Nyingmas, and others who accept the *terma* tradition, that these treasures were concealed for later recovery either physically or from the mindstreams of Padmasambhava's disciples who reincarnate and act as treasure revealers (*gter ston*) at the appropriate time. The *termas* are understood to contain teachings particularly relevant for the time of their discovery or uncovering. Not surprisingly, the status of the *termas* has been controversial in Tibet, as has been the issue of how to identify authentic *termas* and *tertöns*. Along with all the old tantras, all *termas* were excluded from the Tibetan canon compiled by Butön in the fourteenth century.

It was during the fourteenth century that Longchenpa had brought together the Nyingma teachings belonging to the 'long' lineage of oral transmission (*bka' ma*) going back to India and the teachings belonging to the 'short' lineage of treasure teachings (*gter ma*). The essence of Dzogchen, the culmination or pinnacle of Dzogchen, is known as *Nyingthig* (*snying thig*), which means 'heart essence' or 'seminal heart'. At the time of Longchenpa, *Nyingthig* teachings existed in two main streams or collections which Longchenpa brought together and integrated.⁴⁸ He augmented this with material that he collected and some of his own writings. All these collections were then transmitted as one great cycle of teachings known as the *Nyingthig Yabzhi*.⁴⁹

It was Longchenpa who presented a coherent Nyingma view of the entire Buddhist path in nine vehicles (*yāna*) which, as we have seen, culminate in Dzogchen or Atiyoga (the ninth *yāna*).⁵⁰ He understood Dzogchen to be not only the culmination of Nyingma traditions but of all the Buddhist traditions of India and Tibet and, accordingly, he presented Dzogchen in relation to Indian teaching and philosophy, and in the context of both the Old and the New traditions of Tibet. The writings in which Longchenpa did this formed part of his seven treatises, which became known as the *Seven Treasuries* (*mdzod bdun*).

Jigme Lingpa revived the *Nyingthig* teachings that had waned in the centuries following Longchenpa and brought the various Nyingma teachings, which had become fragmented, into a renewed synthesis. In retreat he had a series of visions of Padmasambhava and Longchenpa, and from this a *terma* teaching emerged, not as a physical object (*sa gter*), but as a mind *terma* (*dgongs gter*).⁵¹ Jigme Lingpa did not regard this as his own creation; rather, he understood the origin of his vision to be Padmasambhava and Longchenpa. These teachings are known as the *Longchen Nyingthig*, the *Heart Essence* (*snying thig*) *of the Great Expanse* (*klong chen*). *Longchen* in the title refers not only to the great expanse of reality, the *dharmadhātu*, but also to Longchenpa, the source of the vision. Jigme Lingpa added extensive writings (which he authored himself) to the *terma* and these formed a comprehensive system of practice which acquired similar status to the *terma* itself.

Jigme Lingpa was not a particularly well-known practitioner, and in fact kept these *terma* teachings secret for seven years before he began teaching them in 1764.⁵² They soon became enormously popular, especially in Kham where the Rimé movement originated. The *Longchen Nyingthig* became so widely practised, and was such a complete system in itself, that it became the most practised *Nyingthig* teaching in the Nyingma tradition.⁵³

Jigme Lingpa also introduced certain aspects of Mahāmudrā to the *Longchen Nyingthig*. Notably, he incorporated the 'Four Yogas' belonging to Mahāmudrā into Dzogchen to clarify the stages through which realisation is developed from the initial recognition of the nature of mind up until full confidence in the ultimate state in all situations.⁵⁴ According to Sam van Schaik, Jigme Lingpa's treatment of errors and ways of going astray in meditation also seem to be drawn from

Mahāmudrā tradition, while his discussion of these topics includes terminology commonly found in Mahāmudrā texts, for example, 'ordinary mind' (*tha mal gyi shes pa*) and 'non-distraction' (*yengs med*).[55]

Shabkar Tsogdruk Rangdröl (1781–1851)

Another less direct, but nonetheless important figure, is Shabkar Tsogdruk Rangdröl (1781–1851), who came from Amdo, in northern East Tibet. Although Amdo is not in Central Tibet, the stronghold of the Gelugs, it is nonetheless a very strong Gelug area and was the birthplace of Tsongkhapa. The Gelugs of Amdo were less under the control of the three great Lhasa region monasteries (Ganden, Sera, Drepung) and as a result were more open to other traditions. Shabkar was born into a family of Nyingma yogic practitioners in the Rekong region of Amdo. His autobiography, which is mainly about his travels and teachers, has been translated by Matthieu Ricard and others.[56] Shabkar was drawn to the contemplative and wandering hermit life. Like his predecessor, the Kagyü yogi Milarepa, Shabkar taught mainly through songs. Partly in keeping with his nature, and partly due to the custom in his area, he practised fully in all traditions, including Gelug. His main teacher was a Nyingma who taught at an ex-Gelug monastery that had retained strong Gelug traditions after converting to Nyingma. This guru put Shabkar into his first three-year retreat, which was entirely focused on Tsongkhapa's monumental work on the bodhisattva path, the *Graded Path to Enlightenment* (*lam rim chen mo*). Only after that was Shabkar progressively introduced to Dzogchen.

The three principal figures for Shabkar were Atiśa, who founded the Kadam tradition, Tsongkhapa and Padmasambhava. For Shabkar these three were inseparable. Shabkar experienced visions of Atiśa and Tsongkhapa before he had visionary experience of Padmasambhava. According to his autobiography, he asked Padmasambhava why he had not appeared before, and Padmasambhava said he had, but that he had appeared as Tsongkhapa the last time he had seen him.[57] Shabkar travelled around Tibet as a simple kind of figure, freely teaching all manner of people. There is quite a strong similarity between Shabkar and Patrul Rinpoche, a key figure in the Rimé movement. Both placed a lot of emphasis on altruism and the generation of *bodhicitta*. They also emphasised Avalokiteśvara and the practice of his mantra *oṃ maṇi padme huṃ*. Patrul Rinpoche set off to

Amdo to see Shabkar because he regarded him as the foremost teacher in Tibet of *bodhicitta*, but on the way he heard Shabkar had died. He is reported as saying he had not set out to receive any teachings from Shabkar, he had just wanted to see his face—but unfortunately he did not.[58]

Fourth Panchen Lama, Lobsang Chökyi Gyaltsen (1570–1662) and Khöntönpa (1561–1637)

Two important figures who must be mentioned in regard to the Gelug/Nyingma meeting point in Central Tibet, are the Fourth Panchen Lama, Lobsang Chökyi Gyaltsen (1570–1662), and his younger contemporary Khöntön Peljor Lhündrub (Khöntönpa) (1561–1637). Lobsang Chökyi Gyaltsen was the first of the Panchen Lamas to be recognised as such during his lifetime. The Fourth Panchen Lama was the principal teacher of two Dalai Lamas—the Fourth and Fifth. An essay by E. Gene Smith (who first brought the Rimé movement to Western scholarly attention) contained in the book *Among Tibetan Texts*, discusses the autobiography of the Fourth Panchen Lama and describes him as "the greatest Dge lugs pa scholar of his generation."[59] His Holiness the Fourteenth Dalai Lama frequently teaches from texts of the Fourth Panchen Lama and praises his non-partisan approach. For example, when His Holiness taught from the text *The Gelug/Kagyü Tradition of Mahamudra* written by the Fourth Panchen Lama, he mentioned that various people have wanted to take 'Kagyü' out of the title, but since it was there for a reason it should not be removed.[60] It is also significant that His Holiness the Fourteenth Dalai Lama's published teaching on death and dying is based on the Fourth Panchen Lama's interpretation of the Nyingma *terma* text, the *Bardo Thödröl*, the so-called *Tibetan Book of the Dead*.[61]

The Fourth Panchen Lama was well known for his completely non-sectarian approach and his writings on the unity of all the Tibetan traditions. In the following passage he gives a clear idea of the Tibetan practice traditions (beginning in the first two lines with the names of five Mahāmudrā traditions) as coalescing in a 'single intention':

> Developing Co-emergence, Ga'u ma,
> Fivefold, Single Taste, Four Letters,
> Pacification, Severance, Great Perfection,

Instructions on the Middle View, and others:
There are many names given for each.
And yet if the yogin who is meditatively experienced
and learned in the scriptures of ultimate meaning analyzes [them],
[all these teachings] coalesce in a single intention.[62]

As mentioned above, the Fourth and Fifth Dalai Lamas were both taught by the Fourth Panchen lama. Another important teacher of the Fifth Dalai Lama was Khöntönpa known in his biographies as 'Gsar rnying ris med'.[63] This means: 'one without bias (*ris med*) to the New (*gsar*) and Old (*rnying*) [schools]'. He was born into the Khön clan (which includes the throne holders of the Sakya tradition) and was recognised as a reincarnation of a Nyingma scholar-saint. Khöntönpa became the abbot of Je college of Sera monastery, one of the three great Gelug monasteries in the Lhasa area. He thus had close connections with Sakya, Nyingma and Gelug schools. He also had a profound knowledge of Kagyü teachings. In 2009, His Holiness the Fourteenth Dalai Lama taught on the nature of mind using as his basis Khöntönpa's 1609 work *The Wish-Fulfilling Jewel of the Oral Tradition*.[64] In this work, according to José Ignacio Cabezón, Khöntönpa attempts a reconciliation of Madhyamaka, Mahāmudrā and Dzogchen, taking meditation on the nature of mind as a bridge between these three approaches. Cabezón says: "Certainly no parallel work exists, to my knowledge, in the Gelug school."[65]

It is notable that the Fourth Panchen Lama and Khöntönpa were the principal teachers of the Fifth Dalai Lama. The Fifth Dalai Lama is a major inspiration for His Holiness the Fourteenth Dalai Lama in the present day. The three most influential Dalai Lamas: the Fifth, Thirteenth, and Fourteenth, are each characterised by this unbiased (*ris med*) approach of the Fifth Dalai Lama's principal teachers.

As we consider the various forerunners of the Rimé movement, all of whom embraced a non-sectarian approach, we must keep in mind that at this stage we are not describing an established tradition as explicit as the Rimé movement later was, but rather a range of like-minded individuals acting toward similar ends. Their approach accords with Buddhist teachings on skilful means which recognise that different teachings are suitable for different people and that a single person may require different teachings and methods at various stages of their spiritual journey.

The Rimé movement itself arose as a prominent movement in the nineteenth century at a point in history where sectarian rivalry had become endemic. It had reached a stage that even if one personally did not feel strongly aligned, it was still very much expected that you study exclusively in your own tradition. Within the monasteries the study itself was often quite a formulaic kind of learning. What was being passed off as philosophy was in many cases a rote learning of particular texts, and then engaging in mock debates, which were a kind of ritualised performance of particular points of view. In the various schools, people were often heavily discouraged from taking teachings from other traditions. As we shall see, it was in Kham in East Tibet that this narrow approach was challenged.

Section 3
East Tibet and the Rimé Movement

WE HAVE CONSIDERED the context and background to the Rimé movement in relation to the major schools of Tibetan Buddhism. We have also discussed some antecedents to the Rimé approach going back to the time of the Buddha and have looked at figures in Tibet who may be regarded as forerunners of the movement because of their influence on key figures in the movement or because of their explicitly non-sectarian approach. It now remains to look more closely at the situation in East Tibet, the immediate context of the Rimé movement, and at the main figures involved in the Rimé movement. We will then consider the legacy of the movement through to the present day.

East Tibetan Context

The situation in East Tibet needs to be understood in the broader context of Tibetan culture and, more specifically, in terms of relations between East Tibet and Central Tibet. It is also important to consider some unique local factors. The Tibetan cultural world extends beyond the five areas that are traditionally considered to comprise Tibet (*bod*), namely Ü and Tsang (which comprise Central Tibet), Ngari (West Tibet), and Kham and Amdo (East Tibet). It also embraces Mustang and other parts of present day Nepal, Sikkim, Ladakh and Zanskar in present day India, and the independent kingdom of Bhutan. This explains why Jamgön Kongtrul, in contrast to current usage, refers not so much to 'Tibetan Buddhism' as to the Buddhism of 'the Himalayan region' (*gangs chen rdzong*).[1]

Regional identity has always been important to peoples of the Tibetan cultural and religious world. Thus, although the people of Kham and Amdo might identify themselves generally as 'people of Tibet' (*bod pa*) or 'people of Greater

Tibet' (*bod chen pa*) this did not entail for them recognition of the jurisdiction of the Central Tibetan government. More important to them was their identity as Khampas ('people of Kham') or Amdowas ('people of Amdo').

East Tibet, which is traditionally known as Dokham (*mdo khams*) (a composite of Amdo and Kham), was only ever effectively under centralised control during the late Imperial period in the late eighth and early ninth centuries C.E. For much of Tibetan history East Tibet has been independent or merely under nominal control of the Central Tibet government. Even after the Fifth Dalai Lama unified Tibet in the seventeenth century under the Lhasa-based government (known as the Ganden Phodrang), East Tibet only came under temporary Central Tibetan control and remained largely autonomous thereafter. In the eighteenth century, after the Manchu Chinese intervention in Tibetan affairs, the eastern Tibetan kingdoms, states and tribes became officially removed from direct control of Lhasa and, in theory, owed direct feudal allegiance to Manchu China. However the degree of Chinese control was probably very limited, especially with the decline of the Manchu empire (the Qing dynasty) in the nineteenth century.[2] Within Kham in East Tibet a variety of political formations prevailed comprising some twenty-six 'states'. These were made up of kingdoms, chiefdoms and tribal lands. The largest of these states was the Kingdom of Derge (*sde dge*) which was ruled by hereditary kings.

The hereditary lineage of Derge rulers stretched back to the seventh century. Derge became the capital of the kingdom when the renowned 'iron bridge builder', yogi and eclectic teacher, Thangtong Gyalpo (1361–1485?), was invited to build a monastery in the region in the fifteenth century.[3] The kingdom expanded during the eighteenth century under the reign of Tenpa Tsering, who conquered territories to the north.

The rise in power of Derge and its emergence as a major religious and cultural centre followed the turmoil in Central Tibet which saw the ascendancy of the Dalai Lamas and the Gelug school in the seventeenth century. The upheavals in Central Tibet resulted in the suppression of the Kagyü school (which had been the major rivals to the Gelug School in the political sphere) and lengthy exile of the Tenth Karmapa (who spent much of his time in exile in south-east Tibet). As we have seen, restrictions were placed on printing works of the Jonang school. Restrictions were also placed on the writings of the founders of the Sakya tradition and important Sakya scholars such as Śākya Chokden. This resulted in a weakening of the Sakya scholarly tradition.[4] This suppression and the new conservative 'orthodoxy' also had unfortunate consequences in the Gelug school where the rote learning of Tibetan commentaries and monastic textbooks (*yig cha*) began to replace the study of Sanskrit and even the study of the original texts in Tibetan translation. In the new configuration of religious and political power, the Nyingma school perceived the need to create a monastic base to protect their position.[5] These changes in Central Tibet saw the foundation in East Tibet of new non-Gelug monastic centres, and revitalisation of some old ones, away from the centre of Gelug power.

By the early eighteenth century, four of the six main Nyingma 'mother monasteries' were located in the Kingdom of Derge.[6] Palpung Kagyü monastery, the seat of the Situ Rinpoches (and later also the home monastery of Jamgön Kongtrul), was founded in Derge in 1727. With the decline of Karma Kagyü power in Central Tibet, Palpung became the most important centre of Kagyü learning and culture with the Tai Situ lineage becoming the second most powerful lineage in the Kagyü tradition after the Karmapas.[7]

The patronage of the kings and queens of Derge helped facilitate a cultural renaissance in East Tibet which began in the eighteenth century and extended through the nineteenth century. A significant impetus was the founding of a major printery in Derge at the Gönchen Sakya monastery where, with the patronage of the rulers, an edition of the Tibetan Buddhist canon which is widely regarded as the most reliable in Tibet was produced in the eighteenth century. The Rimé movement may be understood as part of, or perhaps the culmination of, this renaissance. A major shift in the religious and cultural geography of Tibet had taken place. Central Tibet could no longer assume unquestioned ascendancy in the religious and cultural sphere. As Sam van Schaik puts it: "Unnoticed by the powers that be, the cultural vitality of Tibet had shifted eastwards to Kham, a domain of loosely connected kingdoms which had never been convincingly annexed to any empire."[8]

The Derge rulers had converted to Sakya in the thirteenth century and maintained that affiliation. Nevertheless, they were known for their religious tolerance and they patronised and practised within the various religious traditions and schools, both Buddhist and Bon. The Derge king Tsewang Dorje Rigdzin (1786–1847) wrote early in the nineteenth century in his *Royal Genealogy of Sde dge*: "All of the kings, with their compassion and skilful means, were certain that each and every school without distinction—including the Sakya, Gelug, Kagyu, Nyingma and Bon—were genuine sources of benefit and happiness. And thus, regarding them without partiality, they trained in them all with devotion."[9]

An example of religious eclecticism which was significant for the key figures of the Rimé movement can be seen in the royal patronage of the Nyingma yogi Jigme Lingpa and the support given to the propagation of his *terma*, the *Longchen Nyingthig* (discussed in Section 2). Jigme Lingpa lived and wrote in Central Tibet and was perhaps aware of the pressure on the Nyingma traditions there.[10] As we have seen, the *Longchen Nyingthig* is a mind treasure (*dgongs gter*) received in a series of visions of the great Nyingma master Longchenpa, Padmasambhava and others. To this, Jigme Lingpa added over a period of years his own commentaries, guru yogas, aspirational prayers and the like, and these were probably completed by the 1780s.[11] The King and Queen of Derge, who had been in correspondence with Jigme Lingpa for several years, travelled to Central Tibet and received teachings directly from him. Although the King died shortly thereafter, the Queen, Tsewang Lhamo, and her son, Tsewang Dorje Rigdzin, remained the principal patrons of Jigme Lingpa throughout the rest of his life.[12] The *Longchen Nyingthig* was published in Derge as part of Jigme Lingpa's collected works shortly after his death around 1800. The printing was supervised by Jigme Lingpa's close disciple, the first Dödrupchen Rinpoche (Jigme Trinle Özer), and the Queen of Derge, and edited by Getse Tulku of Kathok Nyingma monastery. This became the normative edition of Jigme Lingpa's collected works.[13] The *Longchen Nyingthig* was very widely practised, especially in Kham.

The context within which these publications were completed was a difficult one. The Queen's favouritism towards the Nyingmas had led to resentment and she fell out of favour with the dominant Sakyas.[14] The prince, Tsewang Dorje Rigdzin, who had been educated by the Sakyas, became king in 1804. He reasserted the Derge tradition of tolerance and non-sectarianism. In 1826, after he had ensured the royal succession, the King renounced the throne and became a Sakya monk. According to Smith, Tsewang Dorje Rigdzin's *Royal Genealogy of Sde dge* (see above quote) was "in many ways, the first document of the non-sectarian movement."[15]

Three important incarnations of Jigme Lingpa were enthroned in Derge. An immediate incarnation (*sprul sku*), Do Khyentse Yeshe Dorje (1800–1866), was born in East Tibet and was enthroned as a *tulku* of Jigme Lingpa in the presence of the royal household and dignitaries of Kathok, Shechen and Dzogchen monasteries. The procession was led by the head of the Sakya school.[16] Another recognised incarnation of Jigme Lingpa was Patrul Rinpoche (1808–1887), who lived in Derge and who became a key Rimé teacher. He received the *Longchen Nyingthig* from another of Jigme Lingpa's close disciples, Jigme Gyalwai Nyugu. Later, Jamyang Khyentse Wangpo (1820–1892), who came from a wealthy Derge family, was recognised as another incarnation of Jigme Lingpa.[17]

The production for the first time of a xylographic printed edition of the *Nyingma'i Gyübum*, the collection of Nyingma tantras which had been excluded from the Tibetan canon, was directly inspired by Jigme Lingpa. Getse Tulku (the editor of Jigme Lingpa's collected works) utilised the handwritten edition of Jigme Lingpa which he had studied with him in Central Tibet.[18] Edited by Getse Tulku, it was printed under the auspices of the Queen of Derge.[19] Prior to this the *Nyingma'i Gyübum* had only been available in handwritten form.

During the eighteenth and nineteenth centuries the Tai Situ Rinpoches played a significant part in the cultural revival of East Tibet. As noted above, the lineage became the second most important incarnation lineage in the Karma Kagyü school and its seat of Palpung became a very powerful monastery in East Tibet. The Eighth Situ Rinpoche, Panchen Situ Chökyi Jungne (1700–1774), was at the centre of the revival and had a major impact on Kham intellectual life for almost fifty years. He was accorded the title 'Panchen', 'great scholar' (S. *mahāpaṇḍita*) because of his prodigious learning. The Eighth Situ Rinpoche was born at a time that produced a number of outstanding thinkers in East Tibet, and although the degree of collaboration was not as great between them as later occurred between Jamyang Khyentse, Jamgön Kongtrul and others of their circle, there was considerable interchange between these lamas who belonged to the Kagyü, Sakya and Nyingma schools.[20] According to E. Gene Smith, it was these thinkers who gave birth to the cultural renaissance which found full flower with the Rimé movement in the nineteenth century.[21]

The Eighth Situ Rinpoche and his collaborators in the Nyingma monasteries of Derge were instrumental in promoting tremendous growth in monasticism and intellectual studies in the Kagyü and Nyingma schools but managed to do so without creating rigid boundaries between the celibate monastic *saṅgha* ('religious community') and the non-monastic *saṅgha* of yogis and lay tantric practitioners.[22] This was to remain a characteristic of religious life in Kham throughout the nineteenth century and even through to the present day. According to Antonio Terrone, "Non-celibate religious personalities, representing mainly the rNying ma and bKa' brgyud schools, traditionally more contemplation-oriented, were valued as much as the officially ordained (*rab tu 'byung ba*), and therefore monastically-oriented, abbots and scholars. Despite the apparently fixed demarcation between ordained and non-celibate institutions, religious life in Kham was in fact never really marked in this way."[23]

The Eighth Situ Rinpoche advocated Sanskritic studies and a return to the study of the original Indian texts. As Smith notes, in Tibet, long before the eighteenth century, rote memorisation of Tibetan commentaries had replaced Sanskritic studies and use of original sources.[24] In 1723 Situ had visited Kathmandu and had come in contact with Buddhists there who maintained Sanskritic learning, as well as Indic artistic traditions which interested him greatly. After his return to Kham his patron, the King of Derge, built him Palpung monastery which was henceforth the seat of the Situ Rinpoches. In the following years Situ Rinpoche was involved in the massive task of editing and correcting the sheets for the printing of the Derge edition of the canonical scriptures, the Kanjur (*bka 'gyur*) which was printed in 1733, and in revising and re-examining the existing translations of the Sanskrit grammatical, lexicographic, and poetic treatises.[25]

On his way to Nepal, Situ Rinpoche had visited Jonang monastery and also the former seat of Tāranātha at a time when printing of Jonang works was still banned and dissemination of Jonang thinking was suppressed. He noted that the tradition had not been fully eradicated there. Situ's visit to Jonang made a great impression on him and he later co-operated with his friend the Nyingma master Kathok Tsewang Norbu (1698–1755) in the revival of Jonang *shentong* 'other-emptiness' teachings in East Tibet. Tsewang Norbu had succeeded in 1728 in receiving the full transmission of Jonang teachings at Jonang despite the ban that was in place at the time. He transmitted the teachings to Situ Rinpoche when the two of them spent time together in Nepal in 1748.[26] According to Cyrus Stearns, an authority on Dölpopa and Shentong Madhyamaka: "In the end it would be Situ, more than anyone, who would create the environment for the widespread acceptance of the *shentong* teachings in Tibet during the next century."[27] It was also Situ Rinpoche who blended *shentong* and Mahāmudrā and spread them throughout the Karma Kagyü tradition in Kham.[28]

Upheaval in Nineteenth Century Kham

Feuds with neighbours, matrimonial and sibling rivalry, plunder, brigandry, family and local alliances and so on were part of the complex political scene in East

Tibet, as small political units attempted to enhance their power and wealth. A particularly protracted and disturbing series of troubles in which important monasteries such as Palpung (Jamgön Kongtrul's home monastery) became embroiled took place in Kham between 1837 and 1865. At the centre of the conflict was a chieftain, Gönpo Namgyal (d. 1865), from the Nyarong district of Kham who, following a series of raids, had taken control of a large part of eastern Kham, and by 1860 was threatening the kingdom of Derge. Gönpo Namgyal was widely disliked in East Tibet because of his cruelty and by the 1860s was seen as a threat by both the Central Tibetan government and the Chinese authorities in Sichuan. In 1862 Gönpo Namgyal entered Derge and the Queen and Prince, for whom Kongtrul had been performing rituals, prepared to flee, along with many lamas.[29]

In 1863 the Central Tibetan government (with some support from Khampa and Chinese forces) despatched an army to intervene in Kham. The Lhasa government saw this as an opportunity to extend its influence in East Tibet and, unfortunately for the monasteries, the Gelug hierarchy of the time seized this opportunity to settle old scores with non-Gelugs, and proceeded to close down or convert some of the monasteries. Included in their sights was the monastery of Palpung, Situ Rinpoche's very powerful Karma Kagyü monastery, which harboured some who were hostile to the Lhasa-based regime. Enmity and resentment towards the Central Tibetan government was intensified by the misconduct of the Lhasa-based army. With the defeat and death of Gönpo Namgyal in 1865, Central Tibet claimed Derge, Nyarong and surrounding states as part of their jurisdiction.[30]

Fortunately, Jamgön Kongtrul, as well as being a writer, meditator, and teacher, was also a doctor, and was called in as a physician and ritual specialist for someone who had become very sick in the forces fighting alongside the Lhasa army.[31] He made such an impression that he became a guru to the army. The Lhasa army leadership asked him to perform rituals and do divinations to determine where the Nyarong army was going to attack and how the battles were going to go. According to Jamgön Kongtrul's autobiography, having no expertise in this area, he just said whatever came to mind.[32] His divinations proved to be correct though, and his reputation grew, and subsequently he was in a position to save Palpung monastery and play a part in the settlement of the conflict.[33] Jamyang Khyentse, who came from an influential Derge family and who now had a seat on the council of Derge, also played a part in ensuring the restoration of damaged monasteries in Kham.[34]

This long period of political upheaval reveals some of the tensions between Central and East Tibet and forms part of the context within which the Rimé movement should be understood.

Bon in East Tibet

The cultural and religious environment in East Tibet lent itself to close relations and interaction between Bon and Buddhist traditions. As we have seen, East Tibet, situated between Central Tibet and Manchu China, was effectively under the control of neither. This meant that the more conservative monastic institutions of Central Tibet, both Buddhist and Bon, had less control of East Tibetan religious life and institutions. Political power in East Tibet was decentralised through the twenty-six states and was expressed in a variety of political formations. The region was ethnically diverse and included both nomadic and pastoral populations, with family and clan relations having greater importance than in Central Tibet. Bonpos (adherents of Bon) made up a much greater proportion of the population in East Tibet and did not suffer the same minority status as they did in Central Tibet. As a consequence, there were many more possibilities for patronage for Bonpos in East Tibet.[35] Patronage not only came from Bonpo families but also from the ruling families of East Tibet.[36]

There has, until recently, been considerable confusion about the Bon religious tradition. Most ideas about it have come through Buddhist polemical works which were intent on representing Bon as the pre-Buddhist religion of sacrifice and bloody rituals (aimed at the propitiation of gods and demons) which was banned by Buddhist kings in the eighth century. It is claimed in these same works that Bon was transformed by Buddhism into a clerical and monastic tradition (*bsgyur bon*) with a great deal in common with Buddhism. As this representation is inadequate a few words of clarification are necessary.

Firstly, it is essential to distinguish Bon from what R. A. Stein calls the 'nameless religion', that is to say, the popular Tibetan concern with local divinities (especially of mountains and lakes), the concern with spirits and invisible forces that impact on daily life (and one's destiny after death) and the attempt to turn those forces to human benefit.[37] As Matthew Kapstein notes, these concerns and beliefs are common to all Tibetans, both Buddhist and Bon.[38]

What the Bonpos call 'eternal Bon' (*g.yung drung bon*) (which is to be distinguished from local pre-Buddhist ritual practices to avert evil) has its origins in teachings from the ancient past that were introduced into western Tibet when it was an independent kingdom known as Zhang-zhung.[39] This was during the period before Buddhism was officially introduced to Tibet and before western Tibet became part of the Tibetan empire in the seventh century C.E. The Bonpos claim that Bon was transmitted into India, China, and, from western Tibet, throughout the Tibetan plateau. Bonpos say that Bon was persecuted when Buddhism became the religion of the empire during the reign of Trisong Detsen (eighth century) and it became essential at that time to conceal Bon texts and ritual objects for retrieval later when times were better for the tradition. The concealed items or 'treasures' (*gter ma*) were later recovered by 'treasure revealers' (*gter ston*).[40]

'Eternal Bon' or Yungdrung Bon is, like Buddhism, essentially concerned with the immutable (or unconditioned) absolute and its realisation (equivalent to nirvāṇa). It has a nine vehicle scheme (which is different to that of the Nyingmas) that lays out a hierarchy of ways of realising the ultimate. The nine vehicles of Bon culminate in Dzogchen as do the nine vehicles of the Nyingma.[41] The pre-Buddhist Tibetan word *yungdrung* (*g.yung drung*) which means 'eternal' or 'immutable' also refers to the swastika, an important symbol in Bon (and Buddhism). The swastika has a similar significance in Bon to the vajra or dorje (*rdo rje*) in tantric Buddhism. Both represent the immutable principle of reality which is also present in the world of relative reality.[42]

Clearly there is a great deal in common between the Nyingma and Bon traditions. Tibetan Buddhists are inclined to say that much of Bon was taken from Buddhism and that it was transformed into a tradition no different in essentials to Buddhism. Bonpos see the main influence flowing the opposite direction, from Bon to Buddhism. They say this happened not only in Tibet but elsewhere in an earlier period, when Bon influenced other religions including Indian and Chinese Buddhism.

The modern scholarly study of Bon is in its infancy but it is clear that Bon was already a sophisticated tradition in Tibet before the revival of Buddhism in Tibet associated with the 'second dissemination' of Buddhism and the introduction of the 'new' (*gsar ma*) lineages and translations in the eleventh century. Modern scholarship supports the idea of a transmission of Bonpo teachings, originally in a non-Tibetan language (possibly Zhang-zhung language), from western Tibet to central Tibet, which took place before the time of King Trisong Detson (ruled

754–797).⁴³ A written text reflecting this transmission is the *Zhang zhung snyan rgyud*, the *Oral transmission from Zhang-zhung*. Clearly there was considerable mutual influence between Buddhism and Bon especially in relation to the *terma* traditions.⁴⁴

In Central Tibet 'eternal Bon' developed a strong monastic and scholarly tradition similar to the Gelug tradition. This was headquartered in southern Central Tibet at Menri monastery which was established in 1405.⁴⁵ This came to represent a kind of 'orthodox' Bon. Adherents of this 'orthodox' Bon looked with some suspicion on what they called 'new Bon' (*bon gsar*) which flourished outside Central Tibet, especially in East Tibet.⁴⁶ The so-called 'new Bon', was much less monastic in its orientation and was more closely associated with the treasure (*gter ma*) traditions, especially more recent ones. It was also much more inclined to interact with Buddhist traditions. Critics of 'new Bon' claimed that the new Bon *termas* went too far in incorporating Buddhist figures and Buddhist styles of ritual practice. However, adherents of 'new Bon' did not see it as distinct from, or in any way antithetical to, 'eternal Bon'.⁴⁷

It was not uncommon in nineteenth century East Tibet for Bonpos to study with Buddhist teachers and vice versa. Jamgön Kongtrul had Bon teachers and students, as did Jamyang Khyentse and Chokgyur Lingpa. The culture and practice associated with the discovery of *termas* in the two traditions is very similar, and some nineteenth century Bonpo *tertöns* had close ties with Buddhists.⁴⁸ At a much earlier period there were certain *tertöns* who were simultaneously Bonpo and Nyingma.⁴⁹ Jamgön Kongtrul included five Bon *termas* in his *Treasury of Precious Termas*, although this did cause some controversy.⁵⁰ In the catalogue to this *Treasury* he wrote that some of the well-known Buddhist treasure revealers "discovered Bon treasures, received Bon oral lineages and were generally of great benefit to the Bon tradition." He added that "some Bon treasures seem to be united with [i.e., intended for simultaneous use as] Buddhist treasures."⁵¹

Acceptance of Dzogchen as the pinnacle of all spiritual paths provided a further avenue for exchange between Bonpos and Buddhist followers of Dzogchen. Additional common ground between Buddhist and Bon traditions was found in the person of Padmasambhava whose name in Tibetan is Pemajungne ('born from a lotus'). To the consternation of some of their more conservative counterparts in Central Tibet, some Bonpos in East Tibet, followers of 'new Bon', identified an ambiguous figure in their own tradition named Pemajungne with the Buddhist Pemajungne, that is to say, with Padmasambhava. This identification was accepted by Jamyang Khyentse, Jamgön Kongtrul and others. Indeed, a biography of Padmasambhava authored by Jamyang Khyentse, but written from a Bon perspective, was included in the collection of *termas* which Jamgön Kongtrul assembled and edited.[52]

At a deeper level, an acceptance of a common rootedness in eternal truths and an acceptance of many commonalities between Buddhism and Bon is illustrated by the Bonpo belief that one of their own 'Nine Victorious Ones', or enlightened teachers, appeared as Śākyamuni Buddha in order to subjugate Indians by means of Dharma.[53] Jamgön Kongtrul, from the Buddhist side, expresses the belief that the Buddhas (whose compassion is immeasurable and impartial) manifest to aid beings who follow diverse traditions. He writes: "In fact, in the three worlds, the victors' enlightened activity is present in even the most minor form of virtuous spiritual paths."[54] Referring to the specific Tibetan situation of Buddhism and Bon, Kongtrul perceives the activity of the Precious Guru, Padmasambhava, in both traditions: "Therefore, I have gained firm confidence in the amazing, inconceivable life of the second Buddha from Oddiyana, and in the excellent manner in which his mysterious magical display of skillful means impartially guides his disciples."[55]

Before moving on to the major Rimé figures, Jamyang Khyentse, Chokgyur Lingpa and Jamgön Kongtrul, it is necessary to look a little deeper at the subject of the treasure tradition, since all three were deeply involved in the discovery, collection, classification and promulgation of *termas*.

Termas (*gter ma*) and tertöns (*gter ston*)

Treasures (*gter ma*) and treasure revealers (*gter ston*) have been mentioned at various stages in this book. It has been noted that *termas* may be closely related to substantial physical objects and are thus known as 'earth *termas*' (*sa gter*) or they may come from the mindstreams of *tertöns* and are thus known as mind *termas*.

As mentioned previously, within Buddhism, *termas* are associated predominantly, but not exclusively, with the Nyingma tradition.[56] According to the Nyingmas, teachings may be classified as belonging to one of three transmissions: the long lineage (*ring brgyud*) of oral teachings (*bka' ma*), the short or close lineage (*nye brgyud*) of *termas* (*gter ma*), and the profound Pure Vision teachings (*dag snang*). The boundaries between these three are somewhat fluid.⁵⁷

Recapitulating some earlier explanations given in this book, the idea behind *termas* is one of concealing texts, objects, teachings and so forth for retrieval at a later more favourable time. There are two related aspects in this: firstly, that the time at which a *terma* is initially produced is not the most propitious time for its dissemination; secondly, when a *terma* is revealed it will be appropriate to the time and circumstances. This is further linked with the universally accepted idea in Buddhism that the Dharma declines over time.⁵⁸ The notion is that this decline may be slowed, or even partially reversed, by the introduction of new teachings that are still fresh and full of blessings. Being from a 'short lineage' there is less possibility of the lineage (and the flow of blessings which accompany it) being broken or corrupted. It is further believed that enlightened teachers, such as Padmasambhava, foresaw the inevitable decline of the tradition and made aspirational prayers to bring about its periodic renewal.

Termas are understood to recover some of the potency of an earlier and better time. In the Tibetan Buddhist case, this is usually the period of the initial promulgation of Buddhism in Tibet during the glorious Imperial age, the time of the Yarlung dynasty. This is the golden age of Padmasambhava, the Dharma King Trisong Detsen, and Padmasambhava's twenty-five principal disciples. Included among these are such luminaries as the King himself, Padmasambhava's Tibetan consort Yeshe Tsogyal, the translator Vairocana, and the Dzogchen master Namkhai Nyingpo, to name a few. The majority of *termas* belonging to the Nyingma tradition are understood to be related to teachings given by Padmasambhava to his Tibetan disciples but then concealed by Padmasambhava or Yeshe Tsogyal for later recovery. The destined revealers of the treasures are understood to be later incarnations of these same disciples who act as the medium by which the *termas* appear in the world of humans. Many of the most important *termas* are 'mind *termas*' (*dgongs gter*) understood to be 'concealed' within the mindstream of the disciple who originally received the teaching. Thus in the context of nineteenth century Derge, Jamyang Khyentse was regarded as an incarnation of King Trisong Detsen, Jamgön Kongtrul as an incarnation of the translator Vairocana and Chokgyur Lingpa as an incarnation of the King's son, Prince Damdzin.

As mentioned previously, the Tibetan acceptance of *termas* had a precedent in India. We see it, for example, in the Mahāyāna claim that the *Perfection of Wis-*

dom Sūtras (*prajñāpāramitāsūtra*) were concealed in India for later recovery when circumstances were right for their promulgation, and also in relation to the tantras, many of which are understood to have been promulgated long after their initial teaching. In the case of the *Perfection of Wisdom Sūtras*, it is said that these scriptures were entrusted to the protection of *nāgas* (semi-divine serpent protectors of hidden wisdom) before full revelation and explication by the philosopher-saint Nāgārjuna ('Lord of Serpents').

The early history of *termas* in India and its significance for the Tibetan tradition has been examined by Dan Martin. He asserts that "many of the basic elements of the *gter-ma* complex were already in place by the second century CE, including the possibility that texts might be placed in the care of a supernatural being, a 'protector' during their periods of occultation."[59] What is unique about the Tibetan *terma* tradition of the Bon and Nyingma is not the idea of *termas* as such but its institutionalisation and the particular form it took as a continuing source of teachings accepted as authoritative by significant segments of the population.[60] In the case of the Nyingma this began in the eleventh century and continues into the present time. The institutionalisation of the *terma* tradition in Tibet may have been given further impetus by the establishment of a fixed canon of Buddhist texts in Tibet in the fourteenth century. There was no such closed Mahāyāna canon in India, which meant that texts came to be regarded as authoritative principally through acceptance of them as such by the majority of the Mahāyāna Buddhist community. The closed canon in Tibet engendered controversy over the authority of the treasure teachings.[61]

Although the Tibetan Buddhist *terma* tradition has been a continuous one spanning almost a thousand years it has undergone a number of developments which are beyond the scope of this book to explore.[62] An important period in this development seems to be the time of Longchenpa in the fourteenth century which saw greater recognition of and emphasis given to 'mind *termas*', especially in relation to the innermost or heart essence (*snying thig*) teachings of Dzogchen. By the period of the Rimé movement a more standardised understanding of treasures was accepted which placed them within seven lines of descent or transmission. This is most thoroughly presented by Jamgön Kongtrul in his *Precious Lapis Lazuli Rosary that Briefly Presents the Emergence of the Profound Treasures and the Accomplished Treasure Revealers* which introduces his *Treasury of Precious Termas*.[63]

We will now focus more closely on the central figures in the Rimé movement.

Jamgön Kongtrul Lodrö Thaye (1813-1899)

The life of Jamgön Kongtrul

We will begin our discussion with Jamgön Kongtrul, as he was the main writer of the group. Jamgön Kongtrul seems to have been the first to use the term *rimé* to describe a deliberate and self-conscious non-partisan approach to all the Buddhist traditions of Tibet. He was also the first to articulate that approach while giving a comprehensive overview of Tibetan Buddhist practice and theory. In doing this he was actively encouraged by Jamyang Khyentse who saw the need to preserve the teachings and make them available with commentaries and explanations for practice. Jamyang Khyentse and Jamgön Kongtrul were particularly concerned to save rare and endangered lineages. As Kongtrul wrote: "The continuity of the Shangpa teachings, Zhijé, Dorjé Sumgyi Nyendrup, and some others are extremely rare and nearly going extinct ... so that the frayed rope of those long lineages would at least not break, we must pay some attention to them."[64] This approach was adopted not only towards the 'long' lineages which could be traced back to India but also to the 'short' lineages of the *terma* visionary teachings. As 'spokesperson' for Padmasambhava, who was recognised as the source of most of the visionary teachings, Chokgyur Lingpa encouraged and mandated the collection and organisation of the *termas*.[65] This process, involving collection and explanation of both the 'long' and 'short' lineages, found expression in Jamgön Kongtrul's *Five Treasuries*.

Not only did Jamgön Kongtrul write comprehensively on all the different practice lineages, he also practised them and attained sufficient realisation in them to be able to transmit them. One of his closest students, Tashi Chöpel, commented that considering all Kongtrul wrote, it seems he did nothing other than write, and looking at his meditation practice it appears he did nothing other than spend his entire life in retreat, and seeing all he taught, he seems to have spent a lifetime teaching.[66] Jamgön Kongtrul did all three prolifically and at a very advanced level. Tashi Chöpel adds, "This master's life of freedom can only be understood by awakened persons; [to persons like us] it is inconceivable."[67]

Jamgön Kongtrul was born in 1813 in Kham in East Tibet, into a middle-class Bon family.[68] He was trained in Bon by his nominal father and by a yogi who was master of the nearby Bon monastery where Kongtrul became skilful in

Bon ritual practice and medicine.[69]

When Jamgön Kongtrul was sixteen years old he became a secretary to a district chief who had recognised him as extremely brilliant and clearly destined to go beyond clerical duties. Kongtrul was sent by the chief to Shechen Nyingma monastery to study the traditional secular arts and sciences including poetics, Tibetan grammar and Sanskrit, which he quickly mastered. According to his autobiography, Kongtrul had a deep faith in Padmasambhava from an early age and an intense interest in the religious life, so it was quite natural that at twenty years of age he took full ordination as a monk at Shechen monastery.

Kongtrul came to the attention of the powerful Karma Kagyü monastery of Palpung. Its leaders were very keen to bring him to Palpung and secure him for the monastery. At the insistence of the district chief and with sadness at leaving Shechen, Kongtrul moved to Palpung.[70] At Palpung monastery Kongtrul was required to re-ordain. This was in fact unnecessary since Kongtrul had already ordained at Shechen and there is no such thing as a specifically Kagyü ordination. (Monastic ordination has nothing to do with schools or even the Mahāyāna, for that matter, as ordinations pass through ordination lineages.)[71] Nevertheless, it was insisted upon that Jamgön Kongtrul be ordained by the Kagyü despite his protestations.[72] Very much against his inclination Kongtrul went along with it all and notes in his autobiography that "I did not feel that I had truly received the ordination."[73] E. Gene Smith suggests that "This small experience of intolerance seems to have been significant in channelling Kong sprul's interests toward a nonsectarian approach to Buddhist practice and scholarship."[74]

Furthermore, Jamgön Kongtrul was recognised by the Kagyü as a *tulku* primarily for political reasons. In those days the Derge government could requisition monks into government service but *tulkus* were excluded from this process. So in order to ensure that Kongtrul not be taken from them by the government or another monastery, Palpung monastery recognised him as a *tulku* connected with Palpung. Some at the monastery wanted to make him a very high *tulku*, but this was rather controversial within the monastery itself. Opponents argued that if the real *tulku*, the legitimate owner of the title, were to appear it would be difficult to recognise him if they had already given away the title. The solution the monastery worked out was to make Kongtrul a minor *tulku* so that the issue of the reincarnation of a higher *tulku* would not arise. They came to the decision to recognise him as minor *tulku* from Kongpo (an area in south-eastern Tibet) and hence Jamgön Kongtrul received the title 'Kongtrul', the reincarnation (*sprul* pronounced 'trul') from Kong po.⁷⁵ One can imagine a man as brilliant and sensitive as Kongtrul being quite upset at being labelled a *tulku* for dubious political reasons. As was common in the Tibetan religious milieu, Kongtrul had many different names. He had a Bon name, a Buddhist ordination name, a bodhisattva name, a *tertön* name, and so forth.⁷⁶ Perhaps not surprisingly, he mainly used his bodhisattva name, Lodrö Thaye (*blo gros mtha' yas*, 'Boundless Wisdom'). Some chose to address him as Jamgön Kongtrul Lodrö Thaye, but he mainly identified himself as Lodrö Thaye.

Despite these perhaps rather inauspicious beginnings, Kongtrul quickly formed a close relationship with the Ninth Situ Rinpoche, Pema Nyinje Wangpo (1774–1853), the most senior *tulku* at Palpung and one of the most important figures in the Karma Kagyü school. Kongtrul henceforth always regarded Pema Nyinje Wangpo as his root guru. Having received many teachings and empowerments from Situ Rinpoche and practised assiduously, Kongtrul entered the three-year Kagyü retreat at the age of twenty-two. However he was unable to complete this retreat because of demands made on him at the monastery: he was required to instruct the Fourteenth Karmapa in Sanskrit grammar.⁷⁷ Only after Situ Rinpoche gave Kongtrul permission at the age of twenty-nine to spend three years away from the monastery was he able to complete a three-year retreat, in an abandoned hermitage that had been used by the previous Situ Rinpoche, about an hour's walk from Palpung monastery. As it turned out, Kongtrul spent most of the rest of his life at this hermitage which he had rejuvenated.⁷⁸ Tai Situ Rinpoche named the hermitage Kunzang Dechen Ösel Ling ('All-good abode of radiant bliss').

Kongtrul had a somewhat difficult relationship with Palpung monastery for most of his life, despite being one of its *tulkus*. He was even accused by people at Palpung of fomenting intrigue against the monastery. The accusation was completely unfounded, but it so upset Kongtrul that he did not visit the monastery for a fourteen-year period.⁷⁹ The area around Kongtrul's hermitage was later identified by Jamyang Khyentse as a sacred place and was 'unveiled' or 'opened' by Chokgyur Lingpa as one of the twenty-five sacred places of East Tibet. The area became known as Tsādra Rinchen Drak ('Jewel Cliff like Tsāri').⁸⁰

Although Kongtrul had received the Nyingma teachings, to which he had great devotion, his devotion to these had diminished somewhat now that he considered himself as belonging to the Kagyü. He wrote that because of his partiality and attachment he became disinterested and even a bit averse to visionary texts and the like.[81] In his autobiography he writes that although he gradually developed devotion towards all the teachings and masters of Buddhist doctrine it was only later at the age of thirty-six through the influence of Jamyang Khyentse (whom he had first met and taught Sanskrit when he was twenty-seven and Khyentse was twenty) that the remaining traces of partisanship were finally eliminated. In his autobiography Jamgön Kongtrul states, "It is due to the kindness of the precious guru, Khyentse Rinpoche, that I have not accumulated the serious karmic consequence of rejecting the dharma."[82] A repeated theme that is found in Kongtrul's writings expresses a fear on his part that he might inadvertently reject the Dharma. He berates his own lack of mental strength that allowed him to be influenced by others.[83] Kongtrul writes: "A sectarian person is not worthy of being a holder of the dharma. Not only that, he is unworthy of upholding even his own tradition."[84]

Jamgön Kongtrul gave extensive Marpa Kagyü and Jonang teachings and empowerments to Jamyang Khyentse. These included the Six Yogas of Niguma from the Shangpa Kagyü tradition and Marpa Kagyü teachings according to the manuals written by Karma Chagme. Jamyang Khyentse urged Kongtrul to produce a more adequate set of practice manuals based on those of Karma Chagme.[85] Shortly thereafter, Jamyang Khyentse, in turn, taught and transmitted to Jamgön Kongtrul and others a very extensive range of teachings and practices which he had recently compiled which covered most of the practice traditions of Tibet.[86] Through this, and other transmissions given shortly thereafter, Jamyang Khyentse transmitted all teachings and lineages he held to Jamgön Kongtrul and enthroned Kongtrul as holder of all his teachings. He recognised Jamgön Kongtrul as an incarnation of Vairocana, the great eighth century translator and close disciple of Padmasambhava.

Jamgön Kongtrul spent a great deal of his life meditating and teaching, but between periods of meditation at his hermitage he began composing works and ended up producing an extraordinary literary output comprising more than ninety volumes. Because of his great scholarship and sagacity the honorary title 'Jamgön' ('Gentle Protector') came to be given to Kongtrul. 'Jamgön' is an epithet for Mañjuśrī, the bodhisattva of wisdom, and the prefixing of it to his *tulku* name (Kongtrul) indicates that Kongtrul was regarded as an emanation of Mañjuśrī.

The Five Treasuries of Jamgön Kongtrul

What was to become Kongtrul's monumental work, the *Five Treasuries*, began with a request from another incarnate lama, the first Dazang *tulku*, Ngedon Tenpa Rabgye, to write a work on the three levels of vows and commitments (relating to Hīnayāna, Mahāyāna and Vajrayāna respectively) that form the basis of Buddhist ethics.[87] Kongtrul then decided to expand this to include an overview of the three paths (Hīnayāna, Mahāyāna and Vajrayāna). He showed this to Jamyang Khyentse who was very impressed and suggested that he write a commentary to it, prophesying that these two (the original text and commentary) would form a 'treasury of knowledge', the first of five treasuries that Kongtrul would write! The first 'treasury' was completed in 1864 and became known as *The Encompassment of All Knowledge* (*shes bya kun khyab*) or, as termed by Jamyang Khyentse, simply the *Treasury of Knowledge* (*shes bya mdzod*). After publication in 1876 Kongtrul bestowed the reading transmission on a group of about twenty lamas including Jamyang Khyentse. He gave this transmission a total of five times during his lifetime. *The Encompassment of All Knowledge* is made up of ten books each containing four sections. Many of the sections make substantial books in themselves.[88] The work ranges from Buddhist cosmology (book 1), the life and enlightenment of the Buddha (book 2), Buddhist doctrine, history and ethics (books 3, 4, 5) secular knowledge and knowledge associated with practice of the Buddhist paths and the views (books 6, 7), the methods of practice, the paths traversed and the final fruition (books 8, 9, 10).[89] Kongtrul does not aim at originality or innovation in this work. In line with the approach of his day, Kongtrul draws heavily on scripture and on predecessors such as Longchenpa (on Dzogchen), Śākya Chokden (1428–1507) (on Madhyamaka), Butön (on history) and Tāranātha (on history and Madhyamaka), sometimes copying entire pages of their work. As Elizabeth Callahan notes, this should be understood in the traditional Buddhist context, "where reliance on scripture is not only laudable but to varying degrees mandatory; where passages may be borrowed in their entirety without attribution; and where original writing—that is, something wholly self-created—is considered a fault."[90] Of the *Encompassment of All Knowledge* it has been said, "In Tibetan religious literature, the work stands out as a unique masterpiece embodying the entirety of the theories and methods of implementation of the Buddhist doctrine as it was preserved in Tibet."[91] It is the most comprehensive presentation of non-sectarian (*ris med*) thought in the Tibetan tradition. The *Encompassment of All Knowledge* comprised the first work of the 'Five Treasuries'. The five are:

1. *Encompassment of All Knowledge* (*shes bya kun khyab*) or *Treasury of Knowledge* (*shes bya mdzod*)
2. *Treasury of Kagyü Mantras* (*bka' bryud sngags mdzod*)
3. *Treasury of Precious Termas* (*rin chen gter mdzod*)
4. *Treasury of Spiritual Instructions* (*gdams ngag mdzod*)
5. *Uncommon Treasury* (*thung mong ma yin pa'i mdzod*)[92]

A table of contents in English for all the 'treasuries' can be found in the Appendix to Richard Barron's translation of *The Autobiography of Jamgön Kontrul*.[93]

The second work, *Treasury of Kagyü Mantras*, began with the need for complete practice materials for the death ceremonies of Jamgön Kongtrul's root guru, the Ninth Situ Rinpoche, Pema Nyinje Wangpo in 1853. Kongtrul compiled practices (*sādhana*) for thirteen cycles of tantric practice used in the Kagyü tradition. As supportive teachings for the *Treasury of Kagyü Mantras*, Kongtrul also wrote medium-length commentaries on three important texts.[94]

The third work, the *Treasury of Precious Termas*, is a compilation of treasures containing empowerments, teachings, rites and instructions on how to apply them in retreat. Jamgön Kongtrul's intention was not to replace collected treasure cycles but rather to give order to the genre and establish criteria of authenticity.[95] He was also intent on preserving rare and threatened treasure teachings. The *Treasury of Precious Termas* includes empowerments and instructions for *termas* from a wide range of well-known treasure discoverers such as the various Lingpas (Rinchen Lingpa, Karma Lingpa, Pema Lingpa, Jigme Lingpa, Chokgyur Lingpa, et al.), Longchenpa, Rigdzin Gödem, Thangtong Gyalpo, the Fifth Dalai Lama and Mingyur Dorje, as well as some Bon *tertöns*.[96] As a result of Kongtrul's efforts these *termas* were transmitted widely in East Tibet and practised as never before. The compilation meant that it was possible from that time on to receive jointly the oral transmission and empowerments for a vast cycle of *termas*.[97]

The fourth work, the *Treasury of Spiritual Instructions*, contains a systematic presentation of spiritual (or 'esoteric') instructions (*gdams ngag*) for the 'eight practice lineages' of Tibetan Buddhism: Nyingma, Kadam, Lamdre, Marpa Kagyü, Shangpa Kagyü, Pacification, Vajra Yoga, and Approach and Accomplishment of the Three Vajras. (The 'eight practice lineages' will be discussed further below in relation to retreat practice at Kongtrul's hermitage retreat centre.) The term *gdams ngag* ('spiritual instruction') refers to pithy spiritual advice of a master communicated directly to a student. This is advice arising from the master's own experience rather than from theoretical textbooks.[98] During the time Kongtrul was writing this treasury Jamyang Khyentse strongly encouraged him to write a commentary on the Sakya *Eight Cycles of the Lamdre Teachings*. Jamyang Khyentse had had an auspicious dream in which it was revealed to him that Jamgön Kongtrul was an incarnation of one of the greatest Sakya lamas, Müchen Sangye Rinchen (1453–1524).[99]

The fifth work, the *Uncommon Treasury*, covers material that does not naturally fit elsewhere. It includes hymns of praise (*stotra*), guru yogas, liturgical works and material on deities and esoteric liturgy, especially of the Nyingma school. Its final section contains Kongtrul's own philosophical exegesis relating to Mahāmudrā and Dzogchen, his autobiography and miscellaneous writings on a wide variety of subjects.

Jamgön Kongtrul and shentong

The other-emptiness *shentong* approach to Madhyamaka (covered by Kongtrul in the *Encompassment of All Knowledge* and the *Uncommon Treasury*) held an important place in Kongtrul's thinking. It is sometimes claimed that this was the philosophical position of Rimé but, as we have seen, there is no set Rimé philosophical position—Rimé is an inclusive idea that accepts a variety of perspectives.[100] Some who embraced the Rimé approach, such as Mipham and Khenpo Shenga, were firm adherents to Prāsaṅgika Madhyamaka and its *rangtong* orientation.

As discussed in Section 1, *shentong* or 'other-emptiness' takes a more positive approach to emptiness than does *rangtong* or 'self-emptiness'. To again recapitulate, adherents of *rangtong* assert that emptiness itself is empty and thus cannot be said to be existent or real. Adherents of *shentong*, in contrast, assert that emptiness is empty of error, but after the negation of error ultimate reality (which cannot be characterised in terms of negation) remains. Thus, as Kongtrul points out, *rangtong* and *shentong* do not differ about conventional reality (which both regard as empty) but differ over their understanding of the ultimate: for *rangtong*, ultimate reality is a non-implicative negation (that is to say, nothing positive is implied), while for *shentong* ultimate reality is primordial wisdom, empty of the error of subject-object dualism.[101]

Kongtrul himself devotes a great deal of space to *shentong* and describes it as "the pinnacle of Madhyamaka systems."[102] He suggests that it is the highest position in 'Sūtra Madhyamaka' and is also in accord with 'Tantra Madhyamaka' (which Kongtrul calls 'Secret Mantra Mahāmudrā'). Some questions emerge: Why does Kongtrul devote so much space to *shentong*? What exactly does Kongtrul mean by *shentong*? Why does he give *shentong* this position? And where does this leave *rangtong* in Kongtrul's thought?

It appears that one reason Kongtrul devoted a great deal of space to *shentong* is that the *shentong* approach to Madhyamaka had been marginalised in Tibet for centuries. To begin, we can say that Kongtrul wanted to rehabilitate *shentong* and see it take what he saw as its proper place alongside *rangtong*. As we have seen in Section 1 of this book, the uncompromising *rangtong* position espoused by Tsongkhapa became the dominant philosophical position in Tibet. With the ascendency of the Gelugs numerically and politically, the schools and individuals that upheld 'other-emptiness' became doctrinally suspect, and even politically suspect. As we have seen, political rivalries and alliances often came into the picture and this had resulted in the suppression of the Jonang writings. Kongtrul held Dölpopa, the leading figure of the Jonang, in high esteem and wished to see him reinstated as one of the great philosophical thinkers of Tibet.

Another important figure for Kongtrul was Śākya Chokden (1428–1507), a great scholar of the Sakya school who was critical of Tsongkhapa's interpretation of Madhyamaka and who adopted a position akin to Dölpopa's which Kongtrul includes under the rubric of *shentong*. Śākya Chokden's works were banned in Central Tibet (but were preserved in Bhutan).[103] Restrictions were also placed on the copying of the works of other important philosophers such as the Sakya scholar Gorampa Sönam Senge (1429–1489), another critic of Tsongkhapa's position. This meant that these works were no longer widely studied, with a consequent weakening of the Sakya teaching tradition.[104] The writings of Tāranātha, the most important figure in the Jonang tradition after Dölpopa and author of the *Essence of Shentong*, were also banned in the seventeenth century. As we have seen, Tāranātha was caught up in the political events surrounding the consolidation of power by the Fifth Dalai Lama. Jamgön Kongtrul drew heavily on Tāranātha's writings.

Even the works of Gelug philosophers who put forward a position sympathetic to *shentong* had suffered the same fate as those of Tāranātha and others. Writings of the founders of both Drepung monastery and Sera Je were banned.[105] According to Smith, "The early Gelugpa school slowly calcified and core syllabi replaced honest debate and disputation."[106] Kongtrul wished to restore philosophical balance. In his *Frameworks of Buddhist Philosophy* Kongtrul explains that *rangtong* is necessary to avoid reification (in this case, turning the absolute into a 'thing' and clinging to it and its expressions in terms of deities and so on) and that *shentong* is necessary to avoid the view of denial (*skur ba 'debs pa*) or excessive negation.[107]

It is important to recognise that Kongtrul uses the term *shentong* in a broader and more inclusive sense than does Dölpopa. He includes figures such as Longchenpa and the Third Karmapa, whose views differ considerably from Dölpopa, within the framework of *shentong*.[108] As Elizabeth Callahan has observed, in Buddhist philosophical discourse, two broad approaches can be identified: a 'refutative' approach and a 'syncretic' approach.[109] The first concentrates on differences and refutation of flaws; the second emphasises the strengths of each philosophical position and attempts to reconcile or accommodate the various positions in a broader picture. Kongtrul, in line with his inclusive *rimé* approach, takes the second approach and his use of the term *shentong* reflects this.

Why then does Kongtrul accord the highest position to *shentong*? Why does he regard it as the 'pinnacle of Madhyamaka systems'? One possible clue lies in his argument for the importance of other-emptiness (*gzhan stong*) as a unifying concept, that is, one that can bridge the philosophical positions of Madhyamaka (with its division into Svātantrika and Prāsaṅgika Madhyamaka) and Yogācara, and the viewpoints of sūtra and tantra.[110]

Madhyamaka and Yogācara are regarded in Tibetan doxography (that is, the systematisation of philosophical positions) as the two main philosophical systems of Mahāyāna Buddhism in India. They are associated closely with the founding figures Nāgārjuna (second century C.E.) and Asaṅga (fourth century C.E.) respectively. Yogācara is usually understood to teach that only mind or consciousness is really existent and that appearances ('the world') are illusion. In line with this, Yogācara is normally identified in Tibet as the Cittamātra or the 'Mind-only' school. However, according to Jamgön Kongtrul this is a misunderstanding: the Yogācara that Asaṅga taught is in fact a variety of Madhyamaka.[111] He says the idea of mind as absolutely real was only added by later followers in the school.[112] The true position of Nāgārjuna and Asaṅga, according to Kongtrul, can be reconciled through *shentong* Madhyamaka which is in line with Asaṅga's position. Kongtrul asserts that the Cittamātra position is correctly refuted by Madhayamaka but such a refutation is not a refutation of Asaṅga's position nor of the position of the foundational texts of the Yogācara school (attributed to Maitreya). These texts and Asaṅga do not say that mind is real but rather that the consummate nature (*pariniṣpanna-svabhāva*), which is primordial wisdom free of duality of subject and object, is real. This is not mind (*citta* or *vijñāna*) as a substratum (*ālaya*) but rather emptiness (*śūnyatā*) in its ultimate sense. For Kongtrul the positions of Nāgārjuna and Asaṅga (and Maitreya) do not contradict each other: "one emphasizes outer principles, the other inner principles. Therefore, the judicious thing to do is equally engage their points for study, reflection and meditation."[113] It is, however, not surprising that for one such as Kongtrul, for whom scholarship (the outer) is, in the end, subordinate to meditation practice (the inner), *shentong* is regarded as 'the pinnacle' of philosophical systems.

Kongtrul also argues that *shentong* bridges sūtra and tantra since, like *shentong*, tantra (or 'secret mantra') emphasises primordial wisdom free of duality. However this is not to the exclusion of *rangtong* since both *shentong* and *rangtong* relate to the two stages of tantric practice, the generation stage (*utpatti-krama*) and the completion stage (*saṃpanna-krama*). That the seed syllables and deities visualised in the generation stage of tantric practice arise from primordial wisdom and are expressions of its intrinsic nature relates to *shentong* (emptiness understood as positive); that they must be of free of conceptual elaboration relates to *rangtong* (which negates reification or objectification of the deities as individually existent).[114] In the completion stage, the dissolution of the visualisation of the deity with the understanding that it is insubstantial relates to *rangtong*; the resting in primordial wisdom relates to *shentong*.

Meditation in its most essential form (or non-meditation) in Mahāmudrā and Dzogchen does not involve stages of practice but does entail both freedom from conceptual elaboration (which can be related to *rangtong*) and remaining in the primordial state (which can be related to *shentong*). Furthermore, an important distinction is made in Dzogchen between mind (*citta*, T. *sems*) and the nature of mind (*citta-dharmatā*, T. *sems nyid*). With this, Dzogchen rejects the Cittamātra idea of the ultimacy of mind or consciousness (*citta* or *vijñāna*, T. *rnam shes*) as a substratum (*ālaya*, T. *kun gzhi*) but recognises primordial wisdom (*jñāna*, T. *ye shes*) as the ultimate nature of mind in line with *shentong* Madhyamaka.

Jamgön Kongtrul and Chokgyur Lingpa

When Jamgön Kongtrul was forty years old he met Chokgyur Lingpa who became the third member of this group which collaborated so closely. As mentioned in the Introduction, there was at this point some doubt about the status of the semi-literate Chokgyur Lingpa as a *tertön*. Chokgyur Lingpa was lampooned and called 'Kyater' (*'tertön* of the Kyasu family') on the basis of his family name 'Kyasu', with the implication was that he was not a real *tertön*. Kongtrul thought that 'Kyater' might be genuine *tertön* and later wrote: "Kyater was a person of such fine character and other qualities that no matter how I considered him, he was quite unlike other people."[115] However, only after 'Kyater' had gone to meet Jamyang Khyentse (with an introductory letter from Kongtrul asking Khyentse "to examine the situation") and Khyentse had recognised Chokgyur Lingpa as an undoubted *tertön* did Chokgyur Lingpa and Jamgön Kongtrul enter into a mutual guru-disciple relationship.[116] Although Chokgyur Lingpa was only twenty-four and Kongtrul was forty, Kongtrul later wrote, "I felt like a child being reunited with his father."[117] Jamyang Khyentse held all the lineages and was a major *tertön* himself; in fact he was regarded as one of the most important *tertöns* in the *tertön* tradition. Jamyang Khyentse's recognition of Chokgyur Lingpa as a *tertön* initiated a ten-year period of revealing of *termas* by Chokgyur Lingpa. This was done mainly in co-operation with Kongtrul and Khyentse, who would write them down along with supplementary liturgies, instruction manuals and so on, and who became the main custodians of these *termas*. Patrul Rinpoche was also on occasion entrusted with this role. Later, Jamyang Khyentse and Chokgyur Lingpa, in recognition of Jamgön Kongtrul's role as a *tertön* himself, enthroned him and gave him the *tertön* name Chime Tennyi Yungdrung Lingpa.[118] They told Kongtrul he should henceforth use this name to repair his damaged relationship with the *termas* (because of his previous partiality to the New schools and disinterest in the visionary teachings after he moved from Shechen to Palpung monastery) and in order to discover new *termas*.[119]

Before compiling the treasure teachings Kongtrul asked Chokgyur Lingpa whether this would be a good idea. Chokgyur Lingpa was the acknowledged pre-eminent *tertön* of the group and was understood to have a very close relationship with Padmasambhava. It is said that Chokgyur Lingpa consulted with

Padmasambhava who told him Kongtrul should go ahead, and whatever he decided to do, it would turn out well.[120] Kongtrul therefore proceeded with the compilation which resulted in the *Treasury of Precious Termas*. Twelve years from this point Kongtrul gave the first transmission of the *Treasury of Precious Termas*, which he in fact gave five times during his lifetime. It is notable that the woodblocks of these *termas* (the main holding of these *termas* in written form) were entrusted to the Fifteenth Karmapa. The Karmapas became the main protectors, shall we say, of this collection even though we usually associate *termas* most closely with the Nyingma school.

Kongtrul actually lived longer than Chokgyur Lingpa and Jamyang Khyentse Rinpoche. He performed the funeral rites for both. Chokgyur Lingpa only lived to age forty-one, and Jamyang Khyentse to seventy-two.

The three-year retreat and the eight practice lineages

Jamgön Kongtrul's commitment to a non-sectarian approach is reflected in the three-year retreat program that he created for use in his retreat centre. In his *Encompassment of All Knowledge* (also known as the *Treasury of Knowledge*) he presents Buddhist practice in the framework of 'Eight Practice Lineages' or 'Eight Chariots of the Practice Lineage' (*sgrub brgyud shing rta brgyad*). The three-year program involved practice of seven of these; only Lamdre was omitted. Lamdre was left out, not because Kongtrul was ill-disposed to Sakya—he was, in fact, an important figure in Sakya tradition and drew heavily on Sakya sources in his own writings—but because of its complexity, which he believed made it impossible to practise adequately in the restricted time frame of a three-year retreat involving multiple practice traditions. He also thought that Lamdre was a secure lineage widely practised in East Tibet where the Sakya school was flourishing.[121] Kongtrul laments the fact that even dedicated practitioners only concern themselves with studying and meditating within their own traditions and do little to learn of other traditions or assist in their continuation. As a consequence, he writes, "some very high lineages of meditation practice are close to disappearing into the void."[122] Of himself, he says, "I hope to be of some small benefit to the continuity of the teachings and a good example for the next generation of fortunate and intelligent masters."[123]

Jamgön Kongtrul wrote a *Retreat Manual* as prescribed reading for all practitioners undertaking the retreat. The manual includes instructions on correct attitude, how the teachings should be approached, what the eight practice lineages are, and so on. As such, it is an excellent introduction to the non-sectarian *rimé* approach and is, fortunately, available in English translation.[124]

The first three-year retreat (apart from Kongtrul's own) began in 1860 with just five retreatants (one of whom focused on practices to protector deities). This number was brought up to eight with the presence of the retreat master, a cook and a woodsman. All seven or eight three-year retreats that took place during Kongtrul's lifetime had the same modest number of participants. Kongtrul composed his *Treasury of Knowledge* at his hermitage over a four-month period during the first three-year retreat held there. It became recommended reading for all future participants in his three-year retreats, especially book five on Buddhist ethics.

As mentioned, practice during the retreat involved seven of the eight 'practice lineages'. The eight are:
    1. Nyingma (Ancient ones)
    2. Kadam (Buddha's Word)
    3. Lamdre (Path and Result)
    4. Marpa Kagyü
    5. Shangpa Kagyü
    6. Shije and Chöd (Pacification and Severance)
    7. Vajra Yoga / Six Branch Yoga
    8. Three Vajras intensive practice

The first five of these have already been covered to some extent in this book and are fairly well-known. The last three require some explanation.

Shije (*zhi byed*) and Chöd (*gcod*) are related lineages deriving from the Indian master Phadampa Sangye (d. 1117) who came to Tibet five times, and the Tibetan woman yogi (*yoginī*) Machig Lapdrön (1031–1129). The lineages are treated by Kongtrul as one because Phadampa Sangye was one of Machig Lapdrön's principal teachers and because the two lineages became intertwined. Both Shije and Chöd are based on cutting away the ego and pacifying suffering through understanding emptiness (*śūnyatā*) as presented in the *Prajñāpāramitā* (*Perfection of Wisdom*) *Sūtras*. Chöd practice, in particular, became diffused through all schools of Tibetan Buddhism and Bon and is also widely practised outside the monastic system. Chöd practice involves both sūtric and tantric aspects bought together in the idea of wisdom (*prajñā*) as feminine. In tantric practice of Chöd, wisdom is embodied as the 'unique mother' (*ma gcig*), the divine feminine (*ḍākinī*) as the source of all wisdom and of all the Buddhas. She is the wisdom which is not separate from our own true nature. She allows us to cut through or sever (*gcod*) clinging to the ego and to individual separateness. As a ritual practice, Chöd involves a self-sacrifice in which we offer ourselves to all beings, including our enemies and those we fear. Elements of shamanic and Bon practice are integrated in the ritual which is also influenced by tantric charnel ground practices. Practice in cemeteries and other 'haunted places' is often recommended.[125] Jamgön Kongtrul writes of Chöd: "It is a radical method for cutting through the inflation of ego-fixation, through the willingness to accept what is undesirable, the disregard of difficult circumstances, the realization that gods and demons are one's own mind, and the understanding that oneself and others are utterly equal."[126] Many systems of Chöd were transmitted in Tibet. The Mahāmudrā Chöd lineages which were founded by Machig Lapdrön were practised in the three-year retreat program at Kongtrul's hermitage as a daily practice.[127]

The seventh of the eight 'practice lineages', Vajra Yoga (*rdo rje rnal 'byor*) and Six Branch Yoga (*'byor drug*), come from the *Kālacakra Tantra* (*Wheel of Time Tantra*) which is regarded as the most complete system of tantric teachings from among the tantras belonging to the New traditions (*gsar ma*). According to Jamgön Kongtrul the practices taught in these instructions "stand at the summit of all yoga practices."[128] Vajra Yoga relates primarily to the generation phase of tantric practice in which visualisation of deities, maṇḍala and so on is generated, while the Six Branch Yoga relates to the completion phase where visualisation is dissolved and vital energy (*prāṇa*) is manipulated to access very subtle mind states and to cause the vital energy to enter the central channel (*avadhūti*) which is, according to tantric physiology, the most important of the subtle energy channels (*nāḍī*) which pervade the physical body. The culmination of the six branches of practice is Mahāmudrā. These meditations bring about a transformation process which, according to the cosmology and physiology of the *Kālacakra Tantra*, can lead to complete enlightenment in a period of 'three years and three fortnights'. The idea of a three-year retreat has its roots in this idea. According to Jamgön Kongtrul:

> All the wisdom energy which circulates [with the breath] during one hundred years equals three years and three fortnights. When all karmic energy is transformed into wisdom energy, enlighten-

ment is attained. This is the reason why it is said that the state of Buddha Vajra Holder [Vajradhara] is achieved [by meditation practice during a period of] three years and three fortnights.[129]

Jamgön Kongtrul considered the Kālacakra lineage from the Jonang tradition as the central transmission of these teachings and he incorporated practice from within this tradition into the three-year retreat program.

The last of the eight 'practice lineages', the Three Vajras intensive practice (*rdo rje gsum gyi bsnyen sgrub*), was introduced to the program by Jamgön Kongtrul after the first three-year retreat, as a supplement to Vajra Yoga. It originates with Orgyen Rinchenpal (1230–1309), the principal teacher of the Third Karmapa. According to Kongtrul, Orgyen Rinchenpal received the teachings directly from Vajrayoginī (the essence of all the Buddhas in female form) in Oddiyana, the land 'in the West' associated with Padmasambhava (perhaps located in the Swat Valley in present day northern Pakistan).[130] The 'three vajras' relate to training the body, speech and mind through the indestructible reality (*vajra*) of the buddha-body, buddha-speech and buddha-mind. The retreat manual does not provide detail on this practice.

Each three-year retreat began with the preliminary practices (*sngon 'gro*) as taught in the Karma Kagyü tradition. These included both the four 'ordinary preliminaries' (meditation on the preciousness of a fully-endowed human existence, impermanence, karma, and the unsatisfactory nature of conditioned existence) and the 'special preliminaries' (refuge and generation of *bodhicitta*, purification practice of Vajrasattva, maṇḍala offering, and guru yoga). Instructions for the practice of these were set out by Jamgön Kongtrul in his *Torch of Certainty* which was written as a supplement to the Ninth Karmapa's *Mahāmudrā: The Ocean of Certainty.* Practice included the mind training or lojong (*blo sbyong*) of the Kadam tradition as presented in Gampopa's *Jewel Ornament of Liberation*, Tāranātha's *Stages of the Path for the Three Types of Individual* (or *Essence of Ambrosia*) and Kongtrul's *The Great Path to Awakening*. These three, along with the Ninth Karmapa's *Mahāmudrā: The Ocean of Certainty*, were required reading and served as manuals for the retreat.[131] *The Great Path to Awakening* is Kongtrul's own commentary on the Kadam 'slogans' for training the mind. In his *Retreat Manual*, Kongtrul stresses the importance of developing a helpful and loving attitude (*bodhicitta*), continuous awareness of impermanence and death, and devotion to one's spiritual master (*guru*).[132] The preliminary practices were to be completed within five months.

The five months spent on the preliminaries were followed by fifteen months on meditations from the Shangpa Kagyü tradition including most of the main meditations of the Shangpa tradition. (As previously explained in Section 1 these, for the most part, originated with Niguma, the Indian eleventh century woman master, and were enriched by the Indian woman master Sukhasiddhi.) The Shangpa teachings were first propagated in Tibet by Khyungpo Naljor who, as we have seen, founded the Tibetan Shangpa tradition in West Tibet. The fifteen-month practice included the Six Yogas of Niguma (inner heat, illusory body, dream, clear light, transference of consciousness, intermediate state) and Niguma's Mahāmudrā which is known as Mahāmudrā of the Amulet Box.[133] Mahāmudrā was practised for the final two months of the fifteen months devoted to the Shangpa practices. The transmission lineages used in the retreat were from the Jonang tradition and from Thangtong Gyalpo, the eclectic teacher and 'iron bridge builder' (mentioned early in this Section).

Six months of meditation on the Vajra Yoga instruction lineage followed and this was supplemented by Three Vajras intensive practice.

The final year of the retreat was devoted to practices originating in the Nyingma tradition. Jamgön Kongtrul stresses the importance of Padmasambhava, the Precious Guru (Guru Rinpoche), not only as the wellspring for the Nyingma tradition, but for all Tibetans. He places him at the centre of the configuration of all spiritual masters and writes:

> ...all Tibetans in general and particularly those who are followers of the Oral Instruction Lineage [Kagyü] and the Ancient Instruction Lineage [Nyingma] place their deepest confidence for this life and the next in the second buddha, the sole refuge of beings in these dark times, the great master from Oddiyana [Guru Rinpochay].[134]

The Nyingma tradition includes the 'long' oral lineages (*bka' ma*), and the 'short' treasure lineages (*gter ma*) which, according to Kongtrul, were originally collected (before concealment) by Yeshe Tsogyal, the woman master and Tibetan consort of Padmasambhava. During this part of the retreat, practices were drawn from both the long oral lineage and treasure traditions and included practices from the three highest paths or vehicles of the Nyingma system (Mahāyoga, Anuyoga and Atiyoga/Dzogchen). These culminated in practices belonging to the *Nyingthig* ('innermost essence') of Dzogchen relating to both *trekchö* (*khregs chod*) or 'breakthrough', and *thögel* (*thod rgal*) or 'leapover' practices. The visionary practices of 'leapover' are unique to Dzogchen and are said to potentially lead to transformation of the gross physical elements of the body into a 'rainbow body' or 'body of light' (*'ja' lus*).[135]

Thus we can see that the three-year retreat at Jamgön Kongtrul's retreat centre was divided into four main sections: preliminary practices, the Six Yogas and Mahāmudrā according to the Shangpa Kagyü tradition, Vajra Yoga of the Kālacakra tradition supplemented by the Three Vajras intensive practice, and Nyingma practices of the three highest vehicles with a focus on Dzogchen (Atiyoga). As noted above, Chöd practice was part of the daily schedule. Many additional daily practices and prayers were added including practices to be done immediately on awakening in the morning ('the yoga of waking from sleep'), practices for going to sleep and during sleep ('the yoga of sleep'), prayers of aspiration, confession, prayers to the lineage, and so on. There were also daily group practices involving prayers to Guru Rinpoche (Padmasambhava), prayers to the Dharma protectors and recitation of the mantras of the deities, long-life prayers, recitation of the *Perfection of Wisdom Heart Sūtra*, and so on. There were also monthly and yearly observations for the full moon, new moon, seventh, eighth, tenth, thirteenth and other significant days, and special practices for each month.[136]

Practice at the retreat centre, Kunzang Dechen Ösel Ling, was maintained after Jamgön Kongtrul's death in 1899. By 1920 Norbu Döndrup had become the retreat master there and he recognised that the sixteen-year-old retreatant Karma Drubgyu Tenzin (Kalu Rinpoche) was destined to become the lineage holder of the teachings Norbu Döndrup had received directly from Jamgön Kongtrul and two of his most senior disciples. Norbu Döndrup, who was Kalu Rinpoche's root guru, transmitted the complete teachings of the Karma Kagyü and Shangpa Kagyü to Kalu Rinpoche. When Norbu Döndrup retired in the 1940s, Kalu Rinpoche was summoned by the Eleventh Tai Situ Rinpoche and the Sixteenth Karmapa to return from his twelve years of retreat in the mountains of Kham to take Norbu Döndrup's place as retreat master at the centre. Although the centre was destroyed during the 1960s it was rebuilt in the 1980s under the guidance of Kalu Rinpoche and the Third Jamgön Kongtrul Rinpoche (1954–1992). Three-year retreats recommenced at the hermitage in 1988.

Jamgön Kongtrul completed his autobiography in 1894 but continued writing into the final year of his life in 1899. An account of his final days and passing has been left by his close disciple Tashi Chöpel (who later taught Kalu Rinpoche). Tashi Chöpel lists Jamgön Kongtrul's vast achievements, his teachers and his students. Of his literary achievements he mentions his more than ninety volumes of writing and draws particular attention to his *Five Treasuries* which he says "served as a life-support system for the dying transmission of the teachings, without sectarian bias."[137] Among the vast array of his students, Tashi Chöpel writes of two particular masters to whom Jamgön Kongtrul "entrusted his entire transmissions of teachings and who serve as his true regents."[138] They are the Fifteenth Karmapa, Kunzang Khakyab Dorje (1871–1922) and the Eleventh Tai Situ Rinpoche, Pema Wangchok Gyalpo (1886–1952). Jamgön Kongtrul's immediate incarnation, Jamgön Kongtrul Khyentse Özer (1902–1952), was born as the son of the Fifteenth Karmapa.

Jamyang Khyentse Wangpo (1820-1892)

Jamyang Khyentse's inspiration of Rimé

If Jamgön Kongtrul was the main writer, editor and compiler among the leading figures of the Rimé movement, Jamyang Khyentse Wangpo was undoubtedly the inspiration and prime mover. His influence was transformative. Kongtrul spoke of Jamyang Khyentse thus:

> It goes without saying that, from early on in my life, I had not been lacking in an unbiased respect for the teachings, but nothing had actually opened my eyes to the state of pure vision, in which I could hold all of these teachings in my mind without any contradiction. Since I met Khyentsé Rinpoché, however, I have felt a natural sense of freedom, in that I am confident that I can hold any and all of the Sage's teachings in perfect balance, without seeing any inconsistency between them. Meeting him was also, for me, the dawning of my real familiarity with the Buddhadharma.[139]

Jamyang Khyentse inspired Jamgön Kongtrul to produce his *Five Treasuries*, his numerous commentaries, practice manuals, and so on, and was a catalyst for his activities as a *tertön*.[140] It was also Jamyang Khyentse's recognition of

Chokgyur Lingpa as a *tertön* that opened the way to Chokgyur Lingpa's intense ten years of revelation of *termas*. He also inspired his close student, the Sakya master Jamyang Loter Wangpo (1847–1914), to compile the vast *Compendium of Tantras* (*rgyud sde kun btus*) which includes rare teachings from many schools which might otherwise have become extinct.

Jamyang Khyentse's opinion was regarded as definitive by Jamgön Kongtrul, Chokgyur Lingpa and others and in many ways he set the direction for the others to follow. Although he attempted to lead the reclusive life of a meditator and spiritual teacher, he played a significant role in the political life of Derge. He was an indefatigable collector of teachings and transmissions which he received from over one hundred and fifty teachers during a period of thirteen years wandering in Tibet. He is said to have received the reading transmission of over seven hundred volumes, and was, as Sam van Schaik puts it, "like a human library of rare Buddhist texts."[141] He also played a major role as a *tertön*. Like Jamyang Khyentse Chökyi Lodrö in the first half of the twentieth century, and Dilgo Khyentse Rinpoche in the second half of the twentieth century, Jamyang Khyentse Wangpo probably embodied the breadth of Tibetan traditions more fully than anyone else of his generation. Jamyang Khyentse Wangpo was reputedly capable of teaching in the style and manner of all the approaches and schools without confusing them in any way. He was the spiritual master of an entire generation of teachers, treasure revealers and scholars of all schools of Tibetan Buddhism and Bon.

Background and early life of Jamyang Khyentse

Jamyang Khyentse was born in 1820 into a wealthy Derge Sakya family and was given the name Tsering Döndrup ('Long-lived and achieving benefit'). His father was an official at the Derge court and the young Tsering Döndrup seemed destined for a life of government service. To this end Tsering Döndrup received a thorough education in the worldly arts and sciences including calligraphy, poetics, astrology and medicine. However, when he was twelve years old he was recognised as an incarnation of a previous abbot of Ngor Sakya monastery. He travelled to Ngor monastery where he received teachings and was given the name Jamyang Khyentse Wangpo.[142] At the age of twenty-one Jamyang Khyentse elected to receive his full monastic vows not at Ngor but at the Mindröling Nyingma monastery in Central Tibet. However, he did not settle at Mindröling but rather chose to set off on a journey across Tibet during which he studied with a vast range of spiritual masters and collected a treasure trove of teachings and transmissions, especially seeking out those in danger of disappearing. Thirteen years later Jamyang Khyentse returned to Derge where he set about living modestly, but his family connections with the Derge court, his great learning, level of realisation, personal charisma and rapidly spreading fame meant that he was to play a prominent role in Derge religious and public life from that time on.

Jamyang Khyentse had met Jamgön Kongtrul when Khyentse was twenty years old and Kongtrul was twenty-seven but it was only after Khyentse's return from years of wandering that a close relationship developed. At this time Jamyang Khyentse and Jamgön Kongtrul recognised each other as kindred spirits and exchanged teachings. Kongtrul recognised in Jamyang Khyentse the embodiment of the non-sectarian ideal and later contrasted him with others:

> These days, even among famous lamas and teachers, there are not many who have a pure regard for the teachings of the Sage in their totality, apart from their own traditions and a few scriptures. There are few who have been willing to study with everyone, whether exalted or lowly, and there is little real knowledge of the dharma. Especially in these later times there are a great many who, while they themselves are not perfectly upright and lack a spiritual outlook, talk like arrogant bullies about whether a particular teaching tradition is any good or whether a lineage is pure. Never mind other traditions; they are full of qualms and doubts about the basics of their own tradition, like the proverbial one-eyed yak who startles himself.[143]

Jamyang Khyentse and Jamgön Kongtrul entered into a mutual teacher/student relationship, yet it is apparent that, despite his younger years, Khyentse was spiritually speaking the senior. With the death in 1853 of Jamgön Kongtrul's main teacher, the Ninth Tai Situ Rinpoche, Jamyang Khyentse became Kongtrul's most important master.

Jamyang Khyentse was ardent in his desire to perpetuate the teachings of all the practice lineages which he had received. As previously mentioned, soon after his return from thirteen years of collecting teachings and transmissions Khyentse passed on all these teachings to Jamgön Kongtrul and proclaimed him holder and protector of all the transmissions. It may well have been at Jamyang

Khyentse's instigation that Kongtrul adopted the model of the 'eight practice lineages' or 'eight great chariots that are lineages of attainment' (*sgrub brgyud shing rta chen po brgyad*) as a paradigm to present the spiritual instructions and explain the provenance and significance of the practice lineages in his *Treasury of Spiritual Instructions* and in his *Treasury of Knowledge*. These works were compiled at the urging of Khyentse. This formulation was apparently first used in the sixteenth century by Sherab Özer (1518–1584) in his *Meditation's Ambrosia of Immortality*.[144] Jamyang Khyentse annotated a version of this work and it is included in Khyentse's collected works (along with Khyentse's annotations). Khyentse's collected works also include the whole text of another work by Sherab Özer entitled *Study and Reflection's Ambrosia of Immortality*. The latter work deals with the 'ten great pillars', or great figures in Tibet who supported the teaching lineages in the period of development of Tibetan Buddhism from the seventh to thirteenth centuries.[145]

Although Sherab Özer is not as well-known as the figures we have considered as forerunners of the Rimé movement, he is a very interesting figure and could well have been included. Sherab Özer (also known by his Sanskrit name, Prajñāraśmi) was trained in the Gelug and Sakya schools, attaining the highest academic qualification as a Geshe in both the Gelug and Sakya traditions. He then resided at a Drikung Kagyü monastery and received Karma Kagyü and Nyingma teachings there. He also became a *tertön* in the Nyingma tradition and in 1571 founded the Nyingma Palri monastery in Central Tibet. Sherab Özer also practised in the Drikung and Karma Kagyü traditions.[146] This is quite extraordinary, especially given that this was a period in which there was intense rivalry in Central Tibet between the Gelug and Kagyü schools. In his *Meditation's Ambrosia of Immortality* Sherab Özer presents each of the eight lineages in a non-hierarchical model of complete and equally valid paths to enlightenment. The model of the 'eight practice lineages' may have come to East Tibet via Jigme Lingpa who, as we have seen, had strong connections with East Tibet and was born near, and trained as a monk at, the monastery founded by Sherab Özer.[147]

Jamyang Khyentse and the Longchen Nyingthig

Jamyang Khyentse Wangpo is regarded as a body incarnation of Jigme Lingpa. Jamyang Khyentse's close collaborator, Patrul Rinpoche (who will be discussed later in this Section), is regarded as a speech incarnation of Jigme Lingpa. Patrul

Rinpoche and Jamyang Khyentse had the same root guru, Jigme Gyalwai Nyugu (1765–1843), who was one of the main holders of Jigme Lingpa's Dzogchen *Longchen Nyingthig* lineage, and one of his three principal disciples.[148] Jigme Gyalwai Nyugu was originally from Kham and returned there after spending a considerable time with Jigme Lingpa in Central Tibet. Since Jigme Gyalwai Nyugu regarded Jamyang Khyentse and Patrul Rinpoche as incarnations of his own teacher he treated them with great deference, especially Khyentse. Jamyang Khyentse is reported to have understood the whole import of a teaching after hearing only the beginning of it.[149] He received the transmission of the *Longchen Nyingthig* at the age of nineteen before he left Kham on his thirteen-year period of travelling and collecting teachings and transmissions. Jamyang Khyentse was regarded as 'the Sun' of those who followed in Jigme Lingpa's lineage and Patrul Rinpoche as 'the Moon'. Through Jamyang Khyentse and Patrul Rinpoche the *Longchen Nyingthig* spread widely in Kham where it became the central practice of many associated with the Rimé movement. (It will be recalled that Jigme Lingpa's collected works were published in Derge (in Kham) with royal patronage. It was in Derge that Jigme Lingpa's immediate incarnation, Do Khyentse Yeshe Dorje (1800–1866), had been enthroned.)

Although he was a Sakya, the *Longchen Nyingthig* was Jamyang Khyentse's main practice.[150] In Jamyang Khyentse's time, the interchange we have discussed between the Sakya and Nyingma schools in Kham reached a new level. Khyentse's seat was Dzongsar Sakya monastery in Derge, and for this reason Jamyang Khyentse is also known as the First Dzongsar Khyentse Rinpoche. Through to the present day the Second and Third Dzongsar Khyentse Rinpoches (Jamyang Khyentse Chökyi Lodrö (1893–1959) and Jamyang Khyentse Norbu (b. 1961)) have maintained a strong Rimé approach and have been key lineage holders of the *Longchen Nyingthig*, the Sakya Lamdre, and other lineages. This influence has ensured that the *terma* tradition is now widely accepted in the Sakya school.

Jamyang Khyentse and the terma tradition

As an incarnation of Jigme Lingpa, Jamyang Khyentse is also regarded as an incarnation of King Trisong Detsen and as an important *tertön*. Although he did not personally emphasise his role as a discoverer of new *termas*, Jamyang Khyentse was recognised as one of the five 'king' *tertöns* of the Nyingma *terma* tradition.[151] Both he and Chokgyur Lingpa were said to hold and to be able to

transmit all 'seven transmissions' (*bka' babs bdun*) of the teachings recognised in the Nyingma tradition. Regarding the seven transmissions it is said of Jamyang Khyentse:
1. He received the oral transmission of the tantras which come through the 'long' oral lineages (*bka' ma*).
2. He discovered earth *termas* (*sa gter*).
3. He rediscovered earth *termas* that had been discovered and re-concealed by earlier *tertöns* (*yang gter*).
4. His discovered mind *termas* (*dgongs gter*).
5. He recollected or rediscovered many mind *termas* originally discovered by earlier *tertöns* (*rjes dran gter*).
6. He received teachings in Pure Visions (*dag snang*).
7. He received Oral-transmission teachings (*snyan brgyud*) in aural pure visions.[152]

Of these, Pure Visions and Oral transmission teachings are often loosely regarded as *termas* but are not, strictly speaking, *termas* since they do not involve transmission of teachings considered to have been given at a former time. In this scheme of seven transmissions, four types of *termas* are accepted: earth *termas*, rediscovered earth *termas*, mind *termas*, and recollected mind *termas*.[153]

Jamyang Khyentse Rinpoche placed a great deal of emphasis on the rediscovery of lost *termas* and the clarification of *termas* where the meaning or mode of practice had become obscured. This, it is said, was possible because of his unique visionary abilities and due to the fact that he was regarded as an incarnation of several important *tertöns*. Recollected mind *termas* (*rjes dran gter*) are said to arise out of memories from former lives. Through recollecting *termas*, Jamyang Khyentse is said to have revived many teachings that had been lost or which had had their lineages interrupted. Recollected *termas* are, in particular, associated with Jamyang Khyentse.

Jamyang Khyentse's extensive activities as a *tertön* are catalogued in the traditional biographies. Here we will consider just a couple of illustrative examples of revelations which have been of particular significance. Since Jamyang Khyentse was credited with the special abilities to recollect *termas* from past lives and was regarded as an incarnation of Thangtong Gyalpo, the 'iron bridge builder' and eclectic teacher who had founded Gönchen monastery in Derge in the fifteenth century, he is said to have revived many of Thangtong Gyalpo's 're-concealed' *termas*. These had been found, but re-concealed because they "were not suitable for the people of his time."[154] Thangtong Gyalpo is often referred to as the 'Great Adept' (*mahāsiddha*) and is usually pictured in the guise of a wild tantric yogi. It is said that when people came to meet Jamyang Khyentse he sometimes appeared to be Thangtong Gyalpo.[155] According to Jamgön Kongtrul, Jamyang Khyentse received visionary *Nyingthig* ('heart essence') teachings from Thangtong Gyalpo when Khyentse was fifteen years old and subsequently transcribed the manuals for their practice.[156] This is known as the *Heart Essence of the Great Adept* (*grub thob thug thig*) and is regarded as one such recollected *terma* (*rjes dran gter*) which Khyentse 'remembered' from his previous life as Thangtong Gyalpo. According to Cyrus Stearns, Jamyang Khyentse revived all of the essential content of the treasure teachings which Thangtong Gyalpo had re-concealed.[157] These teachings were later included by Jamgön Kongtrul in his *Treasury of Precious Termas*.

Khyentse is also said to have received the transmission of Niguma's Shangpa teachings, (her Six Yogas and Amulet Box Mahāmudrā), in a vision of Thangtong Gyalpo many years before he received the transmission of the same teachings from Jamgön Kongtrul.[158]

Another important *terma* which belongs among Jamyang Khyentse's 're-collected' *termas* is the *Chetsün Nyingthig* (*lce btsun snying thig*), the *Heart Essence of Chetsün*. This was revealed when Jamyang Khyentse was visiting a sacred place in Central Tibet when he was twenty-four. At that time his ordinary perception dissolved and he clearly recalled the place and time when Chetsün Senge Wangchuk (eleventh century) attained the 'rainbow body' (*'ja' lus*).[159] This *terma* is said to be a teaching originally given to Chetsün Senge Wangchuk by Vimalamitra in a vision. Jamyang Khyentse is recognised as an emanation of both Vimalamitra and Chetsün Senge Wangchuk. Jamyang Khyentse kept this *terma* secret and many years later gave it in a one-to-one transmission to Jamgön Kongtrul. Some time later, he transmitted the *terma* to some of his close disciples including Adzom Drukpa (1842-1924), Tertön Sogyal Lerab Lingpa (1856-1926) and Khenchen Tashi Özer (1836-1910). After this, Jamgön Kongtrul wrote a series of texts for practising the cycle.[160]

Jamyang Khyentse Wangpo was also active in building monasteries and stūpas, sponsoring the printing of books and leading public rituals. Through his prodigious activity, and through the transmissions he gave, Jamyang Khyentse gave great impetus to the Rimé movement. When he was seventy-two years old Jamyang Khyentse Wangpo passed away in meditative equipoise after scattering flowers and reciting prayers. Jamgön Kongtrul performed the funeral rites.

The twentieth century master, Nyoshul Khenpo, wrote of Jamyang Khyentse Wangpo:

> In the Land of the Snows, among all of the learned and accomplished masters of the four schools—Sakya, Geluk, Kagyü and Nyingma—as well as the indigenous Bön tradition, there was not one who did not bow at Jamyang Khyentsei Wangpo's feet. All were taken under his care and received his advice, which derived from the eight lineages of accomplishment.[161]

Chokgyur Dechen Lingpa (1829-1870)

Chokgyur Lingpa, the Great Treasure Revealer

As we have seen, Chokgyur Lingpa was a celebrated treasure revealer (*gter ston*). Jamgön Kongtrul referred to him as *Terchen* ('the great *Tertön*') and as 'Padmasambhava's representative' and he consulted him about compilation of his *Treasury of Precious Termas*. Jamyang Khyentse Wangpo expended considerable energy helping him with revealing, deciphering, writing down, cataloguing and propagating his *termas*. Jamyang Khyentse wrote a biography of Chokgyur Lingpa, as did Jamgön Kongtrul. Chokgyur Lingpa was a teacher to Jamyang Khyentse, Jamgön Kongtrul, the Fourteenth Karmapa and other important lamas. He became so famous that large crowds would gather to witness his revelation of earth *termas* (*sa gter*). Chokgyur Lingpa is recognised as the last of 'one hundred great *tertöns*'. His *termas*, known collectively as the *Chokling Tersar* (*New Treasures of Chokgyur Lingpa*), are widely practised today in the Nyingma and Kagyü schools. They comprise thirty-nine volumes including more than a thousand titles. Chokgyur Lingpa is recognised as one of the few *tertöns* (along with Jamyang Khyentse) to receive all 'seven transmissions' of teachings recognised in the Nyingma tradition. Because he produced *termas* covering several different genres and all three series (*sde*) of Dzogchen teachings, (the mind series (*sems sde*), space series (*klong sde*) and instruction series (*man ngag sde*)), Chokgyur Lingpa is considered unique.

Life and principal termas of Chokgyur Lingpa[162]

Although he eventually became very famous, Chokgyur Lingpa began life in obscurity and struggled to find recognition for many years. He was born in 1829 in Nangchen (a kingdom neighbouring Derge) into the Kyasu family which had some aristocratic connections. He was given the name Norbu Tenzin although little reference is made to this name in the tradition.[163] He was not recognised as anyone special and in his early years he herded cattle and learnt a smattering of reading and writing from his uncle; he had no education beyond this.

When he was thirteen, Chokgyur Lingpa entered Parmi (*dpal me*), a Drikung Kagyü monastery in Nangchen, but was later required to move to the Nangchen Drukpa Kagyü monastery (the monastery under the King of Nangchen) because of the local requirement that his family send a son to that monastery. Chokgyur Lingpa had begun having unusual experiences and visions when he was eleven years old and these continued throughout his youth. However, these experiences were confusing to him and to others and he found himself expelled from the Nangchen monastery because of his strange behaviour.[164] At this time there was much scepticism in East Tibet about *tertöns* and the authenticity of *termas*. It was suspected that Chokgyur Lingpa was not a real *tertön* and, as previously noted, he was mocked and called 'Kyater', the (false) *tertön* of the Kyasu family.

Chokgyur Lingpa left Nangchen in the mid-1850s, when he was twenty-five years of age, for Derge. He went to Palpung monastery, perhaps in the hope of gaining recognition as a *tertön*. At Palpung he met Tai Situ Rinpoche, Dazang Tulku (who later urged Jamgön Kongtrul to write about the three levels of vows in a work which eventually became the *Treasury of Knowledge*) and Jamgön Kongtrul. Kongtrul became Chokgyur Lingpa's principal tantric or Vajrayāna teacher. Situ Rinpoche, Dazang Tulku and Kongtrul thought that Chokgyur Lingpa might be a genuine *tertön* but he was only accepted as such after he had been recognised by Jamyang Khyentse. When Chokgyur Lingpa met Jamyang Khyentse he showed Khyentse the 'yellow parchment scroll' of some of his earth *termas* (which he had kept secret for eight years). Earth *termas* can be actual physical objects such as a statue, a vajra or a crown, but more often than not they are discovered as a scroll which contains some writing which is meaningless to all except the *tertön* destined to reveal the *terma*. The writing (which may only be a letter or two) is understood to act as a 'trigger' or 'key' which ignites or unlocks a teaching which may expand into volumes when deciphered and written down. Jamyang Khyentse is said to have understood the yellow scroll of one of Chokgyur Lingpa's *termas* immediately and exclaimed that it was almost identical to one of his mind *termas*, saying: "I too have a terma teaching called Thukdrub Deshek Dupa with the same meaning as yours; even the words are identical. We should make it into one. Mine is a gongter and yours is a sa-ter, which is more auspicious."[165] The two *termas* of Chokgyur Lingpa and Jamyang Khyentse were combined as one and became known as the *Barchey Kunsel, Dispeller of All Obstacles* or, more fully, as *The Guru's Heart Practice, Dispeller of All Obstacles* (*bla ma'i thugs sgrub bar chad kun sel*).[166] This cycle of *terma* teachings takes up the first ten volumes of the *Chokling Tersar*, and involves practice of Amitāyus (Buddha of unlimited life), Avalokiteśvara, and Padmasambhava in combination with twelve manifestations of Padmasambhava. The practice encompasses the three dimensions (*kāya*) of Buddhahood: the absolute dimension (*dharmakāya*) (Amitāyus), the subtle or universal dimension (*saṃbhogakāya*) (Avalokiteśvara), and the embodied dimension (*nirmāṇakāya*) (Padmasambhava).[167]

Following the sharing of their *termas*, Khyentse and Chokgyur Lingpa developed great confidence in each other. Jamyang Khyentse introduced the nature of mind to Chokgyur Lingpa and became his principal Dzogchen teacher and root guru.[168] As mentioned previously, Chokgyur Lingpa was not only a student of Jamyang Khyentse and Jamgön Kongtrul but he was also their teacher.

Now recognised as a true *tertön*, Chokgyur Lingpa (also known by the abbreviated name, Chokling) returned to Nangchen where he established a monastery and began revealing *termas*. After this, he returned to Derge and a period of close co-operation with Khyentse and Kongtrul ensued. Khyentse, Kongtrul and Chokling were involved collectively in the revelation of many of Chokgyur Lingpa's *termas*. Seventy-four colophons indicate collaboration with Khyentse either in the revelation or establishment of a *terma*, and twenty-three colophons indicate similar collaboration with Kongtrul. According to tradition, this level of co-operation and understanding is a reflection of the previous relationship of Chokling, Khyentse and Kongtrul when, at the time of the establishment of Buddhism in Tibet, they were all disciples of Padmasambhava. As we have seen, it is believed that Jamgön Kongtrul was, at that time, the celebrated translator Vairocana, Jamyang Khyentse was King Trisong Detsen and Chokgyur Lingpa was the king's second son, known variously as Prince Damdzin, Murub Tsenpo, Lhase Damzin Drak, and other names.[169]

During this period Chokling gave teachings and transmissions at the major monasteries in Kham (Dzongsar, Palpung, Shechen, Dzogchen, Palyul, Kathok and others) and travelled to Central Tibet at the invitation of the Fourteenth Karmapa (to whom he had previously given empowerments in Kham). In Central Tibet he visited Tsurphu (the seat of the Karmapas), Mindröling, Dorje Drak, Lhasa and other places. On his return to Kham he visited Thrangu Kagyü monastery and various Sakya monasteries where he gave many transmissions. According to Orgyen Tobgyal, by the time of his return to Derge everyone considered him a great lama—"Guru Rinpoche in person."[170]

All three masters (Chokling, Khyentse and Kongtrul) collaborated in the production of Chokgyur Lingpa's most important *terma*, the *Three Sections of Dzogchen* (*rdzogs chen sde gsum*). This is the only *terma* known to teach all three series of Dzogchen and contains no less than seven *Nyingthig* ('heart essence') teachings. It marked a shift in Chokgyur Lingpa's career as a *tertön* which saw his revelations of earth *termas* (the *termas* for which he is most renowned) becoming public events (*khrom gter*), and his fame spreading.

In the same year that Chokgyur Lingpa revealed the *Three Sections of Dzogchen* he also revealed a catalogue of twenty-five sacred sites which included the area around Jamyang Khyentse's hermitage near Dzongsar monastery and the area around Jamgön Kongtrul's retreat centre within an interconnected web of sacred sites throughout Kham. This 'location list' and the subsequent 'unveiling' of the sacred sites opened Kham as a sacred realm. Kham was now connected to the sacred places of India and Central Tibet (the sacred sites of which were now understood to be replicated in East Tibet). Kham was now understood to be sacred in its own right (in the sense that it was no longer necessary to go to India or Central Tibet to visit these sites). The audiences for the consecration of these sacred sites included monks, local people and on occasion the King of Derge and his retinue. Jamgön Kongtrul wrote a great deal about the spiritual significance of the sacred sites identified by Chokgyur Lingpa, including *A Pilgrimage Guide to Tsādra*.[171] As we have seen, part of the legacy of the cultural renaissance in East Tibet and of the Rimé movement was an assertion of the autonomy of East Tibet from the political and religious dominance of Central Tibet. This is part of the context in which Chokgyur Lingpa's revelation of sacred sites in Kham may be understood. Ngawang Zangpo's *Sacred Ground: Jamgon Kongtrul on "Pilgrimage and Sacred Geography"* explores the significance of pilgrimage in relation to nineteenth century developments in East Tibet.[172]

One of Chokgyur Lingpa's most celebrated *termas* is the *Lamrim Yeshe Nyingpo* (*lam rim ye shes sning po*) or *Wisdom Essence of the Stages of the Path*. This was transcribed by Jamyang Khyentse, who helped unravel the meaning of the yellow parchment scroll. Later, Jamgön Kongtrul added an elaborate commentary. This commentary was so highly regarded that it came to be classified as a *terma* itself. It is understood to contain the essence of the tantras, explanatory scriptures and oral instructions of all *termas* in general, and more particularly the practice of the guru (*gurusādhana*).[173] According to Andreas Doctor, it has "come to be regarded as the exposition on the paths and practices of the New Treasures and the single most authoritative explanation of the intent of Chokgyur Lingpa's Treasures."[174] A major portion of the commentary has been translated into English and published along with the root text, the *Lamrim Yeshe Nyingpo*, in two volumes under the title *The Light of Wisdom*.[175]

As mentioned above, Chokgyur Lingpa is renowned as one of the few *tertöns* to have received all 'seven transmissions' (or 'spiritual descents') of teachings recognised in the Nyingma tradition. These have been enumerated above in this Section under Jamyang Khyentse Wangpo. This way of classifying the transmission of teachings in the Nyingma School, although prefigured in earlier classifications, was first revealed as such in Chokgyur Lingpa's *terma*, the *Three Sections of Dzogchen*, which prophesied that Chokgyur Lingpa and Jamyang Khyentse Wangpo ('father and son') would receive 'seven descents' (*bka' bad bdun*). It declares:

> The river of seven descents—
> The unbroken spoken lineage,
> Profound actual earth Treasures as well as mind Treasures,
> Rediscovered Treasures and recollected Treasures,
> Pure vision and the hearing lineage—
> Will flow into the fortune of the father and son.
> It will enrich the teachings of the degenerate age
> And spread the sunshine of the profound and vast.[176]

Kongtrul used the 'seven transmissions' classification in his introduction to his *Treasury of Precious Termas*.[177] This enumeration of transmissions also provides the traditional framework for presenting Chokgyur Lingpa's life and spiritual heritage. It is beyond the scope of this work to detail Chokgyur Lingpa's reception of each of the transmissions, however such an account is presented by Andreas Doctor in his *Tibetan Treasure Literature: Revelation, Tradition and Accomplishment in Visionary Buddhism*.[178]

Chokgyur Lingpa and Rimé

As we have seen, Chokgyur Lingpa played a role in the cultural renaissance which had begun in East Tibet prior to his time and which flowered in the second half of the nineteenth century when the Rimé figures we have been discussing were at the centre of cultural and religious life in Kham. This renaissance was part of the eastward shift in Tibetan cultural vitality which saw new growth in learning and publication, in the arts and in monastic life. It also saw the revival of waning lineages of spiritual practice and the revelation of new teachings through the *terma* traditions of both Buddhist and Bon *tertöns*. Ngawang Zangpo describes the eastward shift in the activity of the treasure revealers in this way: "The Sun of Guru Rinpoché's treasures rose in Western Tibet, moved eastward, and reached its zenith over Kham during Kongtrul's lifetime."[179] Chokgyur Lingpa was an important and very public part of this process, and he has left an enduring legacy.

Chokgyur Lingpa wrote a brief autobiography around 1867 or early 1868 which was later combined with his accounts of treasure revelation. In one section of the autobiography he writes of the values of the Rimé tradition and the place of the *terma* tradition within it. He encourages practitioners to abandon prejudiced criticism of other traditions and to be aware of the common ground shared by them while respecting their unique qualities.[180] In regard to the *termas*, he stresses that Nyingmas should not be overly attached to particular treasure revealers and their *termas* but should understand the relationship between all the *termas* and their commonality with the long lineages of oral teachings (*bka' ma*). Thus, as Andreas Doctor puts it, they should "acknowledge that the philosophical roots of the Treasures are firmly planted in the general teachings of sūtra and tantra."[181] Jamgön Kongtrul observed that several of Chokgyur Lingpa's *termas* belong in the lineage of oral teachings in terms of both their words and meaning.[182]

Chokgyur Lingpa shared a cordial relationship with Bonpos. He himself revealed two Bon *termas*[183] and the well-known Bon *tertön*, Dechen Lingpa (who is mentioned several times in Kongtrul's autobiography), lists Chokgyur Lingpa as one of his own teachers.[184] Dechen Lingpa had met Chokling in 1864 and Chokling had given him a secret name.[185] After this, Dechen Lingpa met with Jamgön Kongtrul (who is also listed as one of Dechen Lingpa's teachers), and with Jamyang Khyentse.[186]

Chokgyur Lingpa had three children. His first son, born to his consort, Dekyi Chödron, died in his twenties. They also had a daughter, Könchog Paldrön, who lived to the age of seventy. Chokgyur Lingpa's second son, Tsewang Norbu, born to Jamyang Khyentse's niece, a daughter of the Somo Tsang family, lived to the age of seventy-three.[187] The lineage of Chokgyur Lingpa is both a Dharma lineage (*chos brgyud*) through a line of reincarnations, and a family lineage (*rigs brgyud*) through Könchog Paldrön. More detail on both these lineages of Chokgyur Lingpa will be given in Section 4.

As we have seen, Chokgyur Lingpa was welcome at monasteries of the Nyingma, Kagyü and Sakya schools and gave transmissions at many monasteries in East and Central Tibet. (The Gelug school does not, generally, accept the *terma* tradition.) He was also active in promoting the *terma* tradition to the lay population. Chokgyur Lingpa became a celebrated figure through his public revelations, his patronage by the royal family, and his association with Jamgön Kongtrul and Jamyang Khyentse Wangpo. As will become clearer in the discussion of Patrul Rinpoche and Mipham Rinpoche, the popular dimension was an important aspect of the Rimé movement.

Dza Patrul Rinpoche, Orgyen Jikme Chökyi Wangpo (1808–1887)

Patrul Rinpoche was born into a family of nomads in northern Kham in 1808. At an early age he was recognised as a *tulku* (*sprul sku*), or incarnation, of a teacher called Palge Samten Phüntsok, (the name 'Patrul' is an abbreviated form of Palge Tulku), by the First Dödrupchen Rinpoche, a close disciple of Jigme Lingpa and one of the principal lineage holders of the *Longchen Nyingthig*. Dödrupchen Rinpoche bestowed on Patrul an empowerment of the *Longchen Nyingthig*, and gave him the name Orgyen Jikme Chökyi Wangpo. (It will be recalled that Dödrupchen Rinpoche was a principal teacher of the Queen of Derge and her son, who were also disciples of Jigme Lingpa.)

Patrul Rinpoche studied with many lamas, but his root guru was Jigme Gyalwai Nyugu (1765–1843), another principal lineage holder of the *Longchen Nyingthig* and close disciple of Jigme Lingpa. As previously noted, Jigme

Gyalwai Nyugu was also the root guru of Jamyang Khyentse Wangpo. Patrul Rinpoche and Jamyang Khyentse are regarded respectively as the speech and body incarnations of Jigme Lingpa.

Patrul Rinpoche received the *ngöndro* (tantric preliminary practices) of the *Longchen Nyingthig* twenty-five times from Jigme Gyalwai Nyugu and completed them an equal number of times.[188] Patrul wrote down the words of his teacher on the *ngöndro* which are now well-known as *The Words of My Perfect Teacher* (*kun bzang bla ma'i zhal lung*).[189] Patrul Rinpoche is also famous for his elaboration and commentary on the essentialised Dzogchen teaching of Garab Dorje (the first human Dzogchen teacher) called *Hitting the Essence in Three Words* (*tshig gsum gnad brdegs*).[190] His Holiness the Fourteenth Dalai Lama chose to use Patrul Rinpoche's commentary on this text when giving the Dzogchen teachings referred to Section 2 (under Mahāmudrā and Dzogchen).[191]

Patrul Rinpoche was introduced to the nature of mind in an unconventional way by Do Khyentse Yeshe Dorje (1800–1866) (the immediate incarnation of Jigme Lingpa). One day when Patrul was inside his tent, Do Khyentse yelled out, "O Palge! If you are brave, come out!" When Patrul came out, Do Khyentse threw him on the ground and dragged him around by his hair. Patrul smelled alcohol on Do Khyentse's breath and wondered how, contrary to the Buddha's teachings, a great adept like Do Khyentse could be getting drunk. At that moment Do Khyentse released his grip and shouted, "Alas, that you intellectual people could have such evil thoughts! You Old Dog!" Do Khyentse then spat in Patrul's face, made an insulting gesture with his little finger, and departed. Patrul was shocked and realised that he must have misjudged Do Khyentse. Full of remorse he sat up to meditate and had a deep realisation of the nature of mind, beyond what he had received from his root guru, Jigme Gyalwai Nyugu. After that Patrul kept "Old Dog" as his esoteric or secret name.[192]

Patrul was committed to the teachings of Śāntideva, the eighth century monk from Nālandā monastery in India who is famous as the author of the *Bodhicaryāvatāra* (*The Introduction to the Life of a Bodhisattva*). The *Bodhicaryāvatāra* is a text on the bodhisattva path which places great emphasis on *bodhicitta* (the mind of enlightenment full of loving kindness and compassion). Patrul was so devoted to the practice and propagation of this text that he came to be regarded as a reincarnation of Śāntideva. His Holiness the Fourteenth Dalai Lama received the teachings of the *Bodhicaryāvatāra* in the tradition of Patrul Rinpoche from Khunu Lama Rinpoche and has taught this text many times. His

Holiness says of Patrul Rinpoche:

> Dza Patrul Rinpoche was a great master and a great scholar, ...When he would teach the Bodhicaryāvatāra, special flowers would blossom, which became known as 'Bodhicaryāvatāra flowers.' This I was told by Khunu Rinpoche. It is a story which underlines the uniqueness of his [Patrul's] practice of bodhicitta.[193]

Patrul is said to have taught the *Bodhicaryāvatāra* more than a hundred times, but he never wrote a commentary on it. Fortunately, a commentary by Kunzang Pelden, based on the oral teachings Patrul Rinpoche gave on the text at the monastic college Śrī Siṃha Shedra, at Dzogchen monastery, has been preserved.[194] This commentary is said to retain some of the tone of Patrul's direct uncomplicated speech.[195] His student, the very learned Mipham Rinpoche, was encouraged by Patrul to write a commentary on the Wisdom (*prajñā*) chapter of the *Bodhicaryāvatāra*.[196] This is regarded as the authoritative commentary on Patrul's oral explanation of this chapter. When Patrul read Mipham's commentary he is said to have remarked, "Strange, it is written in the style that I used when I taught at Śrī Siṃha Shedra."[197] Chokgyur Lingpa was also present at Dzogchen monastery for these teachings.[198] (Chokgyur Lingpa had great faith in Patrul Rinpoche and declared him the custodian of a cycle of his *termas*.)[199]

Being recognised as Palge Tulku meant that Patrul was expected to live at Palge monastery. However, at the age of twenty, he closed down his monastic residence and departed from the monastery. From then on he always lived as a very simple monk, or even as a beggar, travelling around teaching the path of the bodhisattva to all manner of people, including, at times, large gatherings of lay people. Patrul always encouraged practice of Avalokiteśvara's mantra, *oṃ maṇi padme huṃ*. Wherever he went he is said to have brought Buddhism into everybody's life and home, whether they be monastic or lay.[200] His biographer Minyak Kunzang Sonam wrote: "And the members of the black-clothed laity, both men and women, by attending for just a few moments the explanation of the *Bodhicharyavatara*, came to understand that the good heart and bodhicitta are the living roots of the Mahayana teachings."[201]

The taking of Buddhist teachings to all, including lay people and monastics, was an important characteristic of the Rimé movement, and Patrul's ability to teach the followers of different traditions within their own frameworks made him an important Rimé teacher. He taught the *Bodhicaryāvatāra* to many great masters of all schools, always in accordance with their own traditions. His close student Kunzang Pelden (Khenpo Kunpal) writes:

> In fact, my kind teacher (Paltrül Rinpoche) had realized all teachings without any contradictions and all texts appeared to him as instructions. Therefore, he became a lineage holder for the teachings of the Early and Later (Translation Periods).
> On this basis, when asked, "How should this text (the Bodhisattvacaryāvatāra) be explained?", I (Khenpo Kunpal) heard him say, "It should be explained to the followers of the Sakya School according to the commentary of the venerable Sönam Tsemo; to the followers of the Genden School with the commentary of Darma (Rinchen); to the followers of the Kagyü School with commentaries such as that of Pawo Tsuglak Trengwa and others; and to the followers of the Old School—and (in particular) for the Śrī Siṃha (Shedra) of the ancient Dzogchen (monastery) —according to their own tradition of the Old School."[202]

Much of the time, Patrul travelled in the guise of a humble traveller or beggar and so he was able teach very ordinary people. He did not seek out or associate with high lamas and dignitaries. As he moved between different places, people were often unaware of his identity. There are stories about Paltrul being taught his own teachings by people who did not recognise him or know who he was. He would gratefully receive his own teachings. Later people would be amazed to discover that they had been teaching Patrul Rinpoche.

Patrul was a very plain speaker who was not awed in any way by nobles or high lamas or anybody else. If pretentious or hypocritical people were present he was quite happy to say so. Although extremely humble, he was not very interested in pleasing people. It was said of him that the high and mighty and hypocritical would run away very quickly as he approached, lest their faults be revealed.

What is surprising about Patrul Rinpoche is that he did not live within a scholarly milieu, yet he was extraordinarily learned. When Jamyang Khyentse Wangpo was asked who was the most learned among the group of lamas that included Khyentse, Kongtrul, Paltrul and others, we might be inclined to think his answer would have been Jamgön Kongtrul, but he actually named Patrul Rinpoche.[203]

Mipham Rinpoche, Jamgön Mipham Gyatso (1846-1912)

Mipham the philosopher

Although Jamgön Kongtrul and Patrul Rinpoche were very learned, it was Mipham (also known as Ju Mipham or Jamgön Mipham Gyatso) who was the great philosopher of the Rimé group in the sense that he utilised the language and methods developed by the great Buddhist scholars (*mahāpaṇḍita*) of India. Mipham studied the Indian logical traditions of Dignāga (ca. 480–540 C.E.) and Dharmakīrti (ca. 600–660 C.E.) and Buddhist epistemology (theory of knowledge) which were central to the scholastic approach of the Sakya and Gelug schools in Tibet. Tibetan scholars had applied logical and epistemological theory to Madhyamaka philosophy and the understanding of emptiness (*śūnyatā*). In this enterprise, logic is used to arrive at a correct conceptual understanding of emptiness. A great deal of emphasis is placed on what constitutes a proper inference, what a valid proof is, and on identifying the 'object of negation' (that is, exactly what is being negated by *śūnyatā*), and so on.

Mipham used these philosophical tools while drawing on the perspective of Dzogchen (which is not usually associated with a conceptual and logical approach). He developed a philosophical approach which embraced both the sūtras and tantras, (usually these were kept apart in philosophical discourse), and mounted a philosophical defence of Dzogchen in a way not previously seen in the Nyingma school. Mipham's philosophy had implications for the practical approach to realising emptiness and for the understanding of what emptiness actually is (and is not). Mipham endeavoured to give an account of reality (ontology) and the way of knowing it (epistemology) which was true to the practice-oriented traditions; he aimed to take proper account of the place they gave to meditation and the emphasis they placed on understanding the nature of the mind and human subjectivity.

Mipham expounded a view from the Dzogchen perspective of the sūtras and the authoritative Buddhist texts (*śāstra*) of India, and was able to develop an alternative to the interpretation of Buddhist thought that had been dominant in Tibet since the Gelug ascendancy in the seventeenth century.

The work of Mipham (and later, the work of Khenpo Shenga) laid the basis for the curriculum of study within the *shedra* (*bshad grwa*) or monastic colleges which were becoming a feature of many of the monasteries in Kham in the second half of the nineteenth century. The foundations for the development of the monastic *shedra* were laid during the revival of intellectual study in East Tibet which had begun in the eighteenth century with the Eighth Situ Rinpoche Chökyi Jungne (1700–1774) and others. It was within the Rimé environment of the nineteenth century that the *shedras* could flourish.[204]

Life of Mipham

Mipham was born in Derge in 1846 into the Ju (*'ju*) clan which is said to be of divine ancestry.[205] His father was a doctor and his mother was the daughter of one of the ministers in the kingdom of Derge. He was a child of prodigious intellect and began study at six years of age by memorising a text on the three levels of vows which form the basis of Buddhist ethics. When he was twelve years old he became a novice monk at a branch monastery of Shechen Nyingma monastery, and around the age of fifteen or sixteen he did an eighteen-month retreat on Mañjuśrī, the bodhisattva of wisdom. After this, it is said, Mipham could easily understand any text just by receiving the 'reading transmission' (*lung*).

During the Nyarong war (discussed earlier in Section 3) when Derge was occupied, Mipham accompanied his uncle on a pilgrimage to Central Tibet and spent a short period in a Gelug monastery where he came in contact with the Gelug scholastic tradition. This made a great impression on him and he went on to master the methods and discourse of Tibetan monastic scholarship. Although it is easy to gain the impression (as it is with Jamgön Kongtrul) that Mipham spent his entire life studying and writing, in fact, most of his time was spent in meditation retreat. Like Kongtrul, he composed texts during breaks from retreat.

Mipham's main teachers were Jamyang Khyentse, Patrul Rinpoche and Jamgön Kongtrul. His root guru was Jamyang Khyentse. Kongtrul, Khyentse and Mipham became known as the "three Jamgöns of Kham" as each was regarded as an emanation of Mañjuśrī, one of whose epithets is 'Jamgön' (*'jam mgon*) ('Gentle Protector'). At an early age, Mipham studied Śāntideva's *Bodhicaryāvatāra* (*The Introduction to the Life of a Bodhisattva*) with Patrul Rinpoche and later composed an important (and controversial) commentary on the Wisdom (*prajñā*) section of this text. With Kongtrul he studied Sanskrit grammar and other subjects, both secular and religious. From Jamyang Khyentse,

Mipham received many empowerments, commentaries and explanations relating to both sūtra and tantra from both the Old and New traditions. According to his own words, as recorded in the biography written by one of his students, it was Khyentse who instructed Mipham to write textbooks from the point of view of "our tradition" (that is, Dzogchen).[206] According to the biography, on one occasion Khyentse Rinpoche placed Mipham on a high throne with sacred texts in front of him and commanded: "From now on, preserve them through teaching, debating, and composition."[207]

Since Mipham combined a Dzogchen perspective with scholastic study, and since he defended the Dzogchen perspective vigorously, it is not surprising that his writings sometimes led to philosophical controversy. Mipham explained his own motivation as follows:

> As for my own motivation, I have been impelled only by the command of my lama, and by the fact that nowadays the Early Translation teaching [Nyingma] is not much more than a painting of a butter lamp. Aside from imitating other systems, there are very few who even wonder what the philosophical system of our school is, much less ask about it. Thus, I have hoped it would be of some benefit to write. Otherwise, I haven't even dreamed of reviling other systems or praising myself. If those who possess the eye of gnosis [direct knowledge] gaze upon me, I have nothing of which to be ashamed. ... So, if someone who possesses the Dharma-eye refutes me in accordance with scripture and reasoning, I should rely upon him as a doctor, and should never refute him out of anger. Thus, with a noble and honest intention, I have debated upon occasion.[208]

One well-documented area of controversy concerned Mipham's commentary on the Wisdom section of the *Bodhicaryāvatāra*.[209] He had studied this text with Patrul Rinpoche and it seems that it was Patrul Rinpoche's suggestion that Mipham produce a commentary on Śāntideva's text from the point of view of Dzogchen.[210] This in itself was controversial as it trespassed, so to speak, on the scholastic territory. The *Bodhicaryāvatāra* was regarded as one of the thirteen main texts of Indian Buddhism, and is one of the five main texts of the Gelug curriculum. It had a prominent place in the commentarial tradition of Tibet and its interpretation was closely linked to Tibetan Buddhist scholasticism which had viewed the *Bodhicaryāvatāra* from the Indian gradualist perspective. For

Mipham to assert that the best way of understanding Śāntideva is from the perspective of Dzogchen could be seen as an inflammatory move.

Mipham's commentary on the *Bodhicaryāvatāra*, (and also his commentary on Śāntarakṣita's *Madhyamakālaṃkāra (Ornament of Madhyamaka)*), upset some conservative elements, especially in the Gelug school, prompting heated correspondence and debates.[211] Fortunately, some of Mipham's correspondence with the Gelug scholar Geshe Palri Rabsel has been preserved. Although they disagreed, Geshe Palri Rabsel and Mipham Rinpoche actually became firm friends and often visited each other.[212] However, some of the rebuttals of Mipham's views by others were quite acrimonious.[213] Even some of his fellow Nyingmas were unhappy with Mipham's views. On one occasion Mipham debated for several days with a Nyingma scholar who was well versed in the New traditions. Patrul Rinpoche acted as adjudicator. Apparently Patrul declined to declare either scholar the winner.[214]

Mipham's philosophical position

It is beyond the scope of this work to give a detailed exposition of Mipham's philosophical position.[215] Mipham's aim was to explain and defend the Nyingma tradition in general, and more specifically the view of Dzogchen. To some extent this gives a sectarian identity to his work. However, in line with the Rimé approach of his teachers, and generally in line with the Nyingma approach, Mipham approaches philosophy within a broadly inclusive framework.[216]

Mipham is usually identified as adhering to Prāsaṅgika Madhyamaka which, by definition, entails a *rangtong (rang stong)* orientation (since Prāsaṅgika proceeds by elimination of intellectual positions, exposing the unwanted logical consequences *(prasaṅga)* that they entail). It is certainly true that Mipham is a Prāsaṅgika insofar as he accepts that the *method* by which emptiness is established is via an absolute negation *(prasajyapratiṣedha)*. However, Mipham believes that the absolute which is realised cannot be characterised as an absolute negation. Rather, it is a non-conceptual ultimate, free of conceptual elaboration *(prapañca)* as 'existent' or 'non-existent'.[217] It is to be understood as the identity (or non-duality) of form *(rūpa)* and emptiness *(śūnyatā)* referred to in the *Perfection of Wisdom Sūtras* and in the works of Nāgārjuna and Candrakīrti. This non-conceptual ultimate is, according to Mipham, realised by buddhas in non-dual awareness or gnosis *(jñāna)*. On the more subtle tantric level this non-duality is realised as the non-duality of emptiness and luminosity (*prabhasvara*).

Mipham's position is very close to the *shentong* understanding and consequently he is sometimes identified as endorsing the *shentong* position, or of being inconsistent in his presentation.[218] In considering this, we need to keep in mind that *shentong* is not a monolithic position and, as we have seen, a variety of thinkers with differing views have been identified as adherents of *shentong*. We can say that Mipham is not an adherent of *shentong* insofar as he rejects the idea that the ultimate can be characterised as 'existent'. For Mipham, it is unacceptable to assert the *existence* of emptiness or the ultimate (as Dölpopa, for example, does) since the ultimate is beyond conceptual elaboration (*prapañca*) as 'existent' or 'non-existent'. For Mipham, it is *conventionally* valid to assert the existence of the ultimate (or its equivalent, Buddha-nature) but not ultimately valid to do so.[219] Thus Mipham can accommodate *shentong* in a broadly inclusive framework while remaining a Prāsaṅgika. His understanding of Prāsaṅgika Madhyamaka is not the same as that of Tsongkhapa but, Mipham argues, it is one true to the position of Nāgārjuna and Candrakīrti.

Mipham, Kongtrul and logic—a short anecdote

Although Mipham has become the acknowledged philosopher of the Rimé movement, there is no doubting how astute Jamgön Kongtrul was in this area. An interesting story is related in Tulku Urgyen's *Blazing Splendour*, which is as follows. Mipham one day showed some logical scholastic writing of his to Kongtrul Rinpoche, and asked Kongtrul to give his opinion of it. Kongtrul responded that he was not the one to judge and said, "I don't know much about Buddhist logic, since I never studied the subject. You are the expert in the art of validating knowledge; I'm sure it is very good." Mipham then asked Kongtrul to give him the reading transmission of the text. Kongtrul declined, saying that it was Mipham who was the author, not him, and asked that Mipham read it to him instead. After Mipham read it, Kongtrul said that although he was not well-versed in the words or meaning of such a piece of writing, he would like to try giving an explanation in response. Kongtrul then launched into an extraordinarily erudite explanation. Mipham was astounded, and said that the explanation was brilliant, especially as Kongtrul had not studied logic. Kongtrul admitted that he had said that he had not studied it much, but that this was not exactly the case, since he had studied it extensively in his previous life as Sakya Paṇḍita. He said, "In fact, it all came flooding back to me while you were reading. I don't usually have that ability, so I wanted to explain it to you while the glimpse lasted."[220]

Mipham's other interests

Mipham had extremely wide-ranging interests, amongst them a keen interest in folk traditions and, like Patrul, he brings a popular dimension to the Rimé Movement. Mipham was particularly interested in the Gesar epic and he collected various oral accounts in the hope of producing a standard version of the epic. He also developed practices (*sādhana*) and wrote liturgies associated with the epic. Mipham tried to integrate local Khampa beliefs and customs into Buddhism, drawing on the oral traditions of humble farmers and nomads.[221]

Like Kongtrul, Mipham was a highly skilled doctor, writing extensively on medicine in works which are still highly regarded. Mipham was a Sanskrit scholar and was well versed in the Indian Hindu epics, the *Rāmāyana* and *Mahābhārata*. Drawing on his knowledge of Sanskrit works he wrote an important work on poetics and a dictionary of Sanskrit and Tibetan concentrating on the philosophical and psychological terminology of Dzogchen.[222] He wrote on technology, and more surprisingly, on the *Kāma Sūtra* (the Indian textbook on the erotic arts), even though he was a monk and there is no evidence that he ever had a consort. (Smith notes that this text is one of his less impressive works.)[223] It seems no topic was beyond the scope of his interests.

With Mipham, and with Khenpo Shenga, to whom we will turn next in Section 4, we are moving toward the present day. Mipham died in 1912 and Shenga in 1927, so we are now reaching the period where many twentieth century lamas knew, were taught by, or at least had some connection with these figures.

Section 4

The Heritage of the Rimé Movement

IN THIS FINAL SECTION we turn to the heritage of the Rimé movement. As the movement has no precise boundaries we begin with Khenpo Shenga as a transitional figure. We will confine ourselves to some figures who have been important in the diaspora of Tibetan Buddhism and for the transmission of Tibetan Buddhism to the West. Of course, there have been those, such as Jikme Phüntsok Rinpoche (1933–2004), who carried on the heritage of Rimé in Tibet and never went into exile. They will not be considered in this Section.[1]

Khenpo Shenga, Shenpen Chökyi Nangwa (1871–1927)

Khenpo Shenga provides an important link between the main figures of the Rimé movement and teachers living into the late twentieth century. The masters Dilgo Khyentse Rinpoche (1910–1991) and Dezhung Rinpoche (1906–1987), who are both well-known in the West, studied with him as young men. The Tibetan system of scholarship as it exists today among the Nyingmas, Sakyas and Kagyüs owes a tremendous amount to the curriculum established by Khenpo Shenga on the basis of the groundwork laid by Patrul Rinpoche, Mipham and others.

The Rimé scholars had been ground-breaking in the inclusive way they embraced the breadth of Tibetan scholarly and philosophical traditions. The task of Mipham, set by his masters, had been to expound and defend the position of Dzogchen. Khenpo Shenga took an original and different course: he put aside the Tibetan commentaries along with the debates and all the controversies associated with them and he turned directly to the study of the fundamental Indian Buddhist texts which pre-date the emergence of the different schools of Buddhism in Tibet.[2] Shenga produced a set of annotated commentaries on thirteen Indian treatises which reveal the doctrinal basis of all traditions and schools in Tibet. In the colophon of his commentary on a key Madhayamaka text, Candrakīrti's *Madhyamakāvatāra*, Khenpo Shenga declares that he wrote his commentary "without mixing even a hair of the individual opinions of the Tibetan masters."[3]

In revising the monastic curriculum, Khenpo Shenga replaced the study of monastic textbooks (*yig cha*) with the study of a selection of original Indian texts (in Tibetan translation) with glosses based primarily on the Indian commentaries. He thereby hoped to encourage students to understand the Indian sources and the principles they expounded. As E. Gene Smith states: "It was Gzhan dga' who explicitly formulated the principle that the easiest way to put an end to sectarian differences was to attempt to understand and expound upon the basic Indic sources as the scholars of the past would have."[4]

Shenga's innovation played an important role in the revival of the scholastic traditions among the non-Gelug schools and in revealing the common ground they shared. Georges Dreyfus notes that the full story of the monastic and scholastic revival of these schools has yet to be told. He adds: "What is clear, however, is the decisive role played by Zhenga and his teaching career, which is reflected in his own commentaries on the thirteen great texts ..."[5]

Khenpo Shenga was born in 1871 into a family of nomadic hereditary chieftains in East Tibet, and his father intended him to become the next chief. David Jackson in his biography of Dezhung Rinpoche relates that once when Shenga was about sixteen years old he went on a horse-rustling expedition with his uncle. When they were making their escape with a herd of stolen horses one mare with a bulging belly was lagging behind. Fearing that releasing her might reveal them to their pursuers they decided to kill the mare. Jackson writes: "Shenga himself took a knife and deeply slashed the animal's belly. Suddenly the unborn foal dropped out, and the mare, though mortally wounded, turned her whole attention to licking and caring for the aborted foal. This poignant scene left a deep impression on him and turned his heart toward things of the spirit."[6] One day soon after, overwhelmed with regret about how he had wasted his life, Shenga left home and set off to find the great Patrul Rinpoche.

Patrul was by this time very elderly and was not taking students, but he gave Shenga a letter of introduction to one of his chief disciples, Orgyen Tendzin Norbu. Orgyen Tendzin Norbu became Shenga's root guru and transmitted the complete tradition of Patrul to him. Being very poor and having had no education, Shenga faced a difficult path in his studies. He worked very diligently and also did a retreat on the deity White Sarasvatī, the female deity of learning. He is said have had a vision of the goddess and thereafter been able to easily master any topic of study.

In his thirties, Shenga went to teach at Śrī Siṃha Shedra at Dzogchen Nyingma monastery (where Patrul had taught). He began as an ordinary teacher but soon his fame began to spread and his pedagogical approach began to be adopted by other schools. Shenga was strongly drawn toward the great Sakya scholars of the past and the whole Sakya scholarly tradition.[7] Some Sakyas considered him to be an emanation of Sakya Paṇḍita. Others considered him to be an emanation of Candrakīrti.[8] Philosophically Shenga lent towards the *rangtong* ('self-emptiness') interpretation of Madhymaka; his principal meditation practice was Dzogchen.

Shenga taught at a number of institutions including Palpung Kagyü monastery. The most important of these institutions was the *shedra* at Dzongsar Sakya monastery where he stayed for four years (1919–1923). Jamyang Khyentse Wangpo (whose seat was at Dzongsar) had instructed his followers to build a *shedra* at Dzongsar in 1871. He had invited Jamgön Kongtrul to come and determine the best site for it. The *shedra* was actually founded by Khyentse Wangpo's incarnation, Jamyang Khyentse Chökyi Lodrö (1893–1959), in 1918.[9] Khyentse Chökyi Lodrö invited Khenpo Shenga to be the first *khenpo* (high ranking teacher) in charge of studies at the *shedra* even before it was completed. During his time at Dzongsar *shedra* Shenga trained a number of students who went on to be great scholars in their own right. These students spread Khenpo Shenga's influence throughout the Sakya school.[10]

Jamyang Khyentse Chökyi Lodrö (1893–1959)

Jamyang Khyentse Chökyi Lodrö (1893–1959) is, like Khenpo Shenga, a link between the main figures of the Rimé movement and lamas of the recent past and the present day. He was born while Jamgön Kongtrul, Mipham Rinpoche, Khenpo Shenga and other important figures associated with the movement were still alive. He was the immediate incarnation of Jamyang Khyentse Wangpo (1820–1892), and in the eyes of many was almost a replica of him.[11] Like Khyentse Wangpo he was the holder of all the Tibetan Buddhist lineages and also some Bon ones, and was the principal teacher of many lamas who were

The Heritage of the Rimé Movement

prominent teachers themselves.[12] More than any other person, Chökyi Lodrö is identified with the Rimé ideal in the first half of the twentieth century.

Jamyang Khyentse Chökyi Lodrö was born in 1893 in Kham south of Derge near Kathok Nyingma monastery. His father, Gyurme Tsewang Gyatso, was a tantric master and a 'heart son' of Jamyang Khyentse Wangpo and Jamgön Kongtrul. From him Khyentse Chökyi Lodrö received most of the profound treasures of Khyentse and Kongtrul.[13] Khyentse Chökyi Lodrö was recognised as the activity incarnation of Jamyang Khyentse Wangpo and taken to Kathok monastery when he was seven years old. There he received an education in a wide range of subjects and also received the transmission of the *Longchen Nyingthig* and other Dzogchen teachings.[14]

When he was fifteen years old, Khyentse Chökyi Lodrö moved to Dzongsar Sakya monastery, the seat of his predecessor Jamyang Khyentse Wangpo, where he received the full range of Sakya teachings and transmissions including the Lamdre ('Path and Result'). In 1919 he established a *shedra* or monastic college at Dzongsar and, as previously mentioned, invited Khenpo Shenga to be its founding principal teacher (*mkhan po*). In 1920 Dilgo Khyentse Rinpoche and Dezhung Rinpoche, who became prominent lamas devoted to Rimé principles and played a significant role in the transmission of Buddhism in the West, studied at a nearby *shedra* with Shenga. They were students of both Shenga and Khyentse Chökyi Lodrö.

Jamyang Khyentse Chökyi Lodrö studied at many monasteries with more than eighty teachers in the Sakya, Nyingma, Gelugpa and Kagyü schools and became a complete Rimé master.[15] According to Nyoshul Khenpo:

> He understood precisely, and without sectarian prejudice, the view, meditation, and conduct taught by all traditions ...and so was able to care for students according to their individual needs. As a matter of course, he served each of those traditions.[16]

Nyolshul Khenpo also writes:

> ...when [Jamyang Khyentse Chökyi Lodrö] taught... he would use vocabulary specific to that teaching, immediately hitting the key point, without contradiction or confusing one system with another. Thus he was no different from a master in any of those traditions.[17]

By the 1940s Khyentse Chökyi Lodrö's fame had spread and many masters were eager to receive teachings from him. Dilgo Khyentse reports that when Chökyi Lodrö gave the empowerments for the *Treasury of Precious Termas* (*rin chen gter mdzod*) in 1945 more than one hundred important masters were present. Referring to Chökyi Lodrö on that occasion, Dilgo Khyentse wrote: "the humble regent of the Lotus-Born Guru carried on the tradition of his former incarnation like yesterday's sun shining today."[18] It was Khyentse Chökyi Lodrö who recognised Sogyal Rinpoche (b. 1947) as the incarnation of Tertön Sogyal Lerab Lingpa. He raised him as if he were his own son.[19] Some of the other important teachers known in the present day who were students of Khyentse Chökyi Lodrö include: the Sixteenth Karmapa Rangjung Rigpai Dorje, Dilgo Khyentse, Shechen Kongtrul (an incarnation of Jamgön Kongtrul and a principal teacher of Chogyam Trungpa), Tulku Urgyen, Chatral Rinpoche, Dezhung Rinpoche, Tarthang Tulku, Chagdud Tulku, Namkhai Norbu Rinpoche, Kalu Rinpoche, Adeu Rinpoche, and many more.[20]

At fifty-six years of age, after a long illness, Khyentse Chökyi Lodrö was urged to give back his monastic vows and to marry. In order to dispel obstacles in his life and to promote his spiritual activities he married Khandro Tsering Chödron (1925–2011), whom he had known since he was a young man, and soon recovered his health.[21]

In 1955, when the situation in East Tibet was worsening, Khyentse Chökyi Lodrö travelled through Lhasa and reached India. He went on pilgrimage to the sacred places of Buddhism in India and Nepal before settling in Sikkim. He passed away in Sikkim in 1959. The Third Dzongsar Khyentse Rinpoche, Khyentse Norbu Rinpoche (b. 1961), is recognised as his primary incarnation. Before passing away Khyentse Chökyi Lodrö is reported to have asked whether Dilgo Khyentse had escaped from Tibet and, on hearing that he had, he said: "In that case, the Nyingma teachings are safe."[22]

Dilgo Khyentse Tashi Peljor, Rabsel Dawa (1910–1991)

Dilgo Khyentse was a close disciple of Jamyang Khyentse Chökyi Lodrö and was also his teacher. As both were recognised as incarnations of Jamyang Khyentse Wangpo, each treated the other with great respect. Like Khyentse Chökyi Lodrö and Jamyang Khyentse Wangpo before him, Dilgo Khyentse embodied the

Rimé ideal. He was universally respected by all traditions of Tibetan Buddhism and was an important teacher for many of the present day masters, including His Holiness the Dalai Lama. After the occupation of Tibet in 1959, his role in preserving Tibetan Buddhism was crucial. He also played a major part in the transmission of Buddhism to the West.

Dilgo Khyentse was born in 1910 into a prominent and wealthy Derge family descended from King Trison Detsen (ruled 754–797 C.E.). Mipham Rinpoche (who died in 1912) recognised Dilgo Khyentse Rinpoche as an emanation of Mañjuśrī when he was still in his mother's womb. At that time, Mipham Rinpoche gave Dilgo Khyentse's mother a small blessed pill to put onto Dilgo Khyentse's tongue as soon as he was born and instructed that the syllable *dhī* (the quintessence of Mañjuśrī's mantra) be written on his tongue before he drank his mother's milk. Mipham took a special interest in the child and gave him the name Tashi Peljor ('Auspicious Glory') when he was three days old. Dilgo Khyentse always felt a special connection with Mipham Rinpoche.

When Dilgo Khyentse (or 'Tashi Peljor', as he was known as the time) was one year old he was recognised by the great Sakya lama, Loter Wangpo, a close disciple of Jamyang Khyentse Wangpo, as the incarnation of Khyentse Wangpo. Mipham declared that it was too early to recognise him as Khyentse Wangpo's incarnation and Dilgo Khyentse's father refused to allow the child to be taken to Dzongsar monastery. Several other monasteries requested that Tashi Peljor be sent to their institutions but his father steadfastly refused permission for him to go to any monastery despite repeated indications that he was an important *tulku*. Various lamas predicted serious obstacles unless Tashi Peljor ordain but his father was intent on him remaining a layman and administering the family's vast estates, especially as his two elder sons had already left home and taken up monastic life. Only after an accident in which Tashi Peljor was seriously burnt and was bedridden for a very long period was he permitted to go to Shechen Nyingma monastery (with which Mipham had been associated).

At Shechen, Tashi Peljor (Dilgo Khyentse) was enthroned by Gyaltsab Rinpoche, the Dharma heir of Mipham, as the mind incarnation of Jamyang Khyentse Wangpo. Gyaltsab became one of Dilgo Khyentse's principal gurus and gave him all the essential empowerments and instruction of the Nyingma school.[23] Another important teacher at Shechen was Shechen Kongtrul (1901–1960), an incarnation of Jamgön Kongtrul. Years later, Dilgo Khyentse spent an extended period of time with Jamyang Khyentse Chökyi Lodrö who became another of his principal teachers.²⁴ As we have mentioned earlier in this Section, when Dilgo Khyentse was very young he also studied with Khenpo Shenga. Khenpo Shenga treated the young Dilgo Khyentse with great deference as he considered him to be a reincarnation of his own root guru, Orgyen Tendzin Norbu. With Khenpo Shenga, Dilgo Khyentse studied the *Bodhicaryāvatāra* and Patrul Rinpoche's *The Words of My Perfect Teacher* as well as Madhyamaka philosophy. Shenga gave Dilgo Khyentse the name, Rabsel Dawa ('Brilliant Moon'). Dilgo Khyentse also studied at Dzogchen and Palpung monasteries and received the transmissions of a host of lineages in both the Old and New traditions.²⁵ In all, he had more than fifty teachers.

After Gyaltsab Rinpoche's death in 1926, Dilgo Khyentse spent an extended time in retreat in a secluded cave. In 1934 when a fever bought him near to death, Dilgo Khyentse was advised to marry, and he took Khandro Lhamo as his spiritual consort. This also marked the beginning of his activities as a treasure revealer (*gter ston*). The following year he revealed the first section of one of his most important *termas*, the *Pema Tseyi Nyingthig* (*padma tshe yi snying thig*). The revelation was completed the next year at the cave used by Jamyang Khyentse Wangpo ('Lotus Crystal Cave') near Dzongsar, which had been 'opened' as a sacred site by Chokgyur Lingpa.²⁶

Dilgo Khyentse Rinpoche became an exemplary Rimé lama, a holder of all lineages who could teach in any style without confusion to students from any tradition. He spent over twenty years in retreat as well as giving extensive teachings, performing group rituals, and so on.

In 1956, when the situation was deteriorating in Kham, Dilgo Khyentse set out for Lhasa. Nangchen Chinese soldiers came looking for him, and his wife, Khandro Lhamo, decided it was no longer safe to remain. Khandro Lhamo joined Dilgo Khyentse and went with him to Lhasa. In Lhasa, Dilgo Khyentse met Dudjom Rinpoche for the first time, and also His Holiness the Fourteenth Dalai Lama. (Dilgo Khyentse later became the Dalai Lama's Dzogchen teacher.) Khandro Lhamo and Dilgo Khyentse remained in Lhasa until the Dalai Lama and the Karmapa had escaped, at which time they made their way to Bhutan. From there Dilgo Khyentse moved to Kalimpong where he stayed with Dudjom Rinpoche. Eventually he established his main residence in Bhutan and became a Bhutanese citizen.

Over the years that followed, Dilgo Khyentse made three trips to North America and many trips to Europe. He established a retreat centre at Chanteloube in the Dordogne region in France. Between 1975 and 1990 Dilgo Khyentse visited Chanteloube many times. In 1980 Dilgo Khyentse established Shechen monastery in exile in Boudhanath, near Kathmandu in Nepal. His grandson, Shechen Rabjam (b. 1966), is the abbot.

In 1985 and again in 1988 Dilgo Khyentse was able to visit Tibet. He reconsecrated the printing house in Derge, re-opened the monastic college at Shechen, and gave public teachings at Dzongsar monastery, as well as visiting Palpung and Kathok monasteries.

Dilgo Khyentse Rinpoche passed away in Bhutan in 1991. His reincarnation, Dilgo Yangsi, was born in 1993. Much more information on the life and teachings of Dilgo Khyentse, along with many photographs, can be found in Matthieu Ricard's *Journey to Enlightenment: The Life and World of Khyentse Rinpoche, Spiritual Teacher from Tibet*.[27]

The Third Dzongsar Khyentse Rinpoche, Khyentse Norbu, has written that the recorded achievements of the great Rimé masters Jamyang Khyentse Wangpo and Jamgön Kongtrul are so vast that they hardly seem credible, but having witnessed Dilgo Khyentse's achievements (only a very small portion of which have been recounted here) he realised that it was possible—he saw what "such prolific, selfless beings" could accomplish in a single lifetime.[28] Khyentse Norbu wrote: "Khyentse Rinpoche was, in my opinion, the sole authentic holder of the Ri-me tradition that was Jamyang Khyentse Wangpo and Jamgon Kongtrül Lodro Thaye's great legacy, and so far in my life, I've not seen or heard of any other master who genuinely upholds the Ri-me spirit as completely as he did. ... He genuinely cared about and cherished every single Buddhist lineage."[29]

Tulku Urgyen Rinpoche (1920–1996)

Tulku Urgyen was regarded as the "life-vein" of the teachings and *termas* of Chokgyur Lingpa.[30] His grandmother, Könchog Paldrön, was Chokgyur Lingpa's daughter. From her Tulku Urgyen heard many stories about Chokgyur Lingpa. His root guru was his uncle, Samten Gyatso, Könchog Paldrön's son. Tulku Urgyen held the complete teachings of Chokgyur Lingpa as well as the complete teachings of Jamyang Khyentse Wangpo and Jamgön Kongtrul. He spent over twenty years in retreat, including four three-year retreats. He is said to have had profound realisation of all the teachings that he held. Tulku Urgyen was regarded as having unparalleled skill in conveying the essence of the teachings and in pointing out the nature of mind.

Tulku Urgyen's four sons, Chökyi Nyima Rinpoche, Tsikey Chokling Rinpoche, Drubwang Tsoknyi Rinpoche and Yongey Mingyur Dorje Rinpoche, all hold his lineage and each is a recognised *tulku*. Tulku Urgyen established six monasteries and retreat centres in the Kathmandu region. His memoirs, which mainly relate to the lineage of Chokgyur Lingpa, have been collected and published under the title *Blazing Splendor: The Memoirs of Tulku Urgyen Rinpoche*.[31]

There was a close relationship between the lineage of Tulku Urgyen and that of the Karmapas. The Fourteenth Karmapa Thekchok Dorje (1798–1868) received Chokgyur Lingpa's *termas* from the great *Tertön* Chokgyur Lingpa himself and became a principal lineage holder of the teachings. The grandson of Chokgyur Lingpa, Samten Gyatso, gave the same transmission to the Fifteenth Karmapa Khakyab Dorje (1871–1922). Tulku Urgyen, in turn, was an important teacher of the Sixteenth Karmapa Rangjung Rigpai Dorje (1924–1981) and passed on the complete *Chokling Tersar*, the *New Treasures of Chokgyur Lingpa*, to him. Tulku Urgyen also passed on transmissions of Chokgyur Lingpa's *termas* to Dudjom Rinpoche and Dilgo Khyentse Rinpoche, as well as to many other important contemporary masters.

There are two incarnation lineages of Chokgyur Lingpa: the Kela lineage and the Neten lineage. The first Kela incarnation was recognised by Jamyang Khyentse and Jamgön Kongtrul and sent to Kela in East Tibet. The Neten incarnation lineage was recognised on the basis of a letter given by Chokgyur Lingpa to his close disciple Karmey Khenpo. The first Neten Chokling was born in the Kyasu family and installed at Neten monastery in Nangchen. The second Chokling incarnation of the Kela lineage, Könchog Gyurme Tenpai Gyaltsen, compiled a uniform collection of the treasures and commissioned the woodblocks for the first edition of the *Chokling Tersar*.[32]

The fourth Neten Chokling Rinpoche was born in 1973 in Bhutan and recognised by the Sixteenth Karmapa and Dilgo Khyentse Rinpoche. He was taken to his monastery in Bir, India, when he was seven years old and enthroned by Dilgo Khyentse Rinpoche. He acted in Dzongsar Khyentse Rinpoche's film *The Cup*, and has directed his own film, *Milarepa*. His son is the reincarnation of Tulku Urgyen Rinpoche.

The second son of Tulku Urgyen Rinpoche (who is known as Tsikey

Chokling Rinpoche or Kela Chokling Rinpoche) was born in 1953 and was recognised by the Sixteenth Karmapa as a reincarnation of the Kela lineage. Tsikey Chokling Rinpoche currently resides in Kathmandu and is the father of the reincarnation of Dilgo Khyentse Rinpoche.

Thus, the heritage of Chokgyur Lingpa is transmitted through both a family lineage (*rigs brgyud*) and a religious lineage (*chos brgyud*). Tulku Urgyen Rinpoche passed away at his hermitage, Nagi Gompa, in Nepal in 1996.

Kalu Rinpoche, Karma Drubgyu Tenzin, Rangjung Kunkhyab (1905–1989)

Although Kalu Rinpoche did not have the title 'Kongtrul' he was recognised as an emanation of Jamgön Kongtrul and played a major role in preserving Kongtrul's heritage. He was chief lineage holder of the Shangpa Kagyü teachings which Jamgön Kongtrul did so much to revive. Kalu Rinpoche promoted widely the practice of three-year retreats, taught impartially in all traditions of Tibetan Buddhism, and achieved much in the transmission of Buddhism to the West.

Kalu Rinpoche was born in 1905 in the Hor region of Kham in East Tibet. Both his mother and father were direct disciples of Jamgön Kongtrul, Jamyang Khyentse Wangpo, and Mipham Rinpoche. Kalu Rinpoche's father had in fact been one of the very small group of retreatants at Jamgön Kongtrul's first three-year retreat held at his hermitage, Kunzang Dechen Ösel Ling, at Tsādra Rinchen Drak (the sacred area 'opened by Chokgyur Lingpa').[33] Kalu Rinpoche was recognised very young by the Fifth Dzogchen Rinpoche as the activity incarnation of Jamgön Kongtrul. Dzogchen Rinpoche said he should be sent to Dzogchen monastery but his father, who was an advanced tantric practitioner and recognised *tulku* himself, would not allow the recognition and chose to bring up Kalu Rinpoche himself.[34]

Kalu Rinpoche was taught by his father until he was thirteen and then went to Palpung Kagyü Monastery, the seat of the Situ Rinpoches. There he was given the ordination name Karma Rangjung Kunkhyab ('Self-Arisen and All-Pervading') and studied under the Eleventh Tai Situ Rinpoche, Pema Wangchuk Gyalpo (1886–1952), who had been a student of Jamgön Kongtrul and Khenpo Shenga. He was also taught by Tashi Chöpel and other direct disciples of Jamgön Kongtrul. The Fifteenth Karmapa, Khakyab Dorje (1871–1922), who was also a close disciple of Jamgön Kongtrul and the father of the Second Jamgön Kongtrul (1902–1952), recognised Kalu Rinpoche as an emanation of Jamgön Kongtrul but declared it would be better if he were not enthroned as this would limit his activity. Ngwang Zangpo writes that Kalu Rinpoche was twice "saved from enthronement and all the leaden responsibilities it entailed in old Tibet. ... Thus, Kalu Rinpoché was a nobody in terms of Tibetan Buddhist hierarchy, yet his lack of confinement to a specific institution allowed him to live his own life to the fullest."[35]

Kalu Rinpoche did a three-year retreat at Jamgön Kongtrul's retreat centre, Kunzang Dechen Ösel Ling, at Tsādra, under Lama Norbu Döndrup, who became his root guru. Norbu Döndrup passed on all the empowerments and instructions of the Shangpa and Karma Kagyü lineages and recognised him as the main future holder of the Shangpa Kagyü lineage.[36] As well as being master of the Karma Kagyü teachings, he became the chief lineage holder and head of the Shangpa Kagyü tradition.

At around the age of twenty-five, Kalu Rinpoche began twelve years of meditating in solitude in the remote regions of East Tibet, living in caves or tents. His fame spread and although he would have been happy to continue the life of a wandering yogi, he was recalled to Palpung by Situ Rinpoche and the Fifteenth Karmapa, so that he could become retreat master. From that point on, no matter where he was, Kalu Rinpoche was leading retreats or building facilities for three-year retreats.

Kalu Rinpoche taught and led retreats for many years at Palpung. In the 1940s he began teaching more widely including in Central Tibet where he taught the Shangpa teachings (the Six Yogas of Niguma) to many Gelug lamas. He also taught the regent of the young Fourteenth Dalai Lama and transmitted the Shangpa teachings at the former seat of the Jonang hierarch, Tāranātha, in Tsang.

In 1955 Kalu Rinpoche was asked by the Sixteenth Karmapa to leave Tibet to prepare in India and Bhutan for the impending exile.[37] He went first to Bhutan were he established two retreat centres and ordained three hundred monks. In 1962 he moved to Darjeeling in India and established his own monastery at Sonada, near Darjeeling in 1965. Soon afterwards he established a retreat centre there. Kalu Rinpoche promoted alternating three-year retreats concentrating in turn on the practices of Shangpa Kagyü and those of Karma Kagyü. He was also the Kālacakra master in the Kagyü school and gave this initiation several times in Tibet, India, Europe and North America.

During this period Bokar Rinpoche (1940–2004), who was to become Kalu Rinpoche's Dharma heir, joined Kalu Rinpoche in Darjeeling and completed two three-year retreats under his direction, one in the Shangpa Kagyü tradition, the other in the Karma Kagyü tradition. Bokar Rinpoche became the retreat master at Kalu Rinpoche's retreat centre at Sonada, retreat master for the Sixteenth Karmapa who in exile established his seat in Sikkim, and retreat master of the two three-year retreat centres at his own monastery which he established in Mirik in the Darjeeling district. On Kalu Rinpoche's passing in 1989, Bokar Rinpoche became head of the Shangpa Kagyü lineage. He also built a retreat centre devoted to Kālacakra practice of the Jonang tradition. These traditions are maintained at Bokar monastery in Mirik by Khenpo Lodrö Donyo Rinpoche (b. 1943), Bokar Rinpoche's Dharma heir.

In the late 1960s Kalu Rinpoche began accepting Western Dharma students and in 1971 began teaching in North America and Europe where he established Dharma centres and several facilities for Westerners to undertake long-term retreats. The first three-year retreat for Westerners took place between 1976–1980 at Kagyü Ling, the centre Kalu Rinpoche had established in central France. In 1982, at the urging of the Sixteenth Karmapa, Kalu Rinpoche gave the complete Kālacakra empowerment in New York City in order to aid the process of transmitting the Dharma to the West.[38] In the same year he performed the ceremonies which marked the beginning of the first three-year retreat held in North America. This retreat followed the traditional Tibetan format.

In 1986, when Kalu Rinpoche was already eighty-one years old and involved in another demanding teaching tour of North America, he announced his intention to have Jamgön Kongtrul's encyclopaedic *Treasury of Knowledge* translated into English. From among his Western students, Kalu Rinpoche gathered a group of experienced translators and meditators (nearly all of whom had completed at least one three-year retreat) and set about conveying to them the great merit of this translation project.[39] Kalu Rinpoche argued that the *Treasury of Knowledge* would provide an ideal springboard for the study and practice of Buddhism because in it the views and practices of the practice lineages of Tibetan Buddhism could be found in context. Kalu Rinpoche wanted the translation to serve as a resource for the generally educated reader who had not specialised in Buddhism. According to Ngawang Zangpo, this seemed to be in line with Jamgön Kongtrul's words that the work be "something that would be of use to people who had not studied much."[40] Furthermore, as Kongtrul had suggested, it would be extremely valuable reading for anyone contemplating a three-year retreat. Sarah Harding (who has taken a central role in the translation of the *Treasury of Knowledge*) explained that Kalu Rinpoche wished that practitioners be exposed to a wide variety of traditions and abandon chauvinistic loyalty to their own main lineage of practice:

> [E]xposure to the vast array of techniques virtually forces one to accept that they are more or less the same, and therefore are all equally valid Buddhist teachings. The differences that are fine-tuned to the individual are, after all, very minor and the similarities in being viable techniques on the path to awakening are dominant. Each tradition is profound and brilliant in its own right, once it is glimpsed. It must be seen to be believed.[41]

Kalu Rinpoche was uncomfortable with the label 'Kagyü lama' as it usually understood. According to Ngawang Zangpo (who often acted as his English translator), when asked about his sectarian identity Kalu Rinpoche would sometimes use the Tibetan word *kagyü* in its literal meaning of 'oral instruction lineage' and say: "'Yes, I'm a Kagyu lama. A Nyingma Kagyu lama, a Kadampa Kagyu lama, a Lamdré Kagyu lama, a Kagyu Kagyu lama, a Shangpa Kagyu lama,' and so on."[42]

Kalu Rinpoche passed away at his monastery in India in May 1989. The young reincarnate Kalu Rinpoche (b. 1990) is carrying the heritage of Kalu Rinpoche into the future.

Dezhung Rinpoche, Kunga Tenpay Nyima (1906–1987)

Dezhung Rinpoche was a Sakya teacher and a profound and eclectic scholar. He was a direct student of Khenpo Shenga and Jamyang Khyentse Chökyi Lodrö. Dezhung Rinpoche took up an academic position in the United States in 1960 and had a major impact on the development of academic study of Tibetan Buddhism. A number of his Western academic students also became his Dharma students. It is primarily due to Dezhung Rinpoche's enthusiasm for the main Rimé figures that his student E. Gene Smith was inspired to write about them and make the movement known in the West. Gene Smith later wrote:

It was in 1960 that I first heard of the *Encompassment of All Knowledge*, the *Shes bya kun khyab* from my guru, Deshung Rinpoche. He described this treatise as one of the greatest masterpieces of later Tibetan scholarship. During my studies, he told me much of the nineteenth-century cultural renaissance, the finest flower of which was the nonsectarian (*ris med*) movement of eastern Tibet. As the names and achievements of Kong sprul, Mkhyen brtse, Mchog gling, 'Ju Mi pham, Gzhan dga', and Rdza Dpal sprul flowed from his mouth, I became convinced that this group of scholar-saints had enormous significance for the cultural history of Tibet. I decided to prepare for research into this period.[43]

Another of Dezhung Rinpoche's students, David P. Jackson (former Professor of Tibetan Studies, Hamburg University), has written a magnificent and comprehensive biography Dezhung Rinpoche entitled *A Saint in Seattle: The Life of the Tibetan Mystic Dezhung Rinpoche*.[44] This book has been described as "a model of how the lives of modern saints should be approached."[45]

Dezhung Rinpoche was born near Tharlam monastery in the Dezhung region in Kham in 1906 and was named Könchog Lhündrub. He showed an early predisposition to the religious life and at five years of age was sent to live with his uncle who was in lifelong retreat. Könchog Lhündrub (hereafter referred to as Dezhung Rinpoche) remained in retreat with him until he was ten and during that time learnt the songs of Milarepa and various other texts by heart. His uncle was a disciple of Gatön Ngawang Lekpa (1864–1941), probably the most famous Lamdre ('Path and Result') practitioner in East Tibet at that time. (Dezhung Rinpoche recounts that his uncle's guru had done the *ngöndro*, the tantric preliminary practices, thirty-two times.) When he was ten years old Dezhung Rinpoche met Gatön Ngawang Lekpa (who had just emerged from a fifteen-year retreat) and Gatön immediately recognised him as heir to his heritage and as the Third Dezhung Rinpoche, the main *tulku* of Dezhung monastery. However, Gatön Rinpoche wanted Dezhung Rinpoche to study with him at Tharlam monastery and succeed him there rather than taking up permanent residence at Dezhung monastery. He became Dezhung Rinpoche's root guru. (Dezhung Rinpoche did not undergo an investiture ceremony whereby he formally became recognised as Dezhung Rinpoche until he was sixteen years old.)

From Gatön Rinpoche at Tharlam monastery, Dezhung Rinpoche (also known as Kunga Tenpay Nyima) received the Lamdre transmission. Gatön

Rinpoche had been a direct student of Jamyang Khyentse Wangpo and Jamgön Kongtrul. According to David Jackson, from among his thirty gurus Gatön had the greatest faith in these two lamas and continually prayed to them.[46] Gatön Rinpoche was insistent that Dezhung Rinpoche receive a thorough training in both scholarly studies and meditation practice. Dezhung Rinpoche studied grammar with a Gelug yogi and scholar, and when he was fourteen years old Gatön sent him to study Mahāyāna philosophy with Khenpo Shenga. Gatön Rinpoche had a very high opinion of Khenpo Shenga and considered him to be a reincarnation of Sakya Paṇḍita, the greatest scholar in the Sakya tradition.[47] When he was eighteen, Dezhung Rinpoche met Jamyang Khyentse Chökyi Lodrö at Dzongsar monastery in Derge for the first time. Gatön Rinpoche wanted Jamyang Khyentse Chökyi Lodrö to organise a Sanskrit teacher for Dezhung Rinpoche and insisted on him learning the language well.[48] Dezhung Rinpoche later studied Sanskrit at Dzongsar monastery with Khunu Lama Tenzin Gyalsten (1895–1977), who was also one of Shenga's students and who later became one of the principal teachers of His Holiness the Fourteenth Dalai Lama. Dezhung Rinpoche remained in Derge for seven years (1924–1930).

On his return to Tharlam, Dezhung Rinpoche did a study retreat with Gatön Rinpoche to review what he had learned in Derge. During this retreat, in addition to his studies, Dezhung Rinpoche performed three and half thousand prostrations daily. (After this, he had knee trouble for the rest of his life.) After this time he did a long Hevajra retreat (Hevajra is the main deity of the Lamdre), a Mahākāla retreat, and others. Following this, Dezhung was sought after to teach and give empowerments (including to Jamyang Khyentse Chökyi Lodrö). Gatön Rinpoche died in 1941. Before his death he instructed Dezhung Rinpoche to look after Tharlam monastery both materially and spiritually.[49]

By the mid 1950s the situation in East Tibet was deteriorating. Restrictions on religious activities were being imposed by the Chinese, and some lamas were talking of leaving Tibet for India. Dezhung Rinpoche spent 1956–1958 in retreat. In late 1958 he left Kham and arrived, via a circuitous route, in Lhasa in 1959. From there he escaped to Bhutan and then went via West Bengal to Sikkim where Jamyang Khyentse Chökyi Lodrö had recently died. When they had been together at Dzongsar, Khyentse Rinpoche had said to Dezhung Rinpoche: "Tulku, you and I are very close. When I die, you definitely must come."[50]

Dezhung Rinpoche moved to Darjeeling and from there went to the United States on a Rockefeller Foundation Grant on the recommendation of

Professor Turrell Wylie of the University of Washington in Seattle. In Seattle, Dezhung Rinpoche worked with a number of noted scholars including Robert Ekvall, Turrell Wylie, Aghenanda Bharati, Leon Hurvitz, Edward Conze, Hugh Richardson, and others. Dezhung Rinpoche met and worked with people from many different backgrounds, and Richard Sherburne, a graduate student from the University and a Jesuit priest said of him: "I always felt that Dezhung Rinpoche was beyond organised religion or dogmatic religion, that he was a truly spiritual man. [To him] it didn't matter what people called themselves or what religion they professed."[51]

Among students at the University who formed a Dharma relationship with Dezhung Rinpoche were E. Gene Smith, Cyrus Stearns and David P. Jackson. These three all did ground-breaking academic work and became well-known scholars. At various times each of them acted as interpreters for Dezhung Rinpoche.

Gene Smith (1936–2010) deserves special mention for his work on the Rimé movement and for his work in preserving all Tibetan Buddhist and Bon traditions in exile. In 1965 Smith, who had completed his PhD in Seattle in 1964, went to India on a Foreign Area Fellowship Program (Ford Foundation) grant to study living Tibetan Buddhist and Bonpo traditions. In India he became a student of Dilgo Khyentse Rinpoche. In 1968 he began a project in India in co-operation with the U.S. Library of Congress and was engaged in this work until 1985. This involved the collection and reprinting of Tibetan books which had been brought by Tibetans into exile. Through this, and through his relationship with numerous lamas in India, Gene Smith played a very important role in the preservation of Tibetan Buddhist traditions. During this time he wrote a number of important papers, including "Jam mgon Kong sprul and the Nonsectarian Movement", "Mi pham and the Philosophical Controversies of the Nineteenth Century", "The Diaries of Si tu Paṇ chen", "The Shang pa Bka' brgyud Tradition" and others. Gene Smith's articles are the starting point for any serious study of the Rimé movement. (The articles have been collected and published by Wisdom Publications under the title *Among Tibetan Texts: History and Literature of the Himalayan Plateau.*[52])

Dezhung Rinpoche remained at the University for more than a decade. In the early 1970s he resumed his public activities as a Dharma teacher, teaching at Dharma centres and giving empowerments, including to many important figures among whom was Sakya Trizin, the head of the Sakya school. In 1981, Dezhung

Rinpoche returned to India for the first time in twenty years, to assist Tharlam monks in exile and to establish Tharlam Monastery in Nepal. He died six years later whilst on a second trip to Nepal.

Dezhung Rinpoche was known for his extraordinary humility and modesty. David Jackson reports that many were of the opinion that if Dezhung Rinpoche had one fault, it was his humility—it was so great that he was reticent to teach.[53] Jackson recounts that on one occasion, at the request of His Holiness the Dalai Lama, Dezhung Rinpoche visited him in New York. His Holiness had many questions to ask Dezhung Rinpoche about meditative practice and the traditions in which he was expert. Apparently, Dezhung Rinpoche repeatedly declined to answer saying he was far too ignorant to be able to do so. Eventually His Holiness, seeing the necessity to apply more vigorous means, playfully grabbed Dezhung Rinpoche and shook him, exclaiming, "What is this? Are you like an old dog who has to be kicked before he barks?" When Dezhung Rinpoche departed after very lengthy discussions (the visit was scheduled for two hours but lasted most of the day), His Holiness is said to have remarked, "I knew he was learned and wise, but I had no idea how much so!"[54]

According to a number of sources, including Jackson's biography, Dezhung Rinpoche's knowledge of all traditions was encyclopaedic. He had a particularly deep knowledge of the Kagyü tradition. In the 1970s, at Kalu Rinpoche's request, Dezhung Rinpoche began teaching at Kalu Rinpoche's centres in North America. In fact, he taught in these centres more than Kalu Rinpoche himself. On one occasion, following the dinner after the teachings, Dezhung Rinpoche was asked a simple question about the Karmapas. Cyrus Stearns, who was interpreting at the time, was astonished when Dezhung Rinpoche spoke about all sixteen Karmapas one by one: each one's parents' names, his birth place, date of birth, visions that led to his discovery, and quoted *verbatim* the prediction letters (if found) that each Karmapa had left concerning his own rebirth, and so on.[55] Many similar stories about Dezhung Rinpoche's comprehensive knowledge are recounted.

Dezhung Rinpoche was completely non-sectarian in his approach. A talk which he gave on this subject in 1983 has been preserved.[56] His deep feelings are clear in the following two extracts:

> The Dharma shows us the way to remove the causes of pain and to attain the experience of supreme well-being. Yet there is the dan-

ger of taking hold of Dharma wrongly. If this danger is not avoided and one's approach to Dharma is faulty, 'Dharma' becomes a cause of harm instead of benefit. This is not the intent of the enlightened ones nor of the masters who have entrusted it to us.

Recognize and avoid this danger: it is called 'narrow-mindedness'. It manifests itself in Saṅgha circles in the form of sectarianism: an attitude of partiality, a tendency to form deluded attachments to one's own order and to reject other schools of Buddhism as inferior.

I have seen this narrow-minded spirit detract from Buddhism in my own land of Tibet, and, during the past twenty years of my stay in America, I have also seen it grow among the many Dharma centers founded here by Tibetan teachers and their disciples. It is always with sorrow that I observe sectarianism take root among Dharma centers. It is my karma, as a representative of Buddhism and as a Tibetan, to have the opportunity and responsibility to speak out, when asked, against this 'inner foe'.[57]

...

All these attitudes are commonly found among Tibetan Buddhist monks and lay people. These attitudes may be common, but they are not Buddhist. The great Kagyü master and proponent of the Nonsectarian (*ris med*) movement, Kongtrul Rinpoche, stated that a wise person will have faith in the teachings of all orders and will love the Dharma found in each, just as a mother cherishes all her children. A wise person's mind is vast like the sky, with room for many teachings, many insights and many meditations. But the mind of an ignorant sectarian is limited, tight, and narrow, like a vase that can only hold so much. It is difficult for such a mind to grow in Dharma because of its self-imposed limitations. The difference between the wise Buddhist and the sectarian Buddhist is like that between the vastness of space and the narrowness of a vase. These are the words of Kongtrul Rinpoche.[58]

Dezhung Rinpoche's talk was addressed to the contemporary situation and illustrates that the issue of sectarianism is a perennial one. We will now turn to His Holiness the Fourteenth Dalai Lama, who is a passionate advocate of nonsectarianism in the present day.

Tenzin Gyatso, His Holiness the Fourteenth Dalai Lama (b. 1935)

His Holiness the Dalai Lama values the Rimé approach greatly, and in many ways embodies it. The non-sectarianism which His Holiness espouses has necessarily taken forms not envisaged by its nineteenth century advocates. These reflect greatly changed circumstances which include a sizeable Tibetan community in exile (with the attendant questions of regional identity and sectarian affiliation), Tibetan Buddhism and traditional culture under threat in Tibet following the Chinese occupation, and the unprecedented confrontation of Tibetan Buddhism and culture with modernity. Inextricably bound up with these factors have been issues of Tibetan identity and questions about Tibet as a modern nation. To examine these matters adequately would require a book in itself. Here we will confine ourselves to some remarks on the Dalai Lama's approach to relations between the Tibetan schools (including Bon) and will make only some passing reference to these wider issues.

As we have seen, the unique position of the Dalai Lamas is connected with the ascendency of the Gelug school in the seventeenth century when the Fifth Dalai Lama, with the Mongol backing of Gushri Khan, reunited Tibet and established the government of the Dalai Lama (the Ganden Phodrang (*dga' ldan pho brang*)) at least temporarily, over Central, West and East Tibet. As well as being the most powerful figures in the Gelug school, the Dalai Lamas are understood to be emanations of Avalokiteśvara (Chenrezig), the bodhisattva of compassion, with a special role as protectors of the Tibetan people. In this capacity, the responsibility of a Dalai Lama reaches beyond his role as a Gelug hierarch or as a political figure.

It is important to note that many Dalai Lamas in effect never ruled. For instance, in Kongtrul's lifetime there were five Dalai Lamas, only one of whom (the Thirteenth) lived beyond twenty years of age. Consequently, for much of the time Tibet was in the control of regents who were selected from the major Gelug monasteries. The Sixth Dalai Lama was not suited to the position while the Seventh deposed the Sixth and was a strict Gelug sectarian strongly opposed to the Nyingmas.[59]

The present Dalai Lama feels "a special connection" with the Fifth and Thirteenth Dalai Lamas.[60] These are often referred to as the 'Great' Dalai Lamas due to their enormous impact. Each of the three has espoused non-sectarianism and, in particular, has had important connections with the Nyingma school. The Fifth Dalai Lama, Ngawang Lobsang Gyatso, in addition to his public role, was also a Dzogchen practitioner and a *tertön*. According to the Fourteenth Dalai Lama, the Fifth was "a great Rimey ... very nonsectarian ... one of the unique things about him was that he was a great scholar of the Nyingma, Sakya and Gelug traditions."[61] The non-sectarianism of the Fifth Dalai Lama and his connections with the Nyingmas led to a certain tension with more conservative elements in the Gelug hierarchy. The same connection and tensions can also be seen in the case of the Thirteenth Dalai Lama, Thubten Gyatso. Thubten Gyatso was a student and friend of Tertön Sogyal Lerab Lingpa (1856–1926), who came from Kham and was a student of Jamyang Khyentse Wangpo, Jamgön Kongtrul and Mipham Rinpoche. (Tertön Sogyal was the predecessor of the present Sogyal Rinpoche). Likewise, the present Dalai Lama is non-sectarian in his approach and has close connections with the Nyingmas and the Dzogchen tradition (evidence of which we have seen in the teachings he gave on Dzogchen quoted from in Section 2 of this book).

Following the Tibetan diaspora in 1959, His Holiness the Fourteenth Dalai Lama quickly realised that a co-operative approach was essential amongst all the different Tibetan schools, including the Bon, to prevent the fracturing of Tibetan religious tradition and culture in exile in India and elsewhere. His Holiness believed it was essential that the Nyingmas appoint a head to represent them, something they had lacked up to that time. Around 1960, Dudjom Rinpoche was appointed to this position by universal acclamation.[62] His Holiness the Fourteenth Dalai Lama also formally recognised Bon as the Fifth Dharma tradition or school (*chos lugs*). So, even though Bon is not Buddhist it has thus been recognised as authentic Dharma.

Another initiative aimed at establishing closer co-operation between the schools and greater engagement with contemporary society was the establishment in 1965 of the Central Institute of Higher Tibetan Studies in Sarnath (the place where Śākyamuni Buddha first taught) as a university within the Indian system. The Dalai Lama established this as a neutral environment where the traditions of all the schools could be studied. This was in line with moves His Holiness had taken in 1959 to implement an education policy in exile for primary and secondary schooling of Tibetan children and young people which included modern subjects such as science and technology. Representatives of the four Tibetan schools and members of the Tibetan government cabinet were asked to come together to prepare a series of textbooks which were to include religion and traditional culture within a framework which counters sectarianism and regional factionalism.[63] The first school for refugee children was established in 1960 in the foothills of the Himalayas in Mussoorie in Uttar Pradesh (now in Uttarkhand), India.

Of course, the Dalai Lama has his own tradition of scholarship, coming from Tsongkhapa, which is fundamental to his Gelug roots. It is interesting to note, however, that when His Holiness teaches he does not emphasise his Gelug identity, and tends to talk about the 'Nālandā tradition' as the origin of the teachings. Nālandā University was a great monastic and scholarly institution located in northern India (in present day Bihar) which flourished between the sixth and twelfth centuries and was home to many of the great Buddhist *paṇḍitas* or scholars such as Śāntideva and Dharmakīrti. These scholar-monks wrote the scholarly texts (*śāstra*) which lie at the heart of Tibetan philosophical and sūtra practice traditions. Nālandā was also important in the development of East Asian Buddhism. Nālandā was part of a network of institutions including Vikramaśīla which followed a similar curriculum and which could be said to belong to the same Nālandā tradition. Śāntarakṣita, who helped King Trisong Detsen establish Buddhism in Tibet in the eighth century, was abbot of Nālandā. Atiśa, the founder of the Kadam tradition in the eleventh century, was abbot of Vikramaśīla.

Thus we can see that in emphasising the earlier roots of Tibetan Buddhism, His Holiness is following a similar strategy to Jamgön Kongtrul and other Rimé figures who listed Kadam as one of the 'eight practice lineages' which predates the founding of the four main schools of Tibetan Buddhism and is part of the common heritage practised in all four schools. In taking a step further back historically, His Holiness locates the teachings shared by all the Tibetan Schools (and shared by East Asian Buddhists) in the 'Nālandā tradition' thus bypassing any sectarian identity to the teachings. As he has said, the Nālandā curriculum also included study of non-Mahāyāna Buddhism and secular subjects. A brief example serves to illustrate how the Dalai Lama places emphasis on the Nālandā tradition. The teachings given by His Holiness in Sydney, Australia in December 2009 on 'Awakening the Mind' included the prayers: *Illuminating the Threefold Faith: An Invocation of the Seventeen Great Scholarly Adepts of Glorious Nalanda* and *A True Melodious Song of the Sage: Prayer for the Spreading of the Ecumenical Buddha's Teachings*, both of which were composed by His Holiness. The latter prayer acknowledges all lineages and includes the words:

In short, the ten great pillars of explanation,
the chariots of practice lineage, in general, and the Shije and so forth,
rich with many quintessential instructions combining sutra and tantra,
may this Victor's doctrine in the Land of Snows flourish for a long time.⁶⁴

The 'chariots of practice lineage' refers to the 'eight practice lineages' discussed in Section 3 in relation to Jamgön Kongtrul's three-year retreat program. The 'ten great pillars of explanation' refers to the early great figures of the teaching lineages in Tibet between the seventh and thirteenth centuries.

The Dalai Lama sees the ultimate unity of the Tibetan traditions firstly in the Madhyamaka understanding of emptiness (*śūnyatā*) which as Cabezón puts it, "forms the basis for *all* the great practice traditions of the view, serving as the ground for Mahamudra and Dzogchen."⁶⁵ Secondly, the Dalai Lama argues, it lies in the understanding of the ultimate nature of mind as being the ultimate nature of all phenomena. In a chapter entitled "Union of the Old and New Translation Schools" in the book *Kindness, Clarity and Insight*, the Dalai Lama explores the meeting point between the Old and New traditions which, he believes, is to be found in the proper understanding of the 'innate mind of clear light'. He states: "It is basic knowledge (*rig pa*), clear light (*'od gsal*), the fundamental innate mind of clear light (*gnyug ma lhan cig skyes pa'i 'od gsal gyi sems*) which is the final status (*gnas lugs*) of things".⁶⁶

With regard to the difference in the approach to emptiness as a non-affirming negative (characteristic of the Gelug 'self-emptiness' approach) and in the approach to emptiness as an affirming negative (characteristic of the 'other-emptiness' approach), His Holiness believes that these could be two ways of approaching the same reality. He states: "I have given much consideration to how these two presentations could be coming down to the same thing, and although I have formed some ideas on this, I cannot explain them with complete decision and clarity."⁶⁷ Interestingly, in offering an explanation, His Holiness uses the writing of the Third Dödrupchen Rinpoche, Jikme Tenpe Nyima (1865–1926), as a key to his analysis. The Third Dödrupchen Rinpoche was a student of Jamyang Khyentse Wangpo, Jamgön Kongtrul and Mipham Rinpoche, and an important Rimé figure himself.

The Dalai Lama's endeavours towards inter-religious understanding are well known. In line with the Buddhist argument for the need for different formulations of the Dharma and modes of practice to suit different people and circumstances, His Holiness argues that the different religions serve the needs of different peoples and different mentalities. In a recent address he has said:

> Of course, most people feel their own form of religious practice is the best. I myself feel that Buddhism is best for me. But this does not mean that Buddhism is best for everyone. What is important is what is suitable for a particular person or group of people.[68]

His Holiness argues, in general, against conversion on the grounds that the religion of one's upbringing and cultural background is usually the most suitable. He does not advocate combining or unifying the various religious traditions. However, he says, we should learn from each other. His Holiness also promotes what he calls 'secular ethics' such as honesty and integrity which, being universal, can be practised by people of any religion or no religion.

The Dalai Lama's approach to non-sectarianism has been put to the test in what is generally referred to as the 'Shukden affair' or 'Shukden controversy'. Dorje Shukden is a controversial protector deity of the Gelug school, a deity known for his role in maintaining the purity of the Gelug tradition and for his ferocity towards any Gelug practitioner whose spiritual practices are deemed impure. The 'affair' began in 1976 when His Holiness the Dalai Lama denounced practice associated with Shukden on the grounds that it engenders sectarianism. This was a very controversial move because many within the Gelug school were devoted to invocation of Shukden, including many important lamas within the tradition. The Dalai Lama's denunciation had followed the publication of a book about Shukden generally known as the 'Yellow Book'. The author of this book, Dzemay Rinpoche (1927–1996), outlined stories heard from his teacher Trijang Rinpoche (who was also a tutor to the Dalai Lama) about the lives of Gelug practitioners that were shortened because of Shukden's anger at their pollution of Gelug practices through their adoption of practices from other schools, in particular the practices of the Nyingma school. For instance, the book recounts Shukden's displeasure at the Sixth Panchen Lama's decision to receive teachings from Jamgön Kongtrul's compilation of *terma* teachings, the *Treasury of Precious Termas*, and the Sixth Panchen Lama's subsequent premature death following his failure to heed Shukden's advice to not practise teachings from other schools.[69]

What was being advocated in the 'Yellow Book' was totally contrary to the approach of the Dalai Lama and furthermore appeared to be a direct attack on him since he had recently begun to take Nyingma Dzogchen teachings from Dilgo

Khyentse Rinpoche. As Georges Dreyfus, a Gelug monk at the time and the first Westerner to attain the high monastic Geshe degree, puts it: "More importantly, he [the Dalai Lama] felt that the Yellow Book was an attack on his role as Dalai-Lama, a rejection of his religious leadership by the Ge-luk establishment, and a betrayal of his efforts in the struggle for Tibetan freedom."[70] This led to a crisis (described by Dreyfus) in the Gelug school and bought to the surface deep divisions within the school concerning orthodoxy, Gelug power and relations with the other schools. The Dalai Lama's efforts to limit practice of Shukden led to accusations against him of religious intolerance and to the breakaway (primarily in England) in 1991 of part of the Gelug School to form the 'New Kadam Tradition'. Things took an even uglier turn in 1996 with the murder in Dharamsala (the seat of the Tibetan Government in exile) of the Principal of the Institute of Buddhist Dialectics, Geshe Lozang Gyatso, along with two of his students. Geshe Lozang Gyatso was an outspoken supporter of the Dalai Lama and critic of Shukden practice. Clearly this was not a polite disagreement over religious preferences. Explaining his own cessation of Shukden practice in the 1970s and his efforts to discourage propitiation of Shukden, His Holiness said: "Sectarian feeling and criticism of other teachings or other sects is very bad, poisonous, and should be avoided."[71]

A few words of clarification on protector deities may be useful at this point. Protector deities in Tibetan Buddhism are usually understood either as manifestations of enlightened beings who take on the form of a protector, or they are understood to be lesser beings (worldly deities) that have been required, usually by Padmasambhava, to take a pledge to protect the Dharma.[72] An instance of the latter is Dorje Lekpa in the Nyingma tradition, who was a pre-Buddhist Tibetan deity, bound by a pledge to protect the Dharma. According to the Dalai Lama and other critics of Dorje Shukden, Dorje Shukden is neither an enlightened being nor a pledge-bound protector. Rather, his origins connect him with a vengeful spirit and an obscure and troublesome worldly deity, Dolgyal, from southern Tibet, originally connected with the Sakya school.[73] Dorje Shukden became connected in the minds of his Gelug followers with the desire to establish a purely Gelug rule in Tibet (which had been rejected by the Fifth Dalai Lama) and a desire to preserve a pure Gelug practice free from the influence of the other schools (also rejected by the Fifth Dalai Lama).

Whatever the provenance of Shukden, the sectarian implications are absolutely clear, as we can see from the way in which the Shukden issue has played itself out. Shukden was initially a very minor deity and his practice appears to have waned even further prior to its revival either shortly before or during the time of the Thirteenth Dalai Lama (1876–1933).[74] This revival was given considerable impetus by the activities of the influential Gelug lama, Pabongka Rinpoche (1878–1941). Pabongka Rinpoche was an ardent devotee of Shukden. Whilst visiting East Tibet in the early 1930s Pabongka became alarmed at how the non-Gelug monasteries were thriving—not only in terms of numbers but also in the domain of scholarship —presenting a challenge to the Gelugs on their own territory, so to speak. His resolve was to strengthen pure Gelug teaching, and prevent further erosion due to non-Gelug influence. To this end he promoted the practice of Shukden. One can see that the very success of the Rimé movement in East Tibet engendered a conservative backlash. Pabongka Rinpoche was a charismatic and obviously powerful teacher, and respected in many ways, but he had a narrowness on this particular point. The Thirteenth Dalai Lama tried to prevent him from pursuing this policy, but on the death of the Thirteenth Dalai Lama in 1933 Pabongka renewed his efforts to 'purify' the Gelug tradition and protect it through Shukden practice. Pabongka Rinpoche promoted Dorje Shukden as the central protector of the Gelug tradition. According to Georges Dreyfus, this was an innovation insofar as Pabongka "transformed a marginal practice into a central element of the Ge-luk tradition."[75] Some of the followers of Shukden vowed to never take a teaching from another school, particularly Nyingma teachings. Pabongka Rinpoche was the principal teacher of many prominent lamas including the two tutors of the Fourteenth Dalai Lama, Ling Rinpoche and Trijang Rinpoche. The present day followers of Pabongka Rinpoche deny charges of sectarianism made against him.

 His Holiness the Fourteenth Dalai Lama took the view that limiting teaching to one school was unacceptable and that Shukden, who had only recently become a prominent protector of the Gelug school, did not fulfil the requirements of a genuine protector. The Dalai Lama therefore decided that if people wanted to take teachings from him, they were not to do this particular practice. During the June 2008 teachings given in Sydney, Australia, (where each day Shukden supporters protested outside), His Holiness said a few words about the issue. He explained his decision and said that many were very upset with him because he seemed to be going against his own teachers who were highly respected monks and Shukden practitioners. He explained that he meant no disrespect and that he thought his tutors who engaged in Shukden practice did so fundamentally out of enormous devotion to the Gelug teachings, without fully realising the sectarian implications of it.⁷⁶ In 1996 His Holiness had said:

> It is well known that my whole approach is non-sectarian and in the Tibetan tradition I am particularly trying to promote simultaneously the practices of Sakya, Nyingma, Kagyu and Gelug. One person can embrace all the teachings. However, in following Dorje Shugden there is a tendency towards sectarianism which does not work well with my non-sectarian approach.⁷⁷

In his conversations with the American journalist Thomas Laird, His Holiness recounted a letter he had recently received from a ninety-year-old Kagyü monk from Kham who wished to make a kind of confession and apology to His Holiness before he died. The monk described the three-hundred-year resentment felt in his area and the negative feelings he himself had harboured towards the Dalai Lama because of the forced conversion of Kagyü monasteries to Gelug monasteries which had occurred in East Tibet during the time of the Fifth Dalai Lama. He explained that this had prevented him taking the Kālacakra initiation from the Dalai Lama in 1954 in Lhasa and had caused him to deliberately avoid meeting with His Holiness when he came to Beijing in the 1950s. The elderly monk wrote in his letter that now he had come to understand the Dalai Lama's true non-sectarian stance he wished to make amends. In the words of His Holiness: "Now he had heard, and realized, that I genuinely follow Rimey, and he wanted to make some kind of confession before his death. So he wrote me the letter."⁷⁸

The old lama's letter is very significant because not only does it place his experience of prejudice within the historical context of what has happened between Buddhist schools in Tibet, but also because it is a clear example of how a genuine Rimé attitude can be transformative in a positive way. It opened his heart.

As is clear from his words and actions, the Dalai Lama embraces non-sectarianism as a way to engage with others and with contemporary society. Through it he actively challenges prejudice and positively affirms the importance of difference.

Conclusion

We have seen in this work that sectarianism and non-sectarianism are strong currents that run through Tibetan Buddhism. We have also seen that sectarianism is a perennial issue: it has been an issue throughout the history of Buddhism in Tibet and is still an issue today among both Tibetan and Western followers of Tibetan Buddhism. This is partly due to the human condition: there is a strong tendency to identify with 'I' and 'mine': my school, my practice; to say I am a Nyingma, a Gelug, a ngakpa (lay tantric practitioner), a Dzogchenpa (practitioner of Dzogchen), a practitioner of Lam Rim (the graduated path), and so on. This easily leads to attachment and partiality. Sectarianism also often arises because of limited exposure to other traditions or lineages. One experiences the benefits of a particular practice and concludes it must be best and the others somehow inferior. Few people are happy to practice anything but 'the best'.

Turning to the specific historical circumstances of Tibet, all except one of the 'eight practice lineages' that Jamyang Khyentse and Jamgön Kongtrul refer to had entered Tibet by the eleventh century. (The eighth of the practice lineages, the 'Three Vajras intensive practice', was introduced into Tibet in the thirteenth century.) In this early period masters and students sought out teachers and teachings from the various lineages. This was true even of the founders of the Schools. Tsongkhapa, for instance, the founder of the Gelug School, studied with Nyingma, Kagyü and Sakya teachers. This is not to suggest there weren't some tensions in this early period, for instance, between the Old traditions (Nyingma) and the New ones (Sarma) but, on the whole, there was considerable cross-fertilisation and flexibility both in terms of practice and philosophy or viewpoint.

Partiality and sectarianism became a more acute problem in Tibet with the clear differentiation of the schools between the fifteenth and eighteenth centuries. Part of this was associated with the clearer definition of doctrinal positions and particular emphases of the various syntheses of theory and practice that occurred in the schools. More significantly, political factors often came into play with the struggles for power which involved alliances between powerful families or foreign powers and religious institutions. Regional factors were also significant, as they were in the drive of Central Tibet to unify the Tibetan cultural world both politically and religiously, and in the determination of the people of East Tibet to be free of the political and religious hegemony of Central Tibet and to keep to more decentralised political arrangements and a more pluralistic approach to religious practice.

We have seen how these factors contributed to a cultural renaissance in East Tibet which provided the conditions in which the Rimé movement could flourish. The conditions in East Tibet provided a relatively open environment for religious eclecticism. There were also the conditions for renewed intellectual life with the revival of Sanskrit learning and a strengthening monastic environment in which study was valued. Royal patronage of the printing press, and the value placed, even at a political level, on visionary revelation also played a part. This cultural renaissance is the context in which the Rimé movement must be understood.

In part, the developments in which the Rimé movement played an important role were driven by the need to redress imbalances. In the preceding centuries the political and religious centre of gravity had been Central Tibet and the Gelug School. With this had gone the suppression of writings and viewpoints which were perceived to present a threat to that dominance. This had the consequence that the Sakya intellectual tradition weakened and the Jonang school with its 'other-emptiness' orientation virtually disappeared. It also resulted in a partial eclipse of some visionary dimensions of Tibetan Buddhism (mostly associated with the *terma* tradition) and severe weakening or disappearance of some practice lineages. The Rimé movement was central to redressing this situation— central to a shift in the religious centre of gravity in Tibet eastwards, and to the revalidation of discredited points of view. It gave impetus to the revitalisation of intellectual traditions in the Sakya and Kagyü traditions and the development of philosophical traditions in the Nyingma where they had previously been largely absent. Failure to grasp the need for this redress has led some to think that the Rimé movement was an anti-Gelug crusade. This is far from the case. In concentrating on the 'eight practice lineages', which, of course, include the Kadam lineage which is the basis for the Gelug tradition, Kongtrul and others were employing a non-hierarchical model to present eight equally valid ways to awakening.

The Rimé movement ought be understood not simply as a reaction, but rather as an expression of genuine devotion towards and appreciation of all the different teachings and lineages of the Buddha and their efficacy in ameliorating suffering and increasing the happiness of oneself and others. Impartiality and absence of prejudice flow naturally from this, as does the aspiration to preserve and promote these teachings. This is really quite straightforward. No more complex agenda needs to be sought.

However, more is required to explain the particular manifestation of features we associate with the Rimé movement. Jamyang Khyentse and Jamgön Kongtrul were driven by a passion to find, preserve and propagate all the lineages present in their day. Combining the inspiration and insight of Jamyang Khyentse (and his passion for acquiring and recovering transmissions) and Jamgön Kongtrul's skills in editing and writing, the pair strove to acquire and transmit all the existing lineages, revive those in danger of dying out, and clarify those that were not understood. They collected the treasure teachings, including the 'New Treasures' revealed by their contemporary, Chokgyur Lingpa, and compiled them in such a way as they could be conveniently transmitted and practised. They explained the different practice lineages so that the relationship between them could be understood and the principles behind them grasped. They presented philosophical ideas as an integrated whole, where the various parts inform each other and the relation between theory and practice is evident, and so on. Their efforts, and those of other Rimé figures, represented the last great synthesis in Tibet before the calamitous upheavals of recent history. This synthesis was broader, more encompassing and more complete than any that preceded it.

What motivated them to do this with such urgency? Could they have sensed that the tradition faced a threat to its very existence? The political turmoil at the time Jamgön Kongtrul was composing his *Treasuries* may have contributed to this sense and may, in some way, have foreshadowed the disasters of the twentieth century.[1] Some Tibetan masters believe that the period of the Rimé movement was a kind of 'summing up' of the Tibetan tradition—that this was a special time, but one which marked the end of a whole religious world. Tulku Urgyen, speaking of the period of the Rimé movement, put it this way:

> In fact, throughout Kham and the rest of Tibet, tulkus of all twenty-five [disciples of Padmasambhava] were identified and

recognized. Paradoxically, this flowering was a portent that the time for Tibet's role as a field of influence to benefit beings was just about to run out.[2]

Whether one accepts this perspective or not, it is certainly fortunate that Jamyang Khyentse, Jamgön Kongtrul and others acted as they did. Speaking of the diaspora of the Tibetans in the 1950s and after, Sam van Schaik wrote:

> When the lamas of Kham prepared to flee their homelands and wondered which were the most important books to save for posterity, the answer was obvious: it had to be the collections of Khyentse and Kongtrul.[3]

Of course, what Khyentse and Kongtrul collected and transmitted were not only books. These other collections and transmissions were also carried into exile.

Notes

Introduction

1. van Schaik (2011), p. 164 including fn. 25. Gardner (2006), p. 136, argues: "What seems to be have been the case in the late nineteenth century, and perhaps the early twentieth as well, was not a 'movement' but simply a sizeable community of scholars who put long-held values of inter-sectarian exploration and respect into a regionally and historically specific practice."
2. Kunsang and Schmidt (2005), pp. 42-43.
3. Samuel (1993), p. 537.
4. When there are multiple *tulkus* they are usually understood to be emanations of different aspects: mind, body, voice, quality and activity.
5. From 1976-1980 at his centre, Kagyü Ling, in central France.

Section 1

1. The term 'sect' is sometimes associated with the idea of a 'cult' or some kind of breakaway movement cut off from society, and often has a negative connotation in modern usage. This is inappropriate when referring to Tibetan schools. However some scholars do not object to the term 'sect' in the Tibetan context. For example, the Tibetologist David Germano uses the term 'sect' (in the same sense that 'school' is used in this book) to mean "a religious movement with the following characteristics: a) a clearly identified founder; b) a distinctive body of literature specific to it; c) statements of identity separate from other religious movements; d) centers with permanent buildings; e) a shared administrative hierarchy; f) common ritual activities such as pilgrimages and festival events." The Tibetan and Himalayan Library, http://tmb.thlib.org/categories/302/children/884. Accessed 6 October 2011.

2   Since Padmasambhava's life is surrounded by legend it is not possible to give precise dates for his life or even for his activities in Tibet.
3   A few monks had maintained the monastic rule (*vinaya*) in Amdo in distant north-eastern Tibet.
4   See Davidson (2008), pp. 84-116. The monastic rule was reintroduced to Central Tibet ca. 978 C.E.
5   The original Kadam School ceased to exist as an independent school by the sixteenth century.
6   Gampopa was also known as Dagpo Lhaje, 'the physician from Dagpo'.
7   Sometimes Drukpa Kagyü is not counted as one of the fourteen schools of Dagpo Kagyü.
8   The new translations are said to begin with the work of the great Tibetan translator Rinchen Zangpo who travelled to India in the final years of the tenth century.
9   Padmasambhava was also regarded as the source of most of the 'treasure teachings' (*gter ma*) which by the twelfth century were coming to be regarded as an important part of the transmission of teachings and practice of the Nyingma school. Andreas Doctor (2005), p. 19, says of Padmasambhava that: "his status and importance retroactively became embedded in a legendary narrative that came to play a pivotal role in the self-conception of the Nyingma School."
10 Translators' Note, Dudjom Rinpoche (2004), p. xii.
11 Ganden or Ganden Namgyal Ling (*dga' ldan rmam rgyal gling*) was established in 1409. The abbot of Ganden, the 'throne holder of Ganden' (*dga' ldan khri pa*), is the official head of the Gelug school.
12 The Third Dalai Lama's name was Sönam Gyatso (*bsod nams rgya mtsho*) which actually means 'Ocean of Merit', so it is possible that Altan Khan was simply translating the name into Mongolian rather than bestowing a title.
13 That this was a widely held perception is illustrated by a statement from Jamyang Khyentse Chökyi Lodrö (1893–1959) who was recognised as an activity emanation (*phrin sprul*) of Jamyang Khyentse Wangpo: "It is also said that the Sakyapa and Gedenpa are entrusted with the order to expound and that the Nyingmapa and Kagyüpa are entrusted with the order to practise." Michael Aris (1977), p. 219. (Note that Gedenpa is equivalent to Gelugpa.) Jamyang Khyentse Chökyi Lodrö goes on to clarify that this

statement does not give a complete picture of the nature of these schools.

14 According to Sakya Paṇḍita the Mahāmudrā system of Gampopa is essentially identical to the Chinese system of Dzogchen: "No substantial difference exists between the present-day Great Seal and the Great Perfection (rDzogs-chen) of the Chinese tradition, other than a change in names..." Sakya Pandita Kunga Gyaltsen (2002), p. 118. For a careful analysis of Sakya Paṇḍita's objections, see David Jackson (1994), pp. 67-90.

15 Geoffrey Samuel argues that "Rimed and Gelugpa can be considered as the two major and contrasting syntheses of clerical and shamanic elements within premodern Tibetan religion." (1993), p. 537.

16 The Fourteenth Dalai Lama says of the Fifth Dalai Lama: "Usually we consider him as a great Rimey. Everyone does except the Kagyupa ... He was very nonsectarian. It's also true that he did not study the Kagyu tradition much and that his relations with the Kagyu and the king of Tsang were not very good." Laird (2006), p. 166.

17 Some Jonang monasteries survived in Amdo in East Tibet.

18 Smith (2001), pp. 90, 250. See also Smith, (2004), p. 191. For more detail on Losel Tenkyong, see Jamgön Kongtrul and Ngawang Zangpo (2003), pp. 345-46. Ngawang Zangpo, p. 346, dates the retrieval of the texts to the late 1850s. Smith (2001), p. 90, had dated it at 1871.

19 Emptiness refers to the idea that all dependently arisen things lack (or are 'empty of') self-existence (*svabhāva*) since they depend on other things (other causes and conditions) and thus do not exist 'by themselves'. This includes all things subject to birth-and-death (*saṃsāra*). The question arises whether there is an absolute or ultimate reality which is self-existent, or whether the absolute truth is the mere fact of non-self-existence.

20 The most famous and influential early opponent of Dölpopa's views was Rendawa Shonu Lodrö (1348-1413), one of Tsongkhapa's principal teachers. According to Cyrus Stearns (2010), p. 98, "Although not generally acknowledged, it is clear that much of Tsongkapa's philosophical doctrine was formulated in direct reaction to the teachings of Dölpopa, which he had learned about during his studies of Mahāyāna treatises under the direction of some of Dölpopa's main disciples."

21 Takten Damchö Ling (*rtag brtan dam chos gling*), also known as Takten Phüntsok Ling (*rtag brtan phun tshogs gling*), was the biggest Jonang monastery in Central Tibet.

22 Cited in Jeffrey Hopkins (2007), pp. 11-12.
23 The Jonang monastery established by Tāranātha, known as Takten Damchö Ling or Takten Phüntsok Ling was converted to Gelug and renamed Ganden Phüntsok Ling (*dga' ldan phun tshogs gling*). It was renamed after Ganden, the oldest Gelug monastery (founded 1409) which is also the seat of Gelug power.
24 The first three vehicles are the so-called Hīnayāna ('lesser vehicle') comprising the first two, and the Mahāyāna ('great vehicle') comprising the third. The next three are the outer tantras, Kriyā-, Carya- and Yogatantra. The last three vehicles are the inner tantras, Mahāyoga and Anuyoga, and Dzogchen (or Atiyoga).
25 On the Shangpa Kagyü see Matthew Kapstein (1980). Kapstein p. 138, notes that the Tibetan word 'kagyü' (*bka' brgyud*) literally means 'a lineage of precepts' and does not necessarily imply any connection with other Kagyü schools: "Thus the Shangs-pa bKa'-brgyud is the 'spiritual succession of Shangs': the name implies only that."

Section 2

1 See Schroeder (2004), pp. 15-17, for examples from the Pāli canon of the variety of ways the Buddha taught.
2 *Majjhima Nikāya 22 Alagaddūpama Sutta*.
3 The 'four noble truths' (suffering, arising of suffering, end of suffering, way to the end of suffering) provide a diagnosis of the human condition, the problem of suffering and a remedy for it. One of the epithets of the Buddha is 'physician' (Pāli. *bhissako*), e.g., *Anguttara Nikāya* iv 340.
4 *Samyutta Nikāya 56:31 Siṃsapa Sutta*.
5 For example in Chapter 2 of the *Lotus Sūtra* (*Saddharmapuṇḍarīka Sūtra*). The *Lotus Sūtra* radically claims that all teachings are provisional skilful means since the ultimate truth is inexpressible.
6 Hīnayāna should be distinguished from the Theravāda tradition which did not reject the bodhisattva ideal. See Rahula (1978).
7 Notably in the *Lotus Sūtra*. See Hurvitz (1976), p. 239. Also Part 2 of the *The Skill in Means* (*Upāyakauśalya*) *Sūtra*. Tatz (1994), pp. 51-70.
8 Cited in Ringu Tulku (2006), p. 5.
9 Karmay (1988), p. 128.

Notes to Section 2

10   Cited in Ringu Tulku (2006), p. 7.
11   Cited in the Preface, Tenzin Gyatso, Dalai Lama XIV (2000), p. 15.
12   Ringu Tulku (2006), p. 11.
13   See Tsele Natsok Rangdröl (1996).
14   Tsele Natsok Rangdröl (1996), pp. 36-37. Tsele Natsok Rangdröl is listed among Jamgön Kongtrul's former incarnations. Jamgön Kongtrul (2003a), p. 448.
15   Dudjom Rinpoche (1991), pp. 572-74.
16   Verse 19. As translations of this verse vary considerably the original Tibetan is included:
      yid byed bral ba 'di ni phyag rgya che
      mtha' dang bral ba dbu ma chen po yin
      'di ni kun 'dus rdzogs chen zhes kyang bya
      gcig shes kun don rtogs pa'i gdengs thob shog
17   The Third Karmapa's sentiment had, in fact, been preceded in the Kagyü tradition by both Milarepa (1052-1135) and Gampopa. Milarepa 'sang':
      The Great Perfection takes no sides.
      If it takes sides, it is not the Great Perfection.
      The Great Seal doesn't negate or affirm.
      If there is negation or affirmation, it is not the Great Seal…
      In the Great Middle Way, there is no identity at which to grasp.
      If identity is grasped at, then it is not the Great Middle Way.
Cited in Tenzin Gyatso the Fourteenth Dalai Lama, Khöntön Peljor Lhündrub and José Ignacio Cabezón (2011), pp. 53-54.
18   Brunnhölzl (2007), pp. 159-93. Brunnhölzl (2009), pp. 113-16, outlines some significant differences between the Third Karmapa and Dölpopa (the principal proponent of *shentong*).
19   Brunnhölzl (2007), p. 184.
20   Brunnhölzl (2007), p. 184.
21   The term 'Great Madhyamaka' is sometimes identified with *shentong* but is, in fact, broader in scope. This point is discussed in more detail in Section 3 in relation to Jamgön Kongtrul's presentation of *shentong*.
22   This classification is used by Jamgön Kongtrul. See Jamgön Kongtrul (2007b), pp. 208-26.
23   Tenzin Gyatso H. H. the Dalai Lama and Alexander Berzin (1997), pp. 113-18.

24 Even Sūtra Mahāmudrā may involve 'direct introduction to the [nature of] mind' (*sems kyi ngo sprod*) which is more usually associated with Essence Mahāmudrā. David Jackson (1994), p. 2, writes: "sGam-po-pa is said to have given such Great Seal instructions sometimes not as secret Vajrayāna precepts in connection with initiation and special yogic practices, but rather as a Sūtra-based Great Seal instruction, or even as a doctrine going beyond both Sūtra and Tantra."

25 For a scholarly discussion of Sūtra Mahāmudrā see Jackson (1994), pp. 17-24.

26 Jackson (1994), pp. 11-12. For a concise presentation of 'inner heat' practices see Ray (2001), pp. 237-44.

27 For example, Dagpo Tashi Namgyal (1512-1587) states that Naropa received the secret oral teachings on the quintessential Mahāmudrā from his guru Tilopa which resulted in his liberation which was "not dependent upon the esoteric path of tantra." He also states that Maitrīpa received the illuminating instructions of quintessential Mahāmudrā from his guru Shavarishvara [Shavaripa] which were "not based on the tantric teachings." Both quotes, Takpo Tashi Namgyal (1993), p. 101. See also Jackson (1994), pp. 24-28.

28 Non-fabrication (or non-conceptuality) is the second of the Four Yogas, and non-meditation is the fourth. The first and third yogas are one-pointedness and one-taste respectively.

29 Dzogchen teachings are classified into three classes or series (*sde*) relating to different approaches to the nature of mind: Mind Series (*sems sde*), Space Series (*klong sde*) and Instruction Series (*man ngag sde*). Mahāmudrā is often said to have most in common with the Mind Series. Dzogchen practice is also divided into *trekchö* (*khregs chod*) or 'breakthrough' and *thögel* (*thod rgal*) or 'leapover'. Mahāmudrā is close in its approach to 'breakthrough' and does not utilise the visionary practices of 'leapover'. According to Karma Chagmé (1998), p. 180, 'breakthrough' is "identical to Mahāmudrā."

30 Dzogchen is often characterised as the path of self-liberation (*rang grol lam*) and contrasted with paths of renunciation (*spong lam*) and purification (*sbyong lam*) (sūtra and lower tantras) and transformation (*sgyur lam*) (higher tantras). See Kennard Lipman's Foreword to Mañjusrīmitra (1987), pp. x-xi. According to Elías Capriles (2004), p. 15, this presentation of paths

is found in the *bka'-thang sde-lnga and bsam-gtan mig-sgron* attributed respectively to early Tibetan Dzogchen masters Namkhai Nyingpo and Nubchen Sangye Yeshe. This principle is also applicable to Mahāmudrā. See Traleg Kyabgon (2004), pp. 11-14.

31 Tenzin Gyatso, Dalai Lama XIV (2000), p. 81.
32 Tenzin Gyatso, Dalai Lama XIV (2000), p. 47.
33 Kapstein (2002), p. 105.
34 The Second Karmapa, Karma Pakshi, says the highest vehicle is, in fact, Anuyoga, and the result or fruition of Anuyoga is Dzogchen. This is in line with the view that Dzogchen, strictly speaking, is not a vehicle at all; it is *ati*, meaning 'beyond'. Kapstein (2002), p. 105. The Sanskrit word *ati* does not mean 'highest', as is often said.
35 Sam van Schaik (2004a), pp. 98-99, writes: "Although mixed with these instructions are rejections of supposition (*yid dpyod*) and deliberate effort (*byas pa'i chos*), the instructions are in effect an establishment of emptiness through the intellect."
36 Dzogchen teachings are classified into three classes or series (*sde*). The Instruction Series (*man ngag sde*) approach is most direct while the less direct Mind Series (*sems sde*) involves more oral explanation and includes practices to develop a calm state (S. *śamatha*, T. *zhi gnas*) and insight (S. *vipaśyanā*, T. *lhag mthong*). See Namkhai Norbu (1986), pp. 80-81, 100.
37 Cited in Traleg Kyabgon (2004), p. 8. See pp. 3-11 of this book for a discussion of the milieu in which Saraha lived and in which the Kagyü approach to Mahāmudrā developed. Traleg Rinpoche, p. 11, notes that Mahāmudrā can be distinguished as a unique vehicle (*yāna*) separate from tantra. See also Jackson (1994), pp. 24-28.
38 Cited in Jackson (1994), p. 12. There was an argument in Tibet as to whether this insight into the nature of mind was *all* that was required to achieve Buddhahood, i.e., is it the 'self-sufficient remedy'?
39 Shortly before the Tenth Karmapa's death a reconciliation with the Fifth Dalai Lama took place at the Potala Palace in Lhasa.
40 These are the dates given in Tsering Lama Jampal Zangpo (1988), pp. 46-51. Other sources give different dates.
41 The other main branch of Karma Kagyü is Surmang. Other traditions of Dagpo Kagyü, including the Drikung and Taklung Kagyü, incorporated Nyingma *terma* and *kama* (long oral) traditions, as did the Drukpa Kagyü.

See Ringu Tulku (2006), pp. 140-42.
42. Karma Chagmé (1998), p. 23. There is a second volume in English: Karma Chagmé (2000).
43. Karma Chakme (2004-2011), 4 volumes. (Vol. 5 will contain the Tibetan text.) The term *ri chos* refers to comprehensive retreat instructions (which are also applicable to practice in general).
44. Karma Chakme (2010).
45. Chökyi Nyima Rinpoche (1986).
46. He completed a second three-year retreat in 1762. Goodman (1992), p. 144.
47. Occasionally *termas* were attributed to others such as Vimalamitra who was important in the transmission of Dzogchen to Tibet.
48. These are the *Bima* (or *Vima*) *Nyingthig* (named after Vimalamitra) and the *Khandro Nyingthig*.
49. van Schaik (2004a), pp. 8-10.
50. The nine vehicle scheme had precedents going back the eighth and ninth centuries but is known in its present form only from the tenth century. van Schaik (2004b), pp. 187-89.
51. Goodman (1992), pp. 139-44.
52. A hiatus between uncovering a *terma* and its promulgation is usual, but Jigme Lingpa seems to have been reluctant to teach the *terma* until he was encouraged to do so by a wandering yogi (who had not been told about the *terma*). van Schaik (2004a), pp. 36-37.
53. The *Longchen Nyingthig* was part of Jigme Lingpa's collected works, publication of which was supervised by the Queen of Derge and Jigme Lingpa's disciple Dödrupchen in Derge in Kham ca. 1800. van Schaik (2004a), p. 39. For the lineage of the *Longchen Nyingthig* see Nyoshul Khenpo Jamyang Dorjé (2005). The principal focus of this book is the lineage holders of the *Longchen Nyingthig*.
54. van Schaik (2004a), pp. 106-8. He also notes (pp. 23, 120-21) the influence of Tsele Natsok Rangdröl (b. 1608), the great Karma Kagyü teacher of Mahāmudrā and Dzogchen, who was the subject (along with Longchenpa and Padmasambhava) of Jigme Lingpa's visions during retreats, and the Karma Kagyü teacher Dagpo Tashi Namgyal (1512–1587). Tsele Natsok Rangdröl is listed as a previous incarnation of Jamgön Kongtrul. See Jamgön Kongtrul (2003a), p. 448.
55. van Schaik (2004a), p. 105.

56 Shabkar and Ricard et. al (2001).
57 Shabkar and Ricard et. al (2001), p. xv.
58 Shabkar and Ricard et. al (2001), p. xv.
59 Smith (2001), p. 127. Smith refers to Lobsang Chökyi Gyaltsen as the 'First Paṇ chen Lama' since he was the first to be recognised with that title.
60 Tenzin Gyatso H. H. the Dalai Lama and Alexander Berzin (1997), pp. 169-70. Mahāmudrā in Gelug tradition derives from the Kagyü school and also from Tsongkhapa.
61 Tenzin Gyatso H. H. the Dalai Lama (2004). *The Bardo Thödröl (bar do thos grol)*, *Liberation Through Hearing in the Intermediate State*, is popularly known in the West as *The Tibetan Book of the Dead* because of its alleged similarity to the *Egyptian Book of the Dead* (itself actually titled *Book of emerging forth into the Light*).
62 Smith (2001), p. 128. The five Mahāmudrās are, in the order given in the verse, associated with the following figures: Gampopa, Khyungpo Naljor, Jigten Gompo, Tsangpa Gyarey, and either Hva Shang Mahāyāna or Saraha. Pacification (*zhi byed*) is associated with Phadampa Sangye; Severance (*gcod*) with Machig Lapdrön. See Samten Karmay (1998), p. 144.
63 Tenzin Gyatso the Fourteenth Dalai Lama, Khöntön Peljor Lhündrup and José Ignacio Cabezón (2011), fn. 10, p. 151.
64 The book *Meditation on the Nature of Mind*, includes the talk by His Holiness, a translation of Khöntönpa's text and a biography of Khöntönpa by José Ignacio Cabezón based on a biography by Khöntönpa's most famous student, the Fifth Dalai Lama. Tenzin Gyatso the Fourteenth Dalai Lama, Khöntön Peljor Lhündrub and José Ignacio Cabezón (2011).
65 Tenzin Gyatso the Fourteenth Dalai Lama, Khöntön Peljor Lhündrub and José Ignacio Cabezón (2011), p. 56. See also p. 59.

Section 3

1 For a discussion of this point see the Preface to Jamgön Kongtrul and Ngawang Zangpo (1994), p. 12.
2 Samuel (1993), pp. 68-71.
3 Thangtong Gyalpo is famous for building many iron suspension bridges in Tibet and Bhutan, some of which are still in use today. He is also regarded as the father of Tibetan opera. Exact dates for Thangtong Gyalpo, who

was renowned for his long life, are uncertain. Cyrus Stearns (2007), p. 15, writes: "Tangtong Gyalpo is said to have mastered the practices of all the religious systems in Tibet, and the transmission of his teachings reflects this eclectic approach. His own blend of the various traditions he inherited, influenced by his numerous visions of the divine, came to be known as the Chaksam, or Iron-Bridge, Tradition (*Lcags zam lugs*). .... The teachings of Tangtong Gyalpo's Iron-Bridge tradition have come down to the present day as currents found in virtually all the major Buddhist schools in Tibet."

[4] Smith (2004), p. 186. "The list of the banned books included the works of such philosophical masters as Dolpopa, Taranatha, the Five Patriarchs of the Sakya, and Karma Mikyo Dorje."

[5] Although the Fifth Dalai Lama was well-disposed to the Nyingma and the Nyingmas flourished under him, many others in the Gelug establishment were not. Smith (2001), pp. 244-45. Mindröling Monastery and Dorje Drak in Central Tibet had been destroyed during the Dzungar Mongol invasion in the early eighteenth century. The Nyingma luminaries Lochen Dharmashri (1654-1717) and Pema Trinle (1641-1717) were assassinated and many Nyingma lineage holders fled to East Tibet. Ronis (2009), p. 93.

[6] Dzogchen and Palyül Nyingma monasteries were established in Derge during the seventeenth century. Kathok Nyingma monastery, which had fallen into disrepair, was rebuilt and revitalised in Derge during the same period. Shechen monastery was founded in Derge in 1734. A 'mother monastery' (*ma dgon*) served as the main monastery for many branch monasteries which came under its jurisdiction.

[7] In 1733 both the Karmapa and the high-ranking Zhamarpa Rinpoche died en route to China leaving a power vacuum in the Karma Kagyü school. Smith (2001), pp. 90-91. The position of the Tai Situs was further strengthened by the ban placed on the Sharmapa lineage by the Central Tibetan government in 1791.

[8] van Schaik (2011), p. 160.

[9] Cited in van Schaik (2011), p. 161.

[10] Following the sacking of Mindröling and Dorje Drak monasteries by Dzungar Mongol invaders in 1717, the Nyingmas came under continuing stress in Central Tibet due to pressure from the new Manchu emperor of China, Yongzheng (ruled 1722-1735), who ordered the suppression of the Nyingmas. van Schaik (2004a), p. 26.

Notes to Section 3

11 van Schaik (2004a), p. 38.
12 Janet Gyatso (1997), p. 371. One of the extracts from Jigme Lingpa's autobiography translated by Gyatso recounts his meeting with the King and Queen of Derge.
13 van Schaik (2004a), p. 39.
14 Recent research suggests that the Queen was not exiled as has been commonly thought by Western scholars. According to a recent article, she acted as regent or dowager Queen until her son assumed full power in 1804. Her loss of favour appears to be connected to criticism of the Sakyas made by her Nyingma personal chaplain, Getse Tulku, and included in his *Catalogue* of the Nyingma tantras (*rnying ma rgyud 'bum*) which had been printed with the Queen's patronage. In the *Catalogue*, Getse Tulku had also eulogised the Queen as a great monarch (*mi'i dbang mo*), as protector of the land (*sa kyong*), and as an emanation of the female Buddha Tārā. She died away from the capital in 1812. Ronis, (2011), pp. 61-81.
15 Smith (2001), p. 25.
16 Nyoshul Khenpo Jamyang Dorjé (2005), p. 396.
17 These three masters (Do Khyentse, Patrul and Jamyang Khyentse) were respectively recognised as mind, speech and activity incarnations of Jigme Lingpa.
18 According to Jean-Luc Achard (2003), p. 46, it was this connection with Jigme Lingpa and the future patronage of the royal house of Derge which allowed Getse Tulku to edit the first xylographic version of the *Nyingma'i Gyübum* following the catalogue drawn up by Jigme Lingpa. The woodblocks of this edition survived the Chinese invasion and subsequent Cultural Revolution in Tibet and the text is now being reprinted in Tibet. It is possible that none of the handwritten manuscripts of the *Nyingma'i Gyübum* survived in Tibet. See Preface to 'The *Rig 'dzin Tshe dbang nor bu* Edition of the *rNying ma'i rgyud 'bum*' at http://ngb.csac.anthropology.ac.uk/csac/NGB/Doc/Preface.xml. Accessed 29 Oct 2011.
19 Jamgön Kongtrul (2003a), fn. 132, p. 301.
20 For a list of significant scholars see Smith (2001), p. 89.
21 Smith (2001), p. 89.
22 Jann Michael Ronis discusses Situ Rinpoche's "lifelong mission to propagate monasticism at Kagyü and Nyingma monasteries in Kham." Ronis (2009), pp. 147-56.

23 Terrone (2008), p. 756.
24 Smith (2001), p. 87.
25 Smith notes these Sanskritic studies constitute the basis for Tibetan philological studies. Smith (2001), p. 89. The Sakya scholar Zhuchen Tshultrims Rinchen (1697-1769) edited the Derge edition of the Indian canonical commentaries, the *Tanjur* (*bstan 'gyur*) which was printed in 1743-44. He was, like Situ Rinpoche, a master of Tibetan poetics and Sanskrit language. Smith (2001), p. 91.
26 Stearns (2010), p. 80.
27 Stearns (2010), p. 80.
28 Smith (2001), p. 250.
29 Jamgön Kongtrul (2003a), pp. 132-35. The Queen, Chöying Zangmo, was, in fact, taken hostage along with many lamas and notable lay people, by Gönpo Namgyal. In 1860-1861, Kongtrul and other lamas had been required to perform ritual services for Gönpo Namgyal. Jamgön Kongtrul (2003a), p. 127.
30 According to Xiuyu Wang (2009), p. 481, "The Qing agreed to the arrangement owing to its inability to offer the Dalai Lama financial compensation, and in the hope that Tibetan rule might pacify Kham by undermining the influence of Nyarong in the surrounding areas."
31 According to Smith (2001), p. 249, Kongtrul was regarded as "the most competent physician in Khams."
32 Jamgön Kongtrul (2003a), p. 139.
33 This period is covered in Jamgön Kongtrul (2003a), pp. 132-43. According to Smith (2001), p. 249, in this period Kongtrul and Khyentse were "the moral leaders for the distressed people of Sde dge." He notes that in the troubled times after 1870 Jamyang Khyentse and later Mipham Rinpoche were required to exercise much temporal authority.
34 van Schaik (2011), p. 169. Rule in Derge had been returned to the royal household but affairs were superintended by a 'high commissioner' appointed by the Lhasa government to administer Nyarong and superintend the affairs of Derge. Teichman (1922), p. 5.
35 Bon institutions in Central Tibet in fact relied on support from East Tibet. See Patrick Gorvine (2006), pp. 44-45.
36 One example is the Bonpo *tertön* Shardza Tashi Gyaltsen (*shar rdza bkra shis rgyal mtshan*) (1859-1934) who enjoyed patronage from a wide variety

of royal houses across East Tibet in the nineteenth and twentieth centuries. Gorvine (2006), pp. 182-83.

37 Kapstein (2006), p. 205.

38 Kapstein (2006), p. 205. For an interesting analysis of pre-Buddhist 'original' Tibetan religion in relation to the 'ancient matrix' or archaic world view, see Samuel (1993), pp. 438-44.

39 Bonpos attribute the original teachings to Tönpa Shenrab (*ston pa gshen rab*) who lived in the distant past. They say Bon was introduced into Zhang-zhung from 'Ta-zig' (*stag gzig*) further west from Tibet—possibly Central Asia, Persia or Iran. In Buddhist tradition Padmasambhava is said to come from Oddiyana in 'the West'. The north-west of the Indian subcontinent and Central Asia were certainly areas of great cultural interchange.

40 Kvaerne (1995), pp. 19-21. He also notes that some *termas* are understood to date from an earlier persecution of Bon.

41 The Dzogchen of Bon and Buddhism are substantially the same in meaning and terminology. See Reynolds (2005), pp. 3-16.

42 See Kvaerne (1995), p. 11.

43 On the language of Zhang-zhung, see Dan Martin (2010).

44 See Martin (2001), pp. 16-29.

45 A Bon scriptural canon was probably established around 1450. Most of the texts were discovered by Bon *tertöns*, beginning in the tenth century. Kvaerne (1996), p. 140.

46 The beginnings of this movement can be traced to Tulku Loden Nyingpo (*sprul sku blo ldan snying po*) (b. 1360). However it really grew in eighteenth century East Tibet. Achard (2004a), pp. xi-xii.

47 According to Jean-Luc Achard (2008), p. xxii: "In fact, the incredible variety or richness of the New Bon tradition lies in the fact that it includes all major cycles of Eternal Bon to which are added the various New Bon lines of transmission, even if some caution is required before generalizing."

48 Examples are Dechen Lingpa (*bde chen gling pa*) (b. 1833) and Shardza Tashi Gyaltsen (*shar rdza bkra shis rgyal mtshan*) (1859-1934). Dechen Lingpa's uncle was Jamgön Kongtrul's Bon teacher in his early years. Achard (2004a), fn. 11, p. xiii. Dechen Lingpa is mentioned several times in Kongtrul's autobiography. Jamgön Kongtrul (2003a). Kongtrul first met him in 1872 at Dzongsar monastery where Jamyang Khyentse was residing. Dechen Lingpa had met Chokgyur Lingpa in 1862. Dechen Lingpa lists

49 Chokgyur Lingpa, the Fourteenth Karmapa and Jamgön Kongtrul among his teachers. Achard (2004a) pp. xxi-xxii, including fn. 38. On Shardza Tashi Gyaltsen see Gorvine (2006) and Shardza Tashi Gyaltsen (1993).

49 Jean-Luc Achard (2004b) has studied the *tertön* Tennyi Lingpa Pema Tsewang Gyalpo (*bstan gnyis gling pa padma tshe dbang rgyal po*) (1480-1535) who, he says, foreshadows the characteristics of the Rimé movement more than three centuries before it occurred. Achard refers to earlier figures from the eleventh and fourteenth centuries, and says of Tennyi Lingpa that he belongs to an 'ambivalent' series of *tertöns*, simultaneously Bonpo and Nyingma, whose works are beyond the sectarian limits of the Tibetan schools: "Il appartient en effet à une série de *gter ston* (Révélateurs de Trésors) ambivalents, à la fois bon po et rnying ma pa, dont l'oeuvre littéraire et rédemptrice échappe aux limites sectaires des écoles tibétaines." Achard (2004b), p. 58. The 'Tennyi' (*bstan gnyis*) in his name means 'the two teachings' i.e., Nyingma Buddhist and Bon. Achard (2004b), p. 66.

50 Blondeau (1988), pp. 55-67.
51 Cited by Ngawang Zangpo (2002), p. 189.
52 An introduction to this work and its translation into English can be found in Ngawang Zangpo (2002), pp. 184-205.
53 Achard (2008), fn. 25, p. xv.
54 From the *Catalogue of the Treasury of Precious Termas*, cited and translated by Ngawang Zangpo (2002), p. 189.
55 Ngawang Zangpo (2002), p. 189.
56 Marpa and Gampopa (in the Kagyü tradition), and many others, are also understood to have concealed *termas*.
57 See Andreas Doctor (2005), p. 18, including fn. 2.
58 See Jan Nattier (1991) for a study of ideas of decline in Buddhism.
59 Martin (2001), p. 24.
60 Doctor (2005), pp. 17-18.
61 Doctor (2005), p. 18.
62 On the historical development of the Nyingma *terma* tradition see Part One, Doctor (2005), pp. 17-30.
63 Doctor (2005), p. 26.
64 From the *Catalogue of the Treasury of Spiritual Instructions*, cited in the Introduction to *Esoteric Instructions*, Jamgön Kongtrul (2007b), p. 33.
65 Kongtrul calls Chokgyur Lingpa "...the representative of the great master

from Oddiyana, his emanated messenger of peace to the world..." Cited in Jamgön Kongtrul and Ngawang Zangpo, (1994), p. 42.

[66] Jamgön Kongtrul and Ngawang Zangpo (1994), pp. 54-55.

[67] Jamgön Kongtrul and Ngawang Zangpo (1994), p. 55.

[68] For a short biography of Jamgön Kongtrul see Ringu Tulku (2006), pp. 15-53. See also Smith (2001), pp. 235-72 and Ngawang Zangpo's Introduction in Jamgön Kongtrul and Ngawang Zangpo (1994), pp. 15-56.

[69] Smith (2001), p. 247.

[70] Jamgön Kongtrul (2003a), pp. 20-21. Jamgön Kongtrul's master's parting advice, was "Always focus your mind, rely on your mindfulness and alertness, and don't be sectarian." Jamgön Kongtrul (2003a), p. 21.

[71] The ordination was different to his previous ordination insofar as it followed the 'Western vinaya' lineage which had been introduced to Tibet in the thirteenth century. His previous ordination had been in the 'Eastern vinaya' lineage which had been introduced to Tibet in the eighth century.

[72] Kongtrul says, "Although I explained to him [Palpung Öngen] the way in which I had received the vows already when I stayed at Zhechen, he spoke very disparagingly of this and said, 'It is essential that you request the vows from the Kagyü hierarchs.'" It was suggested that Kongtrul 'offer back' his previous ordination but the ceremony never occurred. Jamgön Kongtrul (2003a), p. 22. I have added 'Palpung Öngen' in square brackets for clarity.

[73] Jamgön Kongtrul (2003a), p. 23.

[74] Smith (2001), p. 248.

[75] Jamgön Kongtrul (2003a), p. 24.

[76] On the names of Jamgön Kongtrul see Smith (2001), pp. 258-262.

[77] Jamgön Kongtrul (2003a), p. 32. Jamgön Kongtrul also taught Sanskrit and other subjects at Palpung during this period.

[78] Ngawang Zangpo notes that Kongtrul's decision not to return to Palpung may be related to the fact that his root guru, Tai Situ Rinpoche, had passed away in 1842, the year Kongtrul began his three-year retreat. Translator's Introduction to Jamgön Kongtrul and Ngawang Zangpo (1994), pp. 40-41.

[79] Jamgön Kongtrul (2003a), p. 174.

[80] See Ngawang Zangpo (2001), pp. 104-5. 'Unveiling' the area in Kongtrul's words, "marked the beginning of this area's enlightened activity." Zangpo (2001), p. 105. The 'unveiling' is understood to release or activate the latent spiritual power in a sacred place. Tsāri is a sacred mountain in Central Tibet

which is itself identified with two sacred places in India described in the tantras, namely, Cāritra and Devīkoṭa. Thus Tsādra Rinchen Drak is also known as the 'Third Devīkoṭa' (the 'Second' being in Central Tibet). See also Jamgön Kongtrul (2003a), p. 106.

81 Jamgön Kongtrul (2003a), p.457. Cf. Jamgön Kongtrul and Ngawang Zangpo (1994), p. 36.
82 Cited and translated by Ringu Tulku (2006), p. 23. See Jamgön Kongtrul (2003a), p. 86, for alternate translation, which uses the words: "I have not committed the grievous fault of rejecting the teachings."
83 Jamgön Kongtrul (2003a), p. 86.
84 Cited in Ringu Tulku (2006), p. 3.
85 Jamgön Kongtrul (2003a), p. 78.
86 For a list see Jamgön Kongtrul (2003a), pp. 84-85.
87 Jamgön Kongtrul (2003c). These are the vows and commitments of personal liberation (*prātimokṣa*), awakening mind (*bodhicitta*) and of the awareness holder (*vidyādhara*) respectively. For a summary see the Translators' Introduction to Jamgön Kongtrul (2003c), pp. 22-34.
88 For example, Section 4 of Book 8, entitled *Esoteric Instructions*, is approximately 300 pages in the English translation. Jamgön Kongtrul (2007b).
89 For Kongtrul's summary of the contents of the *Treasury of Knowledge* see Jamgön Kongtrul (2003a), pp. 263-64. For a complete breakdown of its contents see the Introduction to Jamgön Kongtrul (2007a), pp. 14-17. A modern Tibetan edition was printed in 1982. For details see Jamgön Kongtrul (2003b), fn. 54, p. 260.
90 Introduction to Jamgön Kongtrul (2007a), p. 14.
91 Translators' Introduction to Jamgön Kongtrul (2003c), p. 20.
92 Also known as the *Treasury of Extensive Teachings* (*rgya chen bka' mdzod*). Jamgön Kongtrul (2003a), p. 527.
93 Jamgön Kongtrul (2003a), pp. 515-31.
94 The texts were the *Sublime Continuum* (*uttaratantra*), the *Profound Inner Meaning* (*zab mo nang don*) by the Third Karmapa Rangjung Dorje, and the *Hevajra tantra*. Ringu Tulku (2006), p. 25.
95 Smith (2001), p. 263.
96 For more detail see the Translators' Introduction to Jamgön Kongtrul (2003b), pp. 33-34.

97 The empowerments and oral transmissions of the *Treasury of Precious Termas* given by Jamgön Kongtrul in 1868-1869 took approximately five months. See Jamgön Kongtrul (2003a), p. 152.
98 According to Matthew Kapstein (1996), p. 275, "*gDams ngag* in this sense is, in the final analysis, a product solely of the interrelationship between master and disciple; it is the non-repeatable discourse event in which the core of the Buddhist enlightenment comes to be manifestly disclosed."
99 Ringu Tulku (2006), p. 38.
100 Smith (2001), p. 237, for instance, describes the *shentong* of Kongtrul as "the mortar that held his eclectic structure together." Some other scholars have mistakenly taken Smith's statement as applicable to Rimé thinking as a whole.
101 Jamgön Kongtrul (2007a), p. 259.
102 Jamgön Kongtrul (2007a), p. 259.
103 See Smith (2004), p. 192.
104 Smith (2004), p. 192.
105 Jamyang Choje and Lodrö Rinchen Senge. Smith (2004), p. 186.
106 Smith (2004), p. 186.
107 Jamgön Kongtrul (2007a), pp. 262-65.
108 As Cyrus Stearns (2010), fn. 328, p. 356, says, further research is required on the differences between the views of Dölpopa and other adherents of views which are often labelled '*shentong*'. One obvious difference between the mainstream Kagyü and Nyingma view upheld by Kongtrul (in line with Longchenpa and the Third Karmapa) and Dölpopa is in the understanding of the relation between the essence of thought and *dharmakāya* which Dölpopa regards as radically different. See also Stearns (2010), fn. 556, p. 396. Stearns (2010), p. 82, says of developments in which Kongtrul played a major role: "What is now taught as the *shentong* view in the Kagyü and Nyingma traditions represents a synthesis that has developed over time, primarily in order to enable Dölpopa's most profound insights to be incorporated into the established doctrines of the Great Seal [Mahāmudrā] and the Great Perfection [Dzogchen]." (I have added the words inside square brackets for clarity.)
109 Introduction to Jamgön Kongtrul (2007a), p. 51.
110 Smith (2001) p. 265. Kongtrul writes that other-emptiness is "the profound view linking the Sūtra and Mantra [systems], the pinnacle of Madhyamaka

systems." Jamgön Kongtrul (2007a), p. 259.
111 Embraced by the term 'Great Madhyamaka'. This term does not refer exclusively to the *shentong* view and is broader in scope. Longchenpa and Mipham for example use the term to include Prāsaṅgika Madhyamaka. The main emphasis in Great Madhyamaka is on a non-conceptual ultimate, not on whether the ultimate is characterised as *rangtong* or *shentong*. See Pettit (1999), p. 113.
112 Kongtrul follows Tāranātha on this point. See the Introduction to Jamgön Kongtrul (2007a), pp. 39-40.
113 Jamgön Kongtrul (2007a), p. 262.
114 Kongtrul says, "the seed syllables and emblems that arise within emptiness are not beyond the primordial wisdom of the dharmadhātu.... Their emptiness is that we do not cling to them in any way nor do we conceptualize them as anything." Jamgön Kongtrul (2007a), p. 270.
115 Jamgön Kongtrul (2003a), p. 100.
116 Jamgön Kongtrul (2003a), p. 100.
117 Jamgön Kongtrul (2003a), p. 458. This quote is from *The Mirage of Nectar: A fragmentary account of the past lives of Pema Gargyi Wangchuk Thrinlé Drodul Tsal, a mere reflection of a renunciant who has only three ideas in mind* (i.e. eating, sleeping and pottering about), translated by Richard Barron and included in Jamgön Kongtrul (2003a), pp. 411-502. On the title see fn. 1, p. 468.
118 'Deathless Place of the Swastika of the Two Doctrines' (*'chi med bstan gnyis g.yung drung gling pa*). The term *yungdrung* (*g.yung drung*) in Kongtrul's name is closely connected with Bon and means 'eternal' or 'immutable' and also refers to the swastika, an important symbol in Bon and Buddhism. The 'two doctrines' here refers to Buddhism and Bon. Kongtrul's own summary of his activities as a *tertön* can be found in Jamgön Kongtrul (2003a), pp. 456-67.
119 Jamgön Kongtrul (2003a), p. 459. See also Translator's Introduction to Jamgön Kongtrul and Ngawang Zangpo (1994), p. 38.
120 Kunsang and Schmidt (2005), p. 50.
121 See Translator's Introduction to Jamgön Kongtrul and Ngawang Zangpo (1994), p. 31.
122 Cited in Translator's Introduction to Jamgön Kongtrul and Ngawang Zangpo (1994), p. 27.

Notes to Section 3

[123] Cited in Translator's Introduction to Jamgön Kongtrul and Ngawang Zangpo (1994), p. 30.
[124] Jamgön Kongtrul and Ngawang Zangpo (1994).
[125] Harding (2003), pp. 47-49.
[126] Cited in Harding (2003), p. 21.
[127] Jamgön Kongtrul and Ngawang Zangpo (1994), pp. 119-21.
[128] Jamgön Kongtrul and Ngawang Zangpo (1994), p. 94.
[129] Cited in Translator's Introduction to Jamgön Kongtrul and Ngawang Zangpo (1994), pp. 19-20. Note that I have added 'Vajradhara' in square brackets for clarity.
[130] Jamgön Kongtrul and Ngawang Zangpo (1994), p. 101.
[131] All of these works are available in translation and with commentaries from contemporary teachers.
[132] Jamgön Kongtrul and Ngawang Zangpo (1994), p. 81.
[133] The name 'Amulet Box' is used because Khyungpo Naljor wrote down Niguma's Mahāmudrā instructions and kept them in a sandalwood amulet box. Jamgön Kongtrul and Ngawang Zangpo (1994), p. 88.
[134] Jamgön Kongtrul and Ngawang Zangpo (1994), p. 103. I have added the words 'Kagyü' and 'Nyingma' in square brackets to Ngawang Zangpo's translation for clarity. 'Kagyü' means 'oral instruction (*bka'*) lineage (*brgyud*)'.
[135] According to the Karma Kagyü Mahāmudrā and Dzogchen master Karma Chagmé (who was discussed in Section 2), on account of this, 'leapover' is "said to be even higher than Mahāmudrā." Karma Chagmé (1998), p. 180. Karma Chagmé identifies Mahāmudrā with *trekchö* and relates it to the Mind Series (*sems sde*) of Dzogchen teachings. Karma Chagmé (1998), p. 180.
[136] For more detail on the daily, monthly and yearly retreat schedule see Jamgön Kongtrul and Ngawang Zangpo (1994), pp. 116-39.
[137] Jamgön Kongtrul (2003a), p. 377.
[138] Jamgön Kongtrul (2003a), p. 394.
[139] As told to his senior student Tashi Chöpel. Jamgön Kongtrul (2003a), p. 393.
[140] Tashi Chöpel notes that "Khyentse was the catalyst who, in a timely manner, awakened in Kongtrul Rinpoché the amazing and profound mystery of his aspirations to discover profound *termas*." Jamgön Kongtrul (2003a), p. 393.

141 van Schaik (2011), p. 166.
142 The full name he was given is Jamyang Khyentse Wangpo Kunga Tenpe Gyaltsen Palzangpo.
143 Translation from Kongtrul's autobiography by Sam van Schaik (2011), p. 166. The same passage can be found translated by Richard Barron in Jamgön Kongtrul (2003a), p. 86. Also by Ringu Tulku (2006), p. 23 and by Ngawang Zangpo in Jamgön Kongtrul and Ngawang Zangpo (1994), p. 39.
144 Kongtrul begins his *Treasury of Spiritual Instructions* (the fourth of his Five Treasuries) with the opening verses of *Meditation's Ambrosia of Immortality*. The Tibetan text and English translation of *Meditation's Ambrosia of Immortality* is included in Deroche (2009).
145 Deroche (2009), fn. 46, p. 17, gives these figures as: "Thon mi sam bho ṭa (early-to-mid-seventh century), Vairocana (eighth to ninth century), sKa ba dpal brtsegs (eighth to ninth century), Cog ro klu'i rgyal mtshan (eighth to ninth century), Zhang ye shes sde (eighth to ninth century), Lo chen Rin chen bzang po (957-1055), 'Brom ston pa rGyal ba'i 'byung gnas (1005-1064) and rNgog lo tsā ba bLo ldan shes rab (1059-1109), Sa skya paṇḍita Kun dga' rgyal mtshan (1182-1251), and 'Gos Khug pa lhas btsas (early eleventh century)."
146 For a short biography see Deroche (2011), pp. 140-42. Deroche is currently (late 2011) working on a biography of Sherab Özer with complementary historical references. This is forthcoming and will be available under the title "'Phreng po gter ston Shes rab 'od zer (1518-1584)." In *The Treasury of Lives: Biographies of Himalayan Buddhist Masters* at http://treasuryoflives.org.
147 Deroche (2009), p. 2.
148 Jigme Lingpa's other two main disciples were Dödrupchen (Jigme Tinle Özer, who was the guru of the Queen of Derge) and Jigme Kundröl (*jigs med kun sgrol*).
149 See Nyoshul Khenpo Jamyang Dorjé (2005), p. 272.
150 According to Dilgo Khyentse, Khyentse Wangpo's main practice was the guru yoga of the *Longchen Nyingthig*. Thondhup (1996), p. 218.
151 For a list of these five *tertöns* see Padmasambhava and Jamgon Kongtrul (1995), fn. 5, p. 208.
152 Thondhup (1996), p. 219. See also Doctor (2005), p. 27.
153 This scheme was presented for the first time in Jamgön Kongtrul's *Precious*

Lapis Lazuli Rosary that Briefly Presents the Emergence of the Profound Treasures and the Accomplished Treasure Revealers which introduces his *Treasury of Precious Termas.* Doctor (2005), p. 26.

154 Stearns (2007), pp. 23-24. These are regarded as 're-concealed' because the original teaching is attributed to Padmasambhava.
155 Stearns (2007), p. 31.
156 Stearns (2007), pp. 31-32.
157 Stearns (2007), p. 24.
158 Stearns (2007), p. 31.
159 Nyoshul Khenpo Jamyang Dorjé (2005), p. 278.
160 http://www.rigpawiki.org/index.php?title=Chetsün_Nyingtik. Accessed 17 December 2011.
161 Nyoshul Khenpo Jamyang Dorjé (2005), p. 279.
162 Andreas Doctor (2005), pp. 75-83, has given an overview of sources of information on Chokgyur Lingpa's life, about which Doctor (2005) and Orgyen Tobgyal (1988) provide much useful material. The latter is an oral account by Orgyen Tobgyal and is available as a downloadable pdf file at http://www.rangjung.com/authors/Chokgyur_Lingpa_Life.pdf. Accessed 11 December 2011.
163 Gardner (2006), p. 25, gives an additional name for Chokgyur Lingpa: Könchog Tenzin (*dkon mchog bstan 'dzin*).
164 Orgyen Tobgyal (1988), says the immediate reason for Chokgyur Lingpa's expulsion was a vision Chokgyur Lingpa had during a dance which caused a major disruption. Gardner (2006), p. 28, surmises that Chokgyur Lingpa may have been expelled for taking a consort, which is not permitted to monks but is common among *tertöns*. The account in Padmasambhava and Jamgon Kongtrul (1995), p. xxxviii, states that Chokgyur Lingpa asked to leave the monastery.
165 Orgyen Tobgyal (1988), p. 10. Andreas Doctor (2005), fn. 210, p. 214, notes that there does not seem to be any consensus within the Nyingma school as to whether earth treasures or mind treasures are superior.
166 Orgyen Tobgyal (1988), p. 10.
167 For a short introduction to the Barchey Kunsel see "Tukdrub Barchey Kunsel: A short introduction to the Barchey Kunsel cycle." At http://www.rangjung.com/gl/Tukdrub_Barchey_Kunsel-introduction.htm. Accessed 11 December 2011. See also Chokling Dewey Dorje, Dudjom Rinpoche,

Tulku Urgyen Rinpoche and Chökyi Nyima Rinpoche (2008).
168 Khyentse and Kongtrul were the two principal teachers of Chokgyur Lingpa's four most important teachers. The other two teachers (Bogpai Khenpo and Dazang Tulku) gave Chokling, respectively, the monastic vows and the Mahāyāna bodhicitta vows.
169 For some of the names of Trisong Detsen's second son see Doctor (2005), fn. 191, p. 212.
170 Orgyen Tobgyal (1988), p. 21.
171 As mentioned earlier in Section 3, the area around Jamgön Kongtrul's retreat hermitage became known as Tsādra Rinchen Drak ('Jewel Cliff like Tsāri').
172 See Ngawang Zangpo (2001).
173 Doctor (2005), p. 93. The guru is regarded as the 'root of blessings'. Padmasambhava and Jamgon Kongtrul (1995), p. 26.
174 Doctor (2005), p. 93.
175 Padmasambhava and Jamgon Kongtrul (1995 & 1998).
176 Doctor (2005), p. 27.
177 Doctor (2005), p. 26.
178 Doctor (2005), pp. 84-97.
179 Ngawang Zangpo (2001), p. 96. Ngawang Zangpo is elaborating on what Kongtrul wrote in his *Lives of the Treasure Revealers*: "These genuine treasure revealers, holy individuals, first began to appear mainly in upper [western Tibet], the Ngari area; then in central [Tibet] – Ü, Tsang, Lo, and Mön; and finally in the upper, middle, and lower parts of Amdo and Kham." Ngawang Zangpo (2001), p. 96.
180 Doctor (2005), p. 76.
181 Doctor (2005), p. 76.
182 Doctor (2005), p. 86.
183 Doctor (2005), p. 91.
184 Achard (2004a), p. xxii.
185 Achard (2004a), p. xxi. The secret name was Rig 'dzin Kun grol gsang ba rtsal.
186 Achard (2004a), p. xxi. Achard notes that Dechen Lingpa may have been responsible for curing a disease from which Kongtrul was suffering. This cure is attributed to Chokgyur Lingpa by Orgyen Tobgyal (1988), p. 11. Achard (2004a), fn. 39, p. xxi, states: "It can't obviously be excluded that the

Notes to Section 3

role played by the two *gter ston* had a combined effect."

187 Kunsang and Schmidt (2005), pp. 70-78. See also Orgyen Tobgyal (1988), pp. 37-39.

188 Each *ngöndro* involves meditation on the value of human rebirth, impermanence, the cause and effect of actions, and suffering, together with one hundred thousand prostrations and an equal number of long Vajrasattva mantras, maṇḍala offerings and guru yoga practices. This means that Patrul Rinpoche did two and a half million prostrations, and so on.

189 Patrul Rinpoche (1998).

190 Patrul's teaching is known as the *Special Teaching of the Wise and Glorious King, with its commentary* (*mkhas pa sri rgyal po'i khyad chos 'grel pa dang bcas pa*).

191 Tenzin Gyatso, Dalai Lama XIV (2000).

192 Thondup (1996), p. 202.

193 Tenzin Gyatso, Dalai Lama XIV (2000), p. 45. I have added the word 'Patrul's' in square brackets for clarity.

194 See Kunzang Pelden (2007) for an English translation.

195 Kunzang Pelden (2007), p. xviii.

196 Smith (2001), p. 229, states that Patrul Rinpoche used the ninth (Wisdom) chapter of the *Bodhicaryāvatāra* as a meditation manual.

197 Khenpo Kunpal (2004), p. 42.

198 Khenpo Kunpal (2004), p. 40.

199 Nyoshul Khenpo Jamyang Dorjé (2005).

200 Thondup (1996), p. 203.

201 Kunzang Pelden (2007), p. xvii. 'Black-clothed' distinguishes the lay people from the 'red-clothed' monastic *saṅgha*. In the Nyingma tradition the committed lay tantric practitioners are sometimes identified as 'white-clothed'.

202 Cited in Translator's Introduction, Khenpo Kunpal (2004), pp. 37-38.

203 Kunsang and Schmidt (2005), p. 51.

204 See Ronis (2009) for a study which includes consideration of the "institutional factors that allowed for the rise of the nonsectarian movement and the efflorescence of Nyingma scholarship at the turn of the twentieth century." Ronis (2009), p. 4.

205 For a good survey of Mipham's life see Duckworth (2011), pp. 3-16. See also Pettit (1999), pp. 19-39.

[206] Pettit (1999), p. 26.
[207] Cited in Pettit (1999), p. 29.
[208] Cited in Pettit (1999), p. 26-27. I have added 'Nyingma' and 'direct knowledge' in square brackets for clarity.
[209] For a list of Sanskrit texts on which Mipham wrote commentaries see Smith (2001), fn. 785, p. 327.
[210] Smith (2001), pp. 229-30.
[211] English translations of this commentary are available: Mipham Jamyang Namgyal Gyatso (2004) and Shantarakshita (2005).
[212] Smith (2001), p. 233.
[213] Smith (2001), pp. 231-33.
[214] This is from a biography of Mipham written by Khetsun Sangbo in Mipam-gya-tso (2006), pp. 23-25. See also Pettit (1999), pp. 30-31.
[215] For a detailed exposition see Pettit (1999), and Duckworth (2008 & 2011).
[216] See Duckworth (2011), p. 135-37.
[217] This allows Mipham to accept 'Great Madhyamaka' since, according to him, the emphasis in Great Madhyamaka is on a non-conceptual ultimate, not on whether the ultimate is characterised as *rangtong* or *shentong*.
[218] Mipham wrote a work defending *shentong*. Pettit (1999), p. 114.
[219] See Pettit (1999), pp. 113-14.
[220] Kunsang and Schmidt (2005), pp. 50-51.
[221] Smith (2001), p. 231. See also Samuel (1993), p. 540.
[222] Smith (2001), p. 231.
[223] Smith (2001), fn. 782.

Section 4

[1] On Jigme Phüntsok Rinpoche (or Jikphun Rinpoche) see Germano (1998).
[2] These texts, the 'thirteen great texts', all had unbroken expository lineages. Jackson (2003), p. 80. Duckworth (2008) fn. 48, p. 196, explains the thirteen: "The thirteen great scriptures include two Vinaya texts: *Vinayasūtra* and *Prātimokṣasūtra*; two Abhidharma texts: *Abhidharmakośa* and *Abhidharmasamuccaya*; four texts of the profound view (of the Middle Way): *Mūlamadhyamakakārikā*, *Madhyamakāvatāra*, *Catuḥśataka*, and *Bodhicaryāvatāra*; and the "five treatises of Maitreya" (*byams chos sde lnga*): *Abhisamayālaṃkāra*, *Mahāyānasūtrālaṃkāra*, *Uttaratantra*,

Dharmadharmatāvibhāga, and *Madhyāntavibhāga*. Although Khenpo Zhenga's Interlinear Commentaries on the Thirteen Great Scriptures (*gzhung chen bcu gsum gyi mchen 'grel*) contains more than thirteen interlinear commentaries, Padma Namgyel (*padma rnam rgyal*, twentieth century) identifies the ones listed above as the thirteen texts."

3   Cited in Duckworth (2008), fn. 49, p. 196.
4   Smith (2001), p. 232.
5   Dreyfus (2005), p. 291. Dreyfus (who trained in Gelug monasteries) stresses the non-Gelug aspect of Shenga's mission: "What we have here is a figure single-mindedly bent on a mission, that of creating a non-Geluk scholastic tradition based on a particular institution, the commentarial school, with its well-defined pedagogy and curriculum."
6   Jackson (2003), p. 27.
7   Jackson (2003), fn. 109, p. 585, quotes a verse from Shenga expressing this sentiment: "Ah! I began religious life in the esoteric Old-Translation Tradition. I studied a bit of the learned masters of India. By examining with an impartial mind, I gained trust in the doctrine of glorious Sakya."
8   Jackson (2003), pp. 28-29.
9   Introduction to Khenpo Kunpal (2004), pp. 97-98.
10 Dreyfus (2005), p. 290.
11 According to Tulku Urgyen (1920-1996), "he was not just a tulku of the first Khyentse but a near replica." Kunsang and Schmidt (2005), p. 296. Cf. p. 307.
12 For example, Khyentse Chökyi Lodrö received transmission of Bon lineages from the Bon *tertön* and Rimé figure Shardza Tashi Gyeltsen (ca. 1859-1933). Achard (2008), p. 418. Shardza and Jamgön Kongtrul had been in communication in the 1890s. Gorvine (2006), p. 188.
13 Dilgo Khyentse (2008), p. 109.
14 For more detail see Nyoshul Khenpo Jamyang Dorjé (2005), pp. 297-98.
15 See Nyoshul Khenpo Jamyang Dorjé (2005), pp. 297-303.
16 Nyoshul Khenpo Jamyang Dorjé (2005), p. 301.
17 Nyoshul Khenpo Jamyang Dorjé (2005), p. 303. I have added 'Jamyang Khyentse Chökyi Lodrö' in square brackets for clarity.
18 Dilgo Khyentse (2008), p. 109.
19 For Sogyal Rinpoche's account of his early life with Chökyi Lodrö see Sogyal Rinpoche (2002), pp. xvi-xviii. Tertön Sogyal Lerab Lingpa (1856-

20 1926) was a student of Patrul, Mipham, Kongtrul and other Rimé teachers in Kham, and an important teacher of the Thirteenth Dalai Lama.
20 The Rigpa Wiki web site lists ninety-two lamas as among the most important students of Khyentse Chökyi Lodrö. http://www.rigpawiki.org/index.php?title=Students_of_Jamyang_Khyentse_Chökyi_Lodrö. Accessed 15 December 2011.
21 Khandro Tsering Chödron became universally acclaimed as a highly realised female Dzogchen master. She recently passed away at Sogyal Rinpoche's principal retreat centre, Lerab Ling, in France where she had been living since 2006. Khandro was Sogyal Rinpoche's aunt.
22 http://www.treasuryoflives.org/biographies/view/Jamyang-Khyentse-Chokyi-Lodro/9990. Accessed 15 December 2011.
23 Dilgo Khyentse (2008), pp. 42-66.
24 Dilgo Khyentse (2008), pp. 102-40.
25 Dilgo Khyentse (2008), pp. 31-39.
26 http://www.treasuryoflives.org/biographies/view/Dilgo-Khyentse-Tashi-Peljor/8825. Accessed 15 December 2011.
27 Ricard (1996).
28 Khyentse Norbu's Foreword to *Brilliant Moon*, Dilgo Khyentse (2008), p. ix.
29 Foreword, Dilgo Khyentse (2008), p. xvi-xvii.
30 Orgyen Tobgyal (1988), p. 44.
31 Kunsang and Schmidt (2005), p. 102.
32 Doctor (2005), p. 101.
33 Jamgön Kongtrul and Ngawang Zangpo (1994), p. 364.
34 "The Life of Kalu Rinpoche" by Dezhung Rinpoche in Jackson (2003), pp. 541-46, p. 542.
35 Jamgön Kongtrul and Ngawang Zangpo (1994), pp. 364-65.
36 Ngawang Zangpo writes that Norbu Dondrup had a dream of the "Six-Armed Protector welcoming the new lineage holder on the eve of Kalu Rinpoché's arrival at Palpung Monastery." Jamgön Kongtrul and Ngawang Zangpo (1994), p. 365.
37 Kalu Rinpoche (1986), p. 3.
38 Kalu Rinpoche (1986), p. 11.
39 See Ngawang Zangpo's Translator's Introduction to Jamgon Kongtrul (2011), pp. 18-35, for detail on this project and Kalu Rinpoche's rationale for undertaking it.

Notes to Section 4

40 Cited in Jamgön Kongtrul (2011), p. 23.
41 Cited in Jamgön Kongtrul (2011), p. 25. The original of the quote is in Jamgön Kongtrul (2007b), p. 34.
42 Jamgön Kongtrul and Ngawang Zangpo (2003), p. 366.
43 Smith (2001), p. 235.
44 Jackson (2003). For a shorter biographical account see Victoria Scott's Introduction in Deshung Rinpoche (1995), pp. xxxiii-lxiii.
45 E. Gene Smith, cited on back cover of Jackson (2003).
46 Jackson (2003), p. 16.
47 For an account of his time with Shenga see Jackson (2003), pp. 25-33.
48 Jackson (2003), p. 46.
49 Jackson (2003), p. 114.
50 Jackson (2003), p. 240.
51 Jackson (2003), p. 326.
52 Smith (2001).
53 Jackson (2003), p. xiii.
54 Jackson (2003), p. 391-92.
55 Jackson (2003), p. 441.
56 Jackson (2003), Appendix A, pp. 485-93. Also available at: http://www.quietmountain.org/links/teachings/nonsect.htm. Accessed 17 December 2011.
57 Jackson (2003), Appendix A, p. 488.
58 Jackson (2003), Appendix A, pp. 489-90.
59 Laird (2006), p. 188.
60 Laird (2006), p. 23.
61 Laird (2006), p. 166.
62 Tsewang Dongyal (2008), p. 111.
63 Young (2010), p. 60.
64 Tenzin Gyatso, His Holiness the Dalai Lama (2009), p. 34.
65 Tenzin Gyatso the Fourteenth Dalai Lama, Khöntön Peljor Lhündrup and José Ignacio Cabezón (2011) p. 56.
66 Tenzin Gyatso, His Holiness The Fourteenth Dalai Lama (2006) pp. 236. See also discussion in Young (2010), pp. 51-55.
67 Tenzin Gyatso, His Holiness The Fourteenth Dalai Lama (2006) pp. 233-34.
68 "Message of His Holiness the Dalai Lama to the Global Buddhist Congregation, New Delhi, November 27-30, 2011." At http://www.

dalailama.com/news/post/767-message-of-his-holiness-the-dalai-lama-to-the-global-buddhist-congregation-new-delhi-november-27---30-2011. Accessed 9 December 2011.
[69] Dreyfus (1998), p. 256.
[70] Dreyfus (1998), p. 257. I have added 'Dalai Lama' in square brackets for clarity.
[71] Cited in McCune (2007), p. 36.
[72] See McCune (2007), pp. 25-28.
[73] Said to possibly be the spirit of Drakpa Gyaltsen (grags pa rgyal mtshan) (1619-1656) a contemporary of the Fifth Dalai Lama and one-time contender for the position of Dalai Lama who was murdered (or committed suicide). For more detail on this question see McCune (2007), pp. 46-63, and Dreyfus (1998), pp. 229-39.
[74] Dreyfus (1998), p. 244.
[75] Dreyfus (1998), p. 246.
[76] Author's personal recollection.
[77] Cited in McCune (2007), p. 36.
[78] Laird (2006), p. 168. See also Young (2010), pp. 44-45.

Conclusion

[1] van Schaik (2011), p. 169.
[2] Kunsang and Schmidt (2005), p. 41. I have added the words 'disciples of Padmasambhava' in square brackets for clarity.
[3] van Schaik (2011), p. 169.

Recommended Reading

Jamgön Kongtrul and Ngawang Zangpo (1994). *Jamgön Kongtrul's Retreat Manual.* Translated by Ngawang Zangpo (Hugh Leslie Thompson). Ithaca, NY: Snow Lion.

Kunsang, Erik Pema (Erik Hein Schmidt) and Marcia Binder Schmidt (2005). *Blazing Splendor: The Memoirs of Dzogchen Yogi Tulku Urgyen Rinpoche.* Compiled, translated and edited by Erik Pema Kunsang and Marcia Binder Schmidt, with Michael Tweed. Hong Kong: Rangjung Yeshe.

Ray, Reginald A. (2000). *Indestructible Truth: The Living Spirituality of Tibetan Buddhism.* Boston: Shambhala.

Ringu Tulku (2006). *The Ri-me Philosophy of Jamgon Kongtrul the Great: A Study of the Buddhist Lineages of Tibet.* Edited by Ann Helm. Boston: Shambhala.

Ricard, Matthieu (1996). *Journey to Enlightenment: The Life and World of Khyentse Rinpoche, Spiritual Teacher from Tibet.* NY: Aperture.

Smith, E. Gene (2001). *Among Tibetan Texts: History and Literature of the Himalayan Plateau.* Boston: Wisdom.

Tenzin Gyatso the Fourteenth Dalai Lama, Khöntön Peljor Lhündrup and José Ignacio Cabezón (2011). *Meditation on the Nature of Mind.* Boston: Wisdom.

Tsele Natsok Rangdröl (2009). *Heart Lamp: Lamp of Mahamudra & The Heart of the Matter.* Translated by Eric Pema Kunsang. Boudhanath, Hong Kong and Esby: Rangjung Yeshe.

Bibliography

Achard, Jean-Luc (2003). "Rig 'dzin Tshe dbang mchog grub (1761-1829) et la constitution du *rNying ma rgyud 'bum* de sDe dge." *Revue d'Etudes Tibétaines*, Number 3, 2003, pp. 43-89.

Achard, Jean-Luc (2004a). *Bon po Hidden Treasures: A Catalogue of gTer ston bDe chen gling pa's Collected Revelations*. Leiden: Brill.

Achard, Jean-Luc (2004b). "bsTan gnyis gling pa et la Révélation du *Yang tig ye shes mthong grol*." *Revue d'Etudes Tibétaines*, Number 5, Avril 2004, pp. 57-96.

Achard, Jean-Luc (2008). *Enlightened Rainbows: The life and works of Shardza Tashi Gyeltsen*. Leiden: Brill.

Aris, Michael (1977). "Jamyang Khyentse's 'Brief Discourse on the Essence of all the Ways': A Work of the *Ris-Med* Movement." *Kailash*, Vol. 5:3. pp. 205-28.

Blondeau, Anne-Marie (1988). "La controverse soulevée par l'inclusion de rituels bon-po dans le *Rin-chen gter-mdzod*. Note préliminaire." In H. Uebach and J. L. Panglung, eds., *Tibetan Studies. Proceedings of the 4th Seminar of the International Association for Tibetan Studies. Schloss Hohenkammer-Munich 1985*, pp. 55-67. Studia Tibetica Band II. München: Kommission für Zentralasiatische Studien, Bayerische Akademie der Wissenschaften.

Brunnhölzl, Karl (2004). *The Center of the Sunlit Sky: Madhyamaka in the Kagyü tradition*. Ithaca, NY: Snow Lion.

Brunnhölzl, Karl (2007). *In Praise of Dharmadhātu by Nāgārjuna and the IIIrd Karmapa, Rangjung Dorje*. Translated and introduced by Karl Brunnhölzl. Ithaca, NY: Snow Lion.

Brunnhölzl, Karl (2009). *Luminous Heart: The Third Karmapa on Consciousness, Wisdom, and Buddha Nature*. Translated and introduced by Karl Brunnhölzl. Ithaca, NY: Snow Lion.

Capriles, Elías (2004). *Clear Discrimination of Views Pointing at the Definitive Meaning: The Four Philosophical Schools of the Sutrayana Traditionally Taught in Tibet (With

Reference to the Dzogchen Teachings). Mérida: Universidad de Los Andes.
Chokling Dewey Dorje, Dudjom Rinpoche, Tulku Urgyen Rinpoche and Chökyi Nyima Rinpoche (2008). *The Great Gate: A Guidebook to the Guru's Heart Practice*. Translated and edited by Erik Pema Kunsang and Marcia Binder Schmidt. Kathmandu: Rangjung Yeshe.
Chokyi Nyima Rinpoche (1986). *The Union of Mahamudra and Dzogchen: A Commentary on The Quintessence of Spiritual Practice, The Direct Instructions of the Great Compassionate One by Karma Chagmey Rinpoche I*. Translated by Erik Pema Kunsang. Edited by Marcia B. Schmidt. Hong Kong: Rangjung Yeshe.
Davidson, Ronald M. (2008). *Tibetan Renaissance: Tantric Buddhism in the Rebirth of Tibetan Culture*. Delhi: Motilal Banarsidass.
Deroche, Marc-Henri (2009). "'Phreng po gter ston Shes rab 'od zer (1518-1584) on the Eight Lineages of Attainment: Research on a *Ris med* Paradigm." In Brandon Dotson, Kalsang Norbu Gurung, Georgios Halkias, and Tim Myatt, eds., *Contemporary Visions in Tibetan Studies: Proceedings of the First International Seminar of Young Tibetologists*. Chicago: Serindia.
Deroche, Marc-Henri (2011). "Instructions on the View (*lta khrid*) of the Two Truths: Prajñāraśmi's (1518-1584) *bden gnyis gsal ba'i sgron me*." *Revue d'Etudes Tibétaines*, Number 22, Novembre 2011, pp. 139-213.
Deshung Rinpoche (1995). *The Three Levels of Spiritual Perception: An Oral Commentary on The Three Visions* (Nang Sum) *of Ngorchen könchog lhündrub*. Translated by Jared Rhoton. Edited, with an Introduction, by Victoria R. M. Scott. Boston: Wisdom.
Dilgo Khyentse (2008). *Brilliant Moon: The Autobiography of Dilgo Khyentse*. Translated by Ani Jinba Palmo. Boston: Shambhala.
Doctor, Andreas (2005). *Tibetan Treasure Literature: Revelation, Tradition and Accomplishment in Visionary Buddhism*. Ithaca, NY: Snow Lion.
Dreyfus, Georges (1994). "Proto-nationalism in Tibet." In Per Kvaerne, ed., *Tibetan Studies: Proceedings of the 6th Seminar of the International Association for Tibetan Studies*, Vol. 1, pp. 205-18. Oslo: Institute for Comparative Research in Human Culture.
Dreyfus, Georges (1998). "The Shuk-den Affair: History and Nature of a Quarrel." *Journal of the International Association of Buddhist Studies*, 21:2, pp. 227-70.
Dreyfus, Georges (2005). "Where Do Commentarial Schools Come From? Reflections on the History of Tibetan Scholasticism." *Journal of the International Association of Buddhist Studies*, 28:2, pp. 273-98.

Duckworth, Douglas S. (2008). *Mipam on Buddha-Nature: The Ground of the Nyingma Tradition*. Albany: State University of New York.

Duckworth, Douglas S. (2011). *Jamgon Mipam: His Life and Teachings*. Boston: Shambhala.

Dudjom Rinpoche, Jikdrel Yeshe Dorje (1991). *The Nyingma School of Tibetan Buddhism: Its Fundamentals and History*. Translated by Gyurme Dorje and Matthew Kapstein. 2 vols. Boston: Wisdom.

Dudjom Rinpoche (2004). *Counsels from My Heart*. Translated by the Padmakara Translation Group. New Delhi: Shechen Publications.

Gardner, Alexander Patten (2006). "The Twenty-five Great Sites of Khams: Religious Geography, Revelation, and Nonsectarianism in Nineteenth-Century Eastern Tibet." PhD. dissertation, University of Michigan.

Germano, David (1998). "Re-membering the dismembered body of Tibet: Contemporary Tibetan visionary movements in the People's Republic of China." in Melvyn Goldstein and Matthew Kapstein, eds. *Buddhism in Contemporary Tibet: Religious Revival and Cultural Identity*. pp. 53-94. Berkeley and Los Angeles: University of California.

Goodman, Steven D. (1992). "Rig-'dzin 'Jigs-med gling pa and the Klong-Chen sNying-Thig." In Ronald M. Davidson and Steven D. Goodman, eds., *Tibetan Buddhism: Reason and Revelation*, pp. 133-207. NY: State University of New York.

Gorvine, William M. (2006). "The Life of a Bonpo Luminary: Sainthood, Partisanship and Literary Representation in a 20th Century Tibetan Biography." PhD. dissertation, University of Virginia.

Guenther, Herbert V., transl. (1971). Sgam.po.pa, *The Jewel Ornament of Liberation*. Berkeley: Shambhala.

Gyatso, Janet (1996). "The gTer ma Literature." In José Ignacio Cabezón and Roger R. Jackson, eds., *Tibetan Literature: Studies in Genre*, pp. 147-69. Ithaca, NY: Snow Lion.

Gyatso, Janet (1997). "From the Autobiography of a Visionary." In Donald S. Lopez Jr., ed., *Religions of Tibet in Practice*, pp. 369-75. Princeton: Princeton University.

Harding, Sarah (2003). *Machik's Complete Explanation: Clarifying the Meaning of Chöd, A Complete Explanation of Casting Out the Body As Food*. Ithaca, NY: Snow Lion.

Hopkins, Jeffrey, transl. (2007). *The Essence of Other-Emptiness by Tāranātha*. Ithaca, NY: Snow Lion.

Hurvitz, Leon (1976). *Scripture of the Lotus Blossom of the Fine Dharma*. Translated from the Chinese of Kumarajiva by Leon Hurvitz. NY: Columbia University.

Jackson, David P. (1994). *Enlightenment by a Single Means: Tibetan Controversies on the 'The Self-Sufficient White Remedy' (dkar po chig thub)*. Wien: Österreichische Akademie der Wissenschaften.

Jackson, David P. (2003). *A Saint in Seattle: The Life of the Tibetan Mystic Dezhung Rinpoche*. Boston: Wisdom.

Jamgön Kongtrul (2003a). *The Autobiography of Jamgön Kongtrul: A Gem of Many Colors*. Translated by Richard Barron. Ithaca, NY: Snow Lion.

Jamgön Kongtrul (2003b). *The Treasury of Knowledge: Book One: Myriad Worlds*. Translated by the Kalu Rinpoché Translation Group. Ithaca, NY: Snow Lion.

Jamgön Kongtrul (2003c). *The Treasury of Knowledge: Book Five: Buddhist Ethics*. Translated by the Kalu Rinpoché Translation Group. Ithaca, NY: Snow Lion.

Jamgön Kongtrul (2005). *The Treasury of Knowledge: Book Six, Part Four: Systems of Buddhist Tantra*. Translated by the Kalu Rinpoché Translation Group (Elio Guarisco and Ingrid McLeod). Ithaca, NY: Snow Lion.

Jamgön Kongtrul (2007a). *The Treasury of Knowledge: Book Six, Part Three: Frameworks of Buddhist Philosophy*. Translated by the Kalu Rinpoché Translation Group (Elizabeth Callahan). Ithaca, NY: Snow Lion.

Jamgön Kongtrul (2007b). *The Treasury of Knowledge: Book Eight, Part Four: Esoteric Instructions*. Translated by the Kalu Rinpoché Translation Group (Sarah Harding). Ithaca, NY: Snow Lion.

Jamgön Kongtrul (2008). *The Treasury of Knowledge: Book Eight, Part Three: Elements of Tantric Practice*. Translated by the Kalu Rinpoché Translation Group (Elio Guarisco and Ingrid McLeod). Ithaca, NY: Snow Lion.

Jamgön Kongtrul (2010). *The Treasury of Knowledge: Books Nine and Ten: Journey and Goal*. Translated by the Kalu Rinpoché Translation Group (Richard Barron). Ithaca, NY: Snow Lion.

Jamgön Kongtrul (2011). *The Treasury of Knowledge: Books Two, Three and Four: Buddhism's Journey to Tibet*. Translated and introduced by Ngawang Zangpo. The Kalu Rinpoché Translation Group. Ithaca, NY: Snow Lion.

Jamgön Kongtrul and Ngawang Zangpo (1994). *Jamgön Kongtrul's Retreat Manual*. Translated by Ngawang Zangpo (Hugh Leslie Thompson). Ithaca, NY: Snow Lion.

Jamgön Kongtrul and Ngawang Zangpo (2003). *Timeless Rapture: Inspired Verse of the Shangpa Masters*. Translated and introduced by Ngawang Zangpo. Ithaca, NY: Snow Lion.

Kalu Rinpoche (1986). *The Dharma that Illuminates All Beings Impartially Like the Light of the Sun and the Moon*. Albany: State University of New York. (Originally

published 1977, Shambhala).
Kapstein, Matthew T. (1980). "The Shangs-pa bka' brgyud, an unknown tradition of Tibetan Buddhism." In Michael Aris and Aung San Suu Kyi, eds., *Tibetan Studies in Honour of Hugh Richardson: proceedings of the International Seminar on Tibetan Studies*, Oxford, 1979, pp. 138-44. Warminster, England: Aris and Phillips.
Kapstein, Matthew (1996). "gDams ngag: Tibetan Technologies of the Self." In José Ignacio Cabezón and Roger R. Jackson, eds., *Tibetan Literature: Studies in Genre*, pp. 275-89. Ithaca, NY: Snow Lion.
Kapstein, Matthew T. (2002). *The Tibetan Assimilation of Buddhism: Conversion, Contestation, and Memory*. NY: Oxford.
Kapstein, Matthew T. (2006). *The Tibetans*. Oxford: Blackwell. (Reprinted 2010).
Karma Chagmé (1998). *A Spacious Path to Freedom: Practical Instructions on the Union of Mahāmudrā and Atiyoga*, with commentary by Gyatrul Rinpoche. Translated by Alan B. Wallace. Ithaca, NY: Snow Lion.
Karma Chagmé (2000). *Naked Awareness: Practical Instructions on the Union of Mahāmudrā and Dzogchen*. Translated by B. Alan Wallace. Ithaca, NY: Snow Lion.
Karma Chakme (2004-2011). *Karma Chakme's Mountain Dharma as Taught by Khenpo Karthar Rinpoche*. 4 vols. Woodstock: KTD.
Karma Chakme (2010). *Quintessence of the Union of Mahamudra and Dzokchen: Karma Chakme and Commentary by Khenpo Karthar Rinpoche*. Woodstock: KTD.
Karmay, Samten Gyaltsen (1988). *The Great Perfection: A Philosophical and Meditative Teaching of Tibetan Buddhism*. Leiden/New York: Brill.
Khenpo Kunpal (2004). *Drops of Nectar: Khenpo Kunpal's Commentary On Śāntideva's Entering the Conduct of the Bodhisattvas (Bodhisattva-caryāvatāra)*. Chapter One. With Oral Explanations by Dzogchen Khenpo Chöga. Volume One. Compiled and translated by Andreas Kretschmar. Edited by Judith S. Amtzis and John Deweese. (Internet publication). http://www.dzogchenlineage.org/bca/bca1comm.pdf. Accessed 13 December 2011.
Kunsang, Erik Pema (Erik Hein Schmidt) and Marcia Binder Schmidt (2005). *Blazing Splendor: The Memoirs of Dzogchen Yogi Tulku Urgyen Rinpoche*. Compiled, translated and edited by Erik Pema Kunsang and Marcia Binder Schmidt, with Michael Tweed. Hong Kong: Rangjung Yeshe.
Kunzang Pelden (2007). *The Nectar of Manjushri's Speech: A Detailed Commentary on Shantideva's Way*. Translated by the Padmakara Translation Group. Boston: Shambhala.
Kvaerne, Per (1995). *The Bon Religion of Tibet*. London: Serindia.

Kvaerne, Per (1996). "The Literature of Bon." In José Ignacio Cabezón and Roger R. Jackson, eds., *Tibetan Literature: Studies in Genre*, pp. 138-46. Ithaca, NY: Snow Lion.

Laird, Thomas (2006). *The Story of Tibet: Conversations with the Dalai Lama*. NY: Grove Press.

Lopez, Donald S., Jr. (1998). *Prisoners of Shangri-la: Tibetan Buddhism and the West*. Chicago/London: University of Chicago.

Mañjuśrīmitra (1987). *Primordial Experience: An Introduction to rDzogs-chen Meditation*. Translated by Namkhai Norbu and Kennard Lipman in collaboration with Barrie Simmons. Boston and London: Shambhala.

Martin, Dan (2001). *Unearthing Bon Treasures: Life and Contested Legacy of a Tibetan Scripture Revealer, with a general bibliography of Bon*. Leiden: Brill.

Martin, Dan (2010). "Zhangzhung Dictionary—Introduction." *Revue d'Etudes Tibétaines*, Number 18, Avril 2010, pp. 5-32.

McCune, Lindsay G. (2007). "Tales of Intrigue from Tibet's Holy City: the Historical Underpinnings of a Modern Buddhist Crisis." M.A. thesis. College of Arts and Sciences, Florida State University.

Mipham Jamyang Namgyal Gyatso (2004). *Speech of Delight: Mipham's Commentary on Śāntarakṣita's Ornament of the Middle Way*. Thomas H. Doctor (Translator). Ithaca, NY: Snow Lion.

Mi-pam-gya-tso (2006). *Fundamental Mind: The Nyingma View of the Great Completeness*. Edited and translated by Jeffrey Hopkins. Ithaca, NY: Snow Lion.

Monier-Williams, Monier (1899). *Sanskrit-English Dictionary*. Oxford: Oxford University Press.

Namkhai Norbu (1986). *The Crystal and the Way of Light: Sutra, Tantra and Dzogchen*. Compiled and edited by John Shane. NY: Routledge & Kegan Paul.

Nattier, Jan (1991). *Once Upon a Future Time: Studies in a Buddhist Prophecy of Decline*. Berkeley, CA: Asian Humanities Press.

Ngawang Zangpo (2001). *Sacred Ground: Jamgon Kongtrul on 'Pilgrimage and Sacred Geography'*. Ithaca, NY: Snow Lion.

Ngawang Zangpo (2002). *Guru Rinpoché: His Life and Times*. Ithaca, NY: Snow Lion.

Ngawang Zangpo (2003). *Timeless Rapture: Inspired Verse of the Shangpa Masters*. Compiled by Jamgon Kongtrul. Ithaca, NY: Snow Lion.

Nyoshul Khenpo Jamyang Dorjé (2005). *A Marvellous Garland of Rare Gems: Biographies of Masters of Awareness in the Dzogchen Lineage*. Translated by Richard Barron. Junction City: Pema.

Orgyen Tobgyal (1988). *The Life of Chokgyur Lingpa as told by Orgyen Tobgyal Rinpoche*. Translated by Tulku Jigmey Khyentse and Erik Pema Kunsang. Kathmandu: Rangjung Yeshe.

Padmasambhava and Jamgon Kongtrul (1995 & 1998). *The Light of Wisdom (Vols I & II)*, root text by Padmasambhava, commentary by Jamgon Kongtrul, translated by Erik Pema Kunsang. Boston: Shambhala.

Patrul Rinpoche (1998). *The Words of My Perfect Teacher (Kunzang Lama'i shelung)*. Translated by Padmakara Translation Group. Boston: Shambhala.

Pettit, John Whitney (1999). *Mipham's Beacon of Certainty: Illuminating the View of Dzogchen, the Great Perfection*. Boston: Wisdom.

Pye, Michael (1978). *Skilful Means: A Concept in Mahayana Buddhism*. London: Duckworth.

Rahula, Walpola (1978). "The Bodhisattva Ideal in Theravāda and Mahāyāna" in *Zen and the Taming of the Bull*. pp. 71-77. London: Fraser.

Ray, Reginald A. (2000). *Indestructible Truth: The Living Spirituality of Tibetan Buddhism*. Boston: Shambhala.

Ray, Reginald A. (2001). *Secret of the Vajra World: The Tantric Buddhism of Tibet*. Boston: Shambhala.

Reynolds, John Myrdhin (2005). *The Oral Tradition from Zhang-Zhung: An Introduction to the Bonpo Dzogchen Teachings of the Oral Tradition from Zhang-zhung known as the Zhang-zhung snyan-rgyud*. Thamel, Kathmandu: Vajra Publications.

Ricard, Matthieu (1996). *Journey to Enlightenment: The Life and World of Khyentse Rinpoche, Spiritual Teacher from Tibet*. NY: Aperture.

Ringu Tulku (2006). *The Ri-me Philosophy of Jamgon Kongtrul the Great: A Study of the Buddhist Lineages of Tibet*. Edited by Ann Helm. Boston: Shambhala.

Ronis, Jann Michael (2009). "Celibacy, Revelations, and Reincarnated Lamas: Contestation and Synthesis in the Growth of Monasticism at Katok Monastery from the 11th through 19th Centuries." PhD. dissertation, University of Virginia.

Ronis, Jann Michael (2011). "Powerful Women in the History of Degé: Reassessing the Eventful Reign of the Dowager Queen Tsewang Lhamo (d. 1812)." *Revue d'Etudes Tibétaines*, Number 21, Octobre 2011, pp. 61-81.

Sakya Pandita Kunga Gyaltshen (2002). *A Clear Differentiation of the Three Codes: Essential Distinctions among the Individual Liberation, Great Vehicle, and Tantric Systems*. Translated by Jared Douglas Rhoton. Albany, NY: State University of New York.

Samuel, Geoffrey (1993). *Civilized Shamans: Buddhism in Tibetan Societies*. Washington/

London: Smithsonian Institution Press.

Schaeffer, Kurtis R. (1995). "The Enlightened Heart of Buddhahood: A Study and Translation of the Third Karma pa Rang byung rdo rje's Work on Tathagatagarbha, the De bzhin gshegs pa'i snying po gtan la dbab pa." M.A. thesis, University of Washington.

Schroeder, John William (2004). *Skillful means: the heart of Buddhist compassion*. Delhi: Motilal Banarsidass.

Shabkar Tsogdruk Rangdrol and Matthieu Ricard et. al (2001). *The Life of Shabkar: The Autobiography of a Tibetan Yogin*. Translated by Matthieu Ricard, Jakob Leschley, Erik Schmidt, Marilyn Silverstone and Lodrö Palmo. Ithaca, NY: Snow Lion.

Shardza Tashi Gyaltsen (1993). *Heart Drops of Dharmakaya; Dzogchen Practice of the Bon Tradition*. Translation and commentary by Lopon Tenzin Namdak. Ithaca, NY: Snow Lion.

Shantarakshita (2005). *The Adornment of the Middle Way: Shantarakshita's Madhyamakalankara with Commentary by Jamgon Mipham*. Translated by Padmakara Translation Group. Boston: Shambhala.

Smith, E. Gene (2001). *Among Tibetan Texts: History and Literature of the Himalayan Plateau*. Boston: Wisdom.

Smith, E. Gene (2004). "Banned Books in the Tibetan Speaking Lands." In *21st Century Tibet Issue, Symposium on Contemporary Tibetan Studies: Collected Papers*. pp. 186-96. Taipei: Mongolian and Tibetan Affairs Commission.

Sogyal Rinpoche (2002). *The Tibetan Book of Living and Dying*. Revised and updated edition. San Francisco: HarperSanFrancisco (Harper Collins).

Stearns, Cyrus (2007). *King of the Empty Plain: The Tibetan Iron-Bridge Builder Tangtong Gyalpo*. Ithaca, NY: Snow Lion.

Stearns, Cyrus (2010). *The Buddha from Dolpo, Revised and Expanded: A Study of the Life and Thought of the Tibetan Master Dolpopa Sherab Gyaltsen* (Tsadra Foundation) Ithaca NY: Snow Lion. (Note this is the revised and expanded edition of the 1999 publication, *The Buddha from Dolpo*. Albany: State University of New York.)

Takpo Tashi Namgyal (1993). *Mahāmudrā: The Quintessence of Mind and Meditation*. Translated by Lobsang P. Lhalungpa. Delhi: Motilal Banarsidass.

Tatz, Mark (1994). *Upāyakauśalya Sūtra, The Skill in Means (Upāyakauśalya) Sūtra*. Translated by Mark Tatz. Delhi: Motilal Banarsidass.

Teichman, Eric (1922). *Travels of a Consular Officer in Eastern Tibet*. Cambridge: Cambridge University Press.

Tenzin Gyatso H. H. the Dalai Lama and Alexander Berzin (1997). *The Gelug/Kagyü*

Tradition of Mahamudra. Ithaca, NY: Snow Lion.

Tenzin Gyatso, Dalai Lama XIV (2000). *Dzogchen: The Heart of the Essence of the Great Perfection*. Ithaca, NY: Snow Lion.

Tenzin Gyatso H. H. the Dalai Lama (2004). *Advice on Dying and Living a Better Life*. Translated and edited by Jeffrey Hopkins. Sydney: Random House, Rider.

Tenzin Gyatso, His Holiness the Fourteenth Dalai Lama (2006). *Kindness, Clarity, and Insight*. Edited and translated by Jeffrey Hopkins. Ithaca, NY: Snow Lion.

Tenzin Gyatso, H. H. the Dalai Lama (2009). *His Holiness the Dalai Lama Presents Teachings on Awakening the Mind: Nagarjuna's Commentary on Bodhicitta. 1st and 2nd December 2009. Sydney–Australia*. Sydney: Dalai Lama in Australia Ltd. www.dalailamainaustralia.org.

Tenzin Gyatso the Fourteenth Dalai Lama, Khöntön Peljor Lhündrup and José Ignacio Cabezón (2011). *Meditation on the Nature of Mind*. Boston: Wisdom.

Terrone, Antonio (2008). "Tibetan Buddhism beyond the Monastery: Revelation and Identity in rNying ma Communities of Present-day Kham." In Monica Esposito, ed., *Images of Tibet in the 19th and 20th Centuries*, pp. 747-79. Coll. «Études thématiques» (22.2). Paris: École Française d'Extrême-Orient (EFEO).

Thondup Rinpoche, Tulku (1986). *Hidden Teachings of Tibet: An Explanation of the Terma Tradition of the Nyingma School of Buddhism*. Edited by Harold Talbott. London: Wisdom.

Thondup, Tulku (1996). *Masters of Meditation and Miracles: The Longchen Nyingthig Lineage of Tibetan Buddhism*. Edited by Harold Talbott. Boston: Shambhala.

Traleg Kyabgon (2004). *Mind at Ease: Self-Liberation Through Mahamudra Meditation*. Boston and London: Shambhala.

Tsele Natsok Rangdrol (1989). *Lamp of Mahamudra: The Immaculate Lamp That Perfectly and Fully Illuminates the Meaning of Mahamudra, The Essence of All Phenomena*. Translated by Erik Pema Kunsang (Erik Hein Schmidt). Boston and Shaftesbury: Shambhala.

Tsele Natsok Rangdröl (1996). T*he Heart of the Matter: The Unchanging Convergence of Vital Points that Shows Exactly How to Apply the View and Meditation of the Definitive Meaning*. Translated by Eric Pema Kunsang. Hong Kong: Rangjung Yeshe.

Tsering Lama Jampal Zangpo (1988). *A Garland of Immortal Wish-fulfilling Trees: The Palyül Tradition of Nyingmapa*. Translated by Sangye Khandro. Ithaca, NY: Snow Lion.

Tsewang Dongyal (2008). *Light of Fearless Indestructible Wisdom: The Life and Legacy of*

H. H. Dudjom Rinpoche. Ithaca NY: Snow Lion.

Tsong-kha-pa (2000-2004). *The Great Treatise on the Stages of the Path to Enlightenment: Lam rim Chen mo*. Translated by the Lamrim Chenmo Translation Committee. 3 vols. Ithaca, NY: Snow Lion.

van Schaik, Sam (2004a). *Approaching the Great Perfection: Simultaneous and Gradual Methods of Dzogchen Practice in Jigme Lingpa's 'Longchen Nyingtig'*. Boston: Wisdom.

van Schaik, Sam (2004b). "The Early Days of the Great Perfection." *Journal of the International Association of Buddhist Studies*, 27:1, pp. 165–206.

van Schaik, Sam (2011). *Tibet: A History*. New Haven: Yale.

Wylie, Turrell V. (1959). "A Standard System of Tibetan Transcription." *Harvard Journal of Asiatic Studies*, Vol. 22, pp. 261-67.

Young, Elena (2010). "The Boundaries of Identity: The Fourteenth Dalai Lama, Nationalism, and Ris med (non-sectarian) Identity in the Tibetan Diaspora." PhD. dissertation, McGill University, Montréal.

Xiuyu Wang (2009). "Lu Chuanlin's 'Great Game' in Nyarong: Moving Frontiers and Power Projection in Qing Tibet, 1865-1897." *The International History Review*, 31:3, pp. 473-498.

Table of Tibetan Names

Adeu Rinpoche	a lde'u rin po che
Adzom Drukpa	a 'dzom 'brug pa
Amdo	a mdo
Bokar Rinpoche	'bo dkar rin po che
Bon	bon
Bonpo	bon po
Butön	bu ston
Chagdud Tulku	lcags mdud sprul sku
Chatral Rinpoche	bya bral rin po che
Chenrezig	spyan ras gzigs
Chetsün Senge Wangchuk	lce btsun seng ge dbang phyug
Chime Tennyi Yungdrung Lingpa	'chi med bstan gnyis g.yung drung gling pa
Chogyam Trungpa	chos rgyam drung pa
Chokgyur Dechen Lingpa	mchog gyur bde chen gling pa
Chokling	mchog gling
Chökyi Jungne	chos kyi 'byung gnas
Chökyi Nyima	chos kyi nyi ma
Chöying Dorje	chos dbyings rdo rje
Dagpo Kagyü	dwags po bka' brgyud
Dalai Lama	dalai bla ma
Damdzin	dam 'dzin
Dazang Tulku	zla bzang sprul sku
Dechen Lingpa	bde chen gling pa
Dekyi Chödron	bde skyi chos sgron
Derge	sde dge
Dezhung Rinpoche	sde gzhung rin po che
Dilgo Khyentse Rinpoche	dil mgo mkhyen brtse rin po che
Do Khyentse Yeshe Dorje	mdo mkhyen brtse ye shes rdo rje

Dödrupchen	rdo grub chen
Dödrupchen Jikme Tenpe Nyima	do grub chen 'jigs med bstan pa'i nyi ma
Dödrupchen Rinpoche	rdo grub chen rin po che
Dokham	mdo khams
Dolgyal	dol rgyal
Dölpopa	dol po pa
Dölpopa Sherab Gyalsten	dol po pa shes rab rgyal mtshan
Dorje Drak	rdo rje brag
Dorje Shukden	rdo rje shugs ldan
Drepung	'bras spungs
Drikung Kagyu	'bri gung bka' brgyud
Drokmi	'brog mi
Dromtön	'brom ston
Drukpa Kagyu	'brug pa bka' brgyud
Dudjom Rinpoche	bdud 'joms rin po che
Dza Patrul Rinpoche	rdza dpal sprul rin po che
Dzemay Rinpoche	dze smad rin po che
Dzigar Kongtrul	'dzi sgar kong sprul
Dzogchen	rdzogs chen
Dzogchen Rinpoche	rdzogs chen rin po che
Dzongsar	rdzong gsar
Dzongsar shedra	rdzong gsar bshad grwa
Gampopa	sgam po pa
Ganden	dga' ldan
Garab Dorje	dga' rab rdo rje
Gatön Ngawang Lekpa	sga ston ngag dbang legs pa
Gelug	dge lugs
Geshe Lobsang Gyatso	dge bshes blo bzang rgya mtsho
Getse Tulku	dge rtse sprul sku
Gönchen	dgon chen
Gönpo Namgyal	mgon po nyam rgyal
Gorampa Sönam Senge	go rams pa bsod nams seng ge
Gyaltsab Rinpoche	rgyal tshab rin po che
Gyurme Tsewang Gyatso	'gyur med tshe dbang rgya mtsho
Hva Shang	hwa shang
Jamgön Kongtrul	'jam mgon kong sprul

Jamgön Kongtrul Khyentse Özer	'jam mgon kong sprul mkhyen brtse'i 'od zer
Jamgön Kongtrul Lodrö Thaye	'jam mgon kong sprul blo gros mtha' yas
Jamgön Mipham Gyatso	'jam mgon mi pham rgya mtsho
Jamyang Khyentse	jam dbyangs mkhyen brtse
Jamyang Khyentse Chökyi Lodrö	jam dbyangs mkhyen brtse'i chos kyi blo gros
Jamyang Khyentse Wangpo	jam dbyangs mkhyen brtse'i dbang po
Jamyang Loter Wangpo	jam dbyangs blo gter dbang po
Jigme Gyalwai Nyugu	'jigs med rgyal ba'i myu gu
Jigme Lingpa	'jigs med gling pa
Jigme Trinle Özer	'jigs med phrin las 'od zer
Jikme Phüntsok Rinpoche	'jigs med phun tshogs rin po che
Jonang	jo nang
Kadam	bka' gdams
Kagyü	bka' brgyud
Kagyü Ling	bka' brgyud gling
Kalu Rinpoche Rangjung Kunkhyab	ka lu rin po che rang byung kun khyab
Karma Chagme	karma chags me
Karma Drubgyu Tenzin	karma sgrub brgyud bstan 'dzin
Karma Kagyü	karma bka' brgyud
Karma Kamtsang Kagyü	karma kam tshang bka' brgyud
Karma Lingpa	karma gling pa
Karma Pakshi	karma pakshi
Karmapa	karma pa
Kathok	kaḥ thog
Kathok Tsewang Norbu	kaḥ thog tshe dbang nor bu
Kela Chokling	ke la mchog gling
Khakyab Dorje	mkha' khyab rdo rje
Kham	khams
Khandro Lhamo	mkha' 'gro lha mo
Khandro Tsering Chödron	mkha' 'gro tshe ring chos sgron
Khenchen Tashi Özer	mkhan chen bkra shis 'od zer
Khenpo Kunpal	mkhan po kun dpal
Khenpo Lodrö Donyo Rinpoche	mkhan po blo gros don yod rin po che

Table of Tibetan Names

Khenpo Shenga	mkhan po gzhan dga'
Khön	'khon
Khöntön Peljor Lhündrub	'khon ston dpal 'byor lhun grub
Khöntönpa	'khon ston pa
Khunu Lama Tenzin Gyalsten	khu nu bla ma bstan 'dzin rgyal mtshan
Khyentse Norbu	mkhyen brtse nor bu
Khyungpo Naljor	khyung po rnal 'byor
Könchog Paldrön	dkon mchog dpal sgron
Könchok Gyalpo	dkon mchog rgyal po
Kongpo	kong po
Kunga Tenpay Nyima	kun dga' bstan pa'i nyi ma
Kunzang Dechen Ösel Ling	kun bzang bde chen 'od gsal gling
Kyasu	skya su
Kyater	skya gter
Lhase Damzin Drak	lha sras dam 'dzin grags
Ling Rinpoche	gling rin po che
Lobsang Chökyi Gyaltsen	blo bzang chos kyi rgyal mtshan
Lodrö Thaye	blo gros mtha' yas
Longchen Rabjam	klong chen rab 'byams
Longchenpa	klong chen pa
Losel Tenkyong	blo gsal bstan skyong
Loter Wangpo	blo gter dbang po
Machig Lapdrön	ma gcig lab sgron
Marpa	mar pa
Marpa Kagyü	mar pa bka' brgyud
Milarepa	mi la ras pa
Mindröling	smin grol ling
Mingyur Dorje	mi 'gyur rdo rje
Minyak Kunzang Sonam	mi nyag kun bzang bsod nams
Mipham Rinpoche	mi pham rin po che
Müchen Sangye Rinchen	mus chen sans rgyas rin chen
Murub Tsenpo	mu rub btsan po
Namkhai Norbu	nam mkha'i nor bu
Nangchen	nang chen
Nedo Kagyü	gnas mdo bka' brgyud
Neten Chokling	gnas brtan mchog gling

Ngari	mnga' ris
Ngawang Lobsang Gyatso	ngag dbang blo bzang rgya mtsho
Ngedon Tenpa Rabgye	nges don bstan pa rab rgyas
Niguma	ni gu ma
Norbu Döndrup	nor bu don grub
Nyarong	nyak rong
Nyingma	rnying ma
Nyoshul Khenpo Jamyang Dorje	smyo shul mkhan po 'jam dbyangs rdo rje
Orgyen Jikme Chökyi Wangpo	o rgyan 'jigs med chos kyi dbang po
Orgyen Rinchenpal	o rgyan rin chen dpal
Orgyen Tendzin Norbu	o rgyan bstan 'dzin nor bu
Orgyen Tobgyal	o rgyan stobs rgyal
Pabongka Rinpoche	pha bong kha rin po che
Palge Samten Phüntsok	dpal dge bsam gtan phun tshogs
Palpung	dpal spungs
Palri Rabsel	dpa' ris rab gsal
Palyül	dpal yul
Panchen Lama	pan chen bla ma
Patrul Rinpoche	dpal sprul rin po che
Pema Lingpa	padma gling pa
Pema Nyinje Wangpo	pad ma nyin byed dbang po
Pema Wangchok Gyalpo	padma dbang phyug rgyal po
Pemajungne	padma 'byung gnas
Phadampa Sangye	pha dam pa sangs rgyas
Phagmodru Kagyü	phag mo gru bka' brgyud
Rangjung Dorje	rang byung rdo rje
Rangjung Rigpai Dorje	rang byung rig pa'i rdo rje
Rechungpa	ras chung pa
Rigdzin Gödem	rig 'dzin rgod ldem
Rinchen Lingpa	rin chen gling pa
Ringu Tulku	ri mgul sprul sku
Rongzom Chökyi Zangpo	rong zom chos kyi bzang po
Sakya	sa skya
Śākya Chokden	shākya mchog ldan
Sakya Paṇḍita Kunga Gyaltsen	sa skya paṇḍita kun dga' rgyal mtshan
Sakya Trizin	sa skya khri 'dzin

Samten Gyatso	bsam gtan rgya mtsho
Samye	bsam yas
Sera	se ra
Shabkar Tsogdruk Rangdröl	zabs dkar tshogs drug ran grol
Shangpa Kagyü	shangs pa bka' brgyud
Shardza Tashi Gyeltsen	shar rdza bkra shis rgyal mtshan
Shechen	zhe chen
Shechen Kongtrul	zhe chen kong sprul
Shechen Rabjam	zhe chen rab 'byams
Shenpen Chökyi Nangwa	gzhan phan chos kyi snang ba
Sherab Özer	shes rab 'od zer
Shigatse	gzhis dkar rtse
Situ Chökyi Jungne	si tu chos kyi 'byung gnas
Sogyal Rinpoche	bsod rgyal rin po che
Tai Situ Rinpoche	tai si tu rin po che
Tarthang Tulku	dar than sprul sku
Tashi Chöpel	bkra shis chos 'phel
Tashi Peljor Rabsel Dawa	bkra shis dpal 'byor rab gsal zla ba
Tenzin Gyatso	bstan 'dzin rgya mtsho
Tertön Sogyal Lerab Lingpa	gter ston bsod rgyal las rab gling pa
Thangtong Gyalpo	thang stong rgyal po
Thekchok Dorje	thek mchog rdo rje
Thubten Gyatso	thub bstan gya mtsho
Traleg Kyabgon Rinpoche	sgra legs skyabs mgon rin po che
Trijang Rinpoche	khri byang rin po che
Trisong Detsen	khri srong lde'u btsan
Tsādra Rinchen Drak	tsā 'dra rin chen brag
Tsang	gtsang
Tsele Natsok Rangdröl	tse le sna tshogs rang grol
Tsering Döndrup	tshe ring don sgrub
Tsewang Dorje Rigdzin	tshe dbang rdo rje rigs 'dzin
Tsewang Lhamo	tshe dbang lha mo
Tsewang Norbu	tshe dbang nor bu
Tsikey Chokling Rinpoche	rtsi khe mchog gling rin po che
Tsongkhapa	tsong kha pa
Tulku Urgyen	sprul sku o rgyan

Ü	dbus
Yarlung	yar lung
Yeshe Tsogyal	ye shes mtsho rgyal
Yongey Mingyur Dorje Rinpoche	yongs dge mi 'gyur rdo rje rin po che
Yungdrung Bon	g.yung drung bon
Zhang-zhung	zhang zhung

Index

A Saint in Seattle, 113
Abhidharma, 26, 32, 154 n2
Adeu Rinpoche, 104
Adzom Drukpa, 83
Amdo, 8, 12, 43-44, 47-48, 132 n3
Amitāyus, 86
Among Tibetan Texts, 44, 115
Anuyoga, 19, 37, 75, 134 n24, 137 n34
Asaṅga, 32-33, 68-69
Aspirations for Mahāmudrā, 30, 33
Atiśa, 9, 13, 20, 43, 120
Atiyoga, 19, 36, 42, 75-76, 134 n24
Australia, xi, 120, 124
Autobiography of Jamgön Kontrul, 53, 61, 63, 65, 143 n48
Avalokiteśvara, 4, 38-39, 43, 86, 92, 118

Barchey Kunsel, 86, 151 n167
Bardo Thödröl, 44, 139 n61
Barron, Richard, 65, 148 n117
Bharati, Aghenanda, 115
Bhutan, 4, 47, 67, 106-8, 110, 114, 139 n3
Blazing Splendor, 98, 108
Bodhicaryāvatāra, 4, 91-93, 95-97, 106, 153 n196
bodhicitta, 43-44, 74, 91-92, 146 n87
body of light. See rainbow body
Bokar Rinpoche, 111
Bon, 3, 19, 49, 54-60, 62, 65, 72-73, 78, 84, 89, 102, 115, 118-19, 142 n35, n36, 143 n39, n40, n41, n45, n48, 144 n49, 148 n118, 155 n12
Eternal (g.yung drung), 54-56, 143 n47, 148 n118
New (bon gsar), 56, 143 n47
orthodox, 56
breakthrough, 76, 136 n29, 149 n135
Brunnhölzl, Karl, 31, 135 n18
Buddha, 1, 2, 23-27, 32, 34, 41, 47, 57, 64, 72, 73-75, 91, 119, 128, 134 n1, n3
Buddha-nature, xi, 32, 34, 98
Buddhahood, 2, 8, 25, 28, 32, 35, 38, 86, 137 n38
Buddhapālita, 33
Butön, 15, 41, 64

Callahan, Elizabeth, 64, 68
Candrakīrti, 15, 31-33, 81-83, 97-98, 101-2
calm state. See tranquillity
canon, 15, 26
Bon, 143 n45
Pāli, 23, 134 n1
Tibetan, 15, 41, 49, 51-52, 59, 142 n25
Central Tibet, 12, 29, 38, 40, 43-44, 47-51, 53-56, 67, 78, 80-81, 83, 87, 90, 95, 110, 127, 132 n4, 133 n21, 140 n5, n7, n10, 142 n35, 145 n80
Chagdud Tulku, 104
Chatral Rinpoche, 104
Chenrezig. See Avalokiteśvara
Chetsün Nyingthig, 83

Chetsün Senge Wangchuk, 83
Chime Tennyi Yungdrung Lingpa, 70
China, 8, 11, 48, 54-55, 125, 140 n7, n10
Chinese, 14-15, 48, 53, 55, 106, 114, 118
    133 n14, 141 n18
Chöd, 72-73, 76
Chogyam Trungpa, 104
Chokgyur Lingpa, 3, 5, 56-58, 60, 62, 65,
    70-71, 78, 81, 84-90, 92, 106, 107-9,
    128, 143 n48, 144 n65, 151 n162,
    n163, n164, 152 n168, n185
Chokling. *See also Chokgyur Lingpa*
    Kela, 108-9
    Neten, 108
Chokling Tersar, 84, 86, 108
Chökyi Jungne. *See Tai Situ*
Chökyi Nyima, 108
Chöying Dorje. *See Karmapa*
Chöying Zangmo. *See Queen of Derge*
Cittamātra, 68-69
Compendium of Tantras, 78
completion stage, 34-35, 69, 73
conceptual elaboration, 69, 97-98
Conze, Edward, 115

Dalai Lama, 11-12, 44-45, 48, 118-19,
    142 n30
    Sonam Gyatso (3rd), 12, 132 n12
    Yonten Gyatso (4th), 12, 44-45
    Ngawang Lobsang Gyatso (5th),
        11-12, 16-18, 44-45, 48, 65, 67,
        118-19, 123, 125, 133 n16, 137 n39,
        139 n64, 140 n5, 158 n73
    Tsangyang Gyatso (6th), 118
    Thubten Gyatso (13th), 118-19, 124,
        156 n19

Tenzin Gyatso (14th), 5, 10, 27-28, 36,
    44-45, 91, 105-6, 110, 114, 116-
    25, 133 n16
Damdzin, 58, 86
Darjeeling, 110-11, 114
Dazang Tulku, 64, 85, 152 n168
Dechen Lingpa, 89-90, 143 n48, 152 n186
definitive, 29, 32-33, 78
Dekyi Chödron, 90
Derge, 48-53, 58, 61, 78-82, 85-87,
    90, 95, 103, 105, 107, 113-14,
    140 n6, 141 n18, 142 n25, n34
Dezhung Rinpoche, 5, 100-1, 103-4,
    112-17
Dharma, xii, 14, 23-24, 27, 32, 57-58,
    63, 77, 79, 90, 96, 105, 111-12,
    115-17, 119, 121, 123
Dharma protector, 27, 59, 72, 76, 123,
    156 n36
Dharmadhātu, 41-42, 148 n114
Dharmadhātustotra, 31
Dharmakīrti, 94, 120
Dignāga, 94
*Dispeller of All Obstacles. See Barchey
    Kunsal*
Dilgo Khyentse, 4, 11, 78, 100, 103-9,
    115, 122-23, 156 n26
Do Khyentse Yeshe Dorje, 50, 81, 91,
    141 n17
Doctor, Andreas, 88-89, 132 n9, 151 n162
Dödrupchen
    Jigme Trinle Özer (1st), 50, 90,
        138 n53, 150 n148
    Jikme Tenpe Nyima (3rd), 121
Dokham, 48
Dolgyal, 123

Dölpopa Sherab Gyalsten, 17-18, 52, 67-68, 98, 133 n20, 135 n18, 140 n4, 147 n108
Dorje Drak, 87, 140 n5, n10
Dorje Shukden, 122-25
Drepung, 16, 43, 68
Dreyfus, Georges, 101, 123-24, 155 n5
Drokmi, 9, 20
Dromtön, 9
dualism, duality, 17, 28, 67, 69, 97
Dudjom Rinpoche, 10-11, 30, 106, 108, 119
Dza Patrul. *See Patrul Rinpoche*
Dzemay Rinpoche, 122
Dzigar Kongtrul. *See Jamgön Kongtrul*
Dzogchen, xii, 4, 14-16, 19-20, 25-31, 33-43, 45, 55-56, 58-59, 64, 66, 69, 75-76, 81, 84, 86-88, 91, 94, 96-97, 99-100, 102-3, 106, 119, 121-22, 126, 133 n14, 134 n24, 136 n29, n30, 137n34, n36, 138 n47, n54, 143 n41, 147 n108, 149 n135, 156 n21
Dzogchen monastery, 13, 50, 87, 92-93, 102, 106, 109, 140 n6
Dzogchen Rinpoche, 109
Dzongsar Khyentse, 81, 104, 107-8. *See also Jamyang Khyentse*
Dzongsar monastery, 81, 87, 102-3, 105-7, 114, 143 n48
Dzongsar *shedra*, 102

East Tibet, 2, 4, 8, 12, 38-40, 43, 46-56, 60-62, 65, 71, 80, 85, 87, 89, 90, 95, 101, 104, 108-9, 113-14, 118, 120, 124-25, 127, 132 n3, 133 n17, 140 n5, 142 n35, 143 n36, n46
eight practice lineages. *See lineage*
Ekvall, Robert, 115
emanation, 5, 27, 38, 40, 63, 83, 95, 102, 105, 109-10, 118, 131 n4, 132 n13, 141 n14
empowerment, 34, 62-63, 65, 87, 90, 96, 104-5, 110-11, 114-15, 147 n97
emptiness (*śūnyatā*), xii, 17, 25, 30-34, 66, 69, 72, 94, 97-98, 121, 133 n19, 137 n35, 148 n114
  other-emptiness (*gzhan stong*), 17-18, 30-31, 52, 66-69, 97-98, 121, 127, 147 n110, 148 n111, 154 n217
  self-emptiness (*rang stong*), 17, 30-31, 33, 66-69, 97, 102, 121, 148 n111, 154 n217
Encompassment of All Knowledge, 64-66, 71, 113. *See also Treasury of Knowledge*
epistemology, 4, 13, 94

fabrication, 29-30, 35, 37, 136 n28
Five Treasuries, 60, 64-65, 77, 150 n144
  Treasury of Kagyü Mantras, 65
  Treasury of Knowledge, 64-65, 71-72, 80, 85, 111-12, 146 n89
  Treasury of Precious Termas, 56, 59, 65, 71, 83-84, 88, 104, 122, 147 n97, 150 n153
  Treasury of Spiritual Instructions, 65, 80, 150 n144
  Uncommon Treasury, 65-66
Four Yogas, 35, 42, 136 n28
France, 106-7, 111, 131 n5, 156 n21

Gampopa, 9, 13-14, 20, 28, 38, 41, 74, 132 n6, 133 n14, 135 n17, 139 n62, 144 n56

Ganden monastery, 11, 15-16, 43, 132 n11, 134 n23

Garab Dorje, 19, 36, 91

Gatön Ngawang Lekpa, 113-14

Gatön Rinpoche. *See Gatön Ngawang Lekpa*

Gelug, 4, 7, 9-13, 15-17, 27-28, 34, 38, 43-45, 48-49, 53, 56, 67-68, 80, 90, 94-97, 101, 103, 110, 114, 118-27, 132 n11, n13, 133 n15, 134 n23, 139 n60, 140 n5, 155 n5

Gelug/Kagyü Tradition of Mahamudra, 44

generation stage, 34, 69

Geshe, 80, 123

Geshe Lozang Gyatso, 123

Geshe Palri Rabsel, 97

Getse Tulku, 50-51, 141 n14, n18

Gönchen monastery, 49, 82

Gönpo Namgyal, 53, 142 n29

Gorampa Sönam Senge, 67

Guru Rinpoche, 8, 75-76, 87, 89. *See also Padmasambhava*

Gyaltsab Rinpoche, 105-6

Gyurme Tsewang Gyatso, 103

Harding, Sarah, 112

heart essence (*snying thig*), 41, 42, 59, 83, 87

Heart Essence of Chetsün, 83

Heart Essence of the Great Adept, 83

Heart Essence of the Great Expanse (Longchen Nyingthig), 4, 40, 42, 50-51, 57, 80-81, 90-91, 103,
138 n53, 150 n150

Heart Essence of the Karmapas (Karma Nyingthig), 30

hermeneutics, 14, 25-26, 32

Hevajra, 114

Hevajratantra, 19, 146 n94

Hīnayāna, 24-25, 64, 134 n24

Hitting the Essence in Three Words, 91

Hurvitz, Leon, 115

Hva Shang, 14, 139 n62

implicit, 25-26

In Praise of Dharmadhātu, 31

incarnation, reincarnation, 4, 5, 28, 40, 45 50-51, 58, 61-63, 66, 77-78, 80-82, 90-91, 102-9, 114, 135 n14, 138 n54

India, Indian, 4, 7-10, 14-15, 19-21, 25, 38, 41-42, 47, 52, 55, 57-60, 68, 72, 75, 87, 91, 94, 96, 99, 101, 104, 108, 110, 112, 114-16, 119-20, 132 n8, 142 n25, 143 n39, 146 n80, 155 n7

inner fire (heat), 35, 75, 136 n26

Jackson, David P., 101, 113-16, 136 n24

Jamgön Kongtrul, 5, 76

Khyentse Özer, 77

Lodrö Thaye, 1, 3, 5, 16. 21, 28, 47, 49, 51, 53, 56-80, 83-90, 93-95, 98-99, 102-5, 107-11, 114, 117-22, 126-29, 135 n14, n21, n22, 138 n54, 142 n29, n31, n33, 143 n48, 144 n65, 145 n68, n70, n72, n76, n77, n78, n80, 146 n82, n89, 147 n97, n100, n108, n110, 148 n112, n114, n118, 149 n140, 150 n144, n153, 152 n179, n185, 155 n12, n19

Index 181

Shechen Kongtrul, 5, 104-5
Dzigar Kongtrul, 5
Jamgön Mipham Gyatso. *See Mipham Rinpoche*
Jamyang Khyentse, 81
   Khyentse Chökyi Lodrö, 4, 27, 78, 81, 102-6, 112, 114, 132 n13, 155 n12, n19, 156 n20
   Khyentse Norbu, 81, 104, 107
   Khyentse Wangpo, 1, 3-5, 16, 20-21, 27, 40, 51, 53, 56-58, 60, 62-64, 66, 70-71, 77-88, 90-91, 93, 95-96, 100, 102-7, 109, 114, 119, 121, 126, 128-29, 132 n13, 141 n17, 142 n33, 143 n48, 149 n140, 150 n142, 150 n150, 152 n168, 155 n11
Jamyang Loter Wangpo, 78, 105
Jigme Gyalwai Nyugu, 51, 81, 90-91
Jigme Lingpa, 40-42, 50-51, 65, 80-81, 90-91, 138 n52, n53, n54, 141 n12, n17, n18, 150 n148
Jigme Trinle Özer. *See Dödrupchen*
Jikme Phüntsok, 100
Jonang, 16-18, 21, 52, 63, 67, 74-75, 110-11, 127, 133 n17, n21, 134 n23
Journey to Enlightenment, 107

kadag. See primordial purity
Kadam, 9, 12-13, 16, 72, 74, 120, 127
Kagyü, xi-xii, 7, 9-10, 12-20, 28-29, 34, 37, 41, 43-45, 48-49, 51, 61-63, 65, 75, 84, 90, 93, 100, 103, 112, 116-17, 125-27, 132 n13, 133 n16, 135 n17, 137 n37, 139 n60, 141 n22, 144 n56, 145 n72, 147 n108, 149 n134

Dagpo, 9, 20, 132 n7, 137 n41
Drikung, 9, 12, 20, 80, 85, 137 n41
Drukpa, 9, 20, 85, 132 n7, 137 n41
Karma (Kamtsang), 3, 9, 12, 20, 29-33, 38-39, 49, 51-53, 61-62, 74, 76, 80, 87, 102, 110-11, 137 n41, 138 n54, 140 n7, 149 n135
Marpa, 9, 13, 21, 63, 65, 72
Nedo, 39
Phagmodru, 12
Shangpa, 21-22, 60, 63, 65, 72, 75-76, 83, 109-12, 134 n25
Kagyü Ling, 111, 131 n5
Kālacakra, 74, 76, 110-11, 125
Kālacakra tantra, 73
Kalimpong, 106
Kalu Rinpoche, 5, 76-77, 104, 109-12, 116, 156 n34, n36, n39
Kapstein, Matthew, 54, 134 n25, 147 n98
Karma Chagme, 38-40, 63, 136 n29, 149 n135
Karma Drubgyu Tenzin. *See Kalu Rinpoche*
Karma Lingpa, 65
Karma Nyingthig. See Heart Essence of the Karmapas
Karma Pakshi. *See Karmapa*
Karmapa, 30, 49, 71, 87, 108, 116, 140 n7
   Karma Pakshi (2nd), 29, 37, 39-40, 137 n34
   Rangjung Dorje (3rd), 29-33, 39-40, 68, 74, 135 n17, n18, 146 n94, 147 n108
   Chöying Dorje (10th), 38, 48, 137 n39
   Thekchok Dorje (14th), 62, 84, 87, 108, 144 n48
   Khakyab Dorje (15th), 5, 71, 77, 108-10

Rigpai Dorje (16th), 5, 76, 104,
106, 108-11
Kathok monastery, 13, 50, 87, 103, 107,
140 n6
Kathok Tsewang Norbu, 52
Khakyab Dorje. See Karmapa
Kham, 2, 12, 42, 46-53, 60, 76, 81, 87,
89-90, 95, 99, 103, 106, 109,
113-14, 119, 125, 128-29, 138 n53,
141 n22, 142 n30, n31, 152 n179,
155 n19
Khan, 11-12, 118, 132 n12
Khandro Lhamo, 106
Khandro Tsering Chödron, 104, 156 n21
Khenchen Tashi Özer, 83
Khenpo Kunpal. See Kunzang Palden
Khenpo Lodrö Donyo, 111
Khenpo Shenga, 4, 66, 94, 99, 100-3,
106, 109, 112, 114, 155 n5, n7,
157 n47
Khön family, 9, 11, 45
Khöntön Peljor Lhündrub, 44-45, 139 n64
Khöntönpa. See Khöntön Peljor Lhündrub
Khunu Lama Tenzin Gyalsten, 91-92, 114
Khyentse Norbu. See Jamyang Khyentse
Khyungpo Naljor, 21, 75, 139 n62, 149
n133
Kings of Derge, 48-50, 52, 87
Tsewang Dorje Rigdzin (19th cent.),
49-50
Könchog Paldrön, 90, 107
Könchok Gyalpo, 9
Kongpo, 61
Kumārarāja, 29
Kunga Tenpay Nyima. See Dezhung
Rinpoche

Kunzang Dechen Ösel Ling, 62, 76,
109-10
Kunzang Pelden, 92, 93
Kyasu, 70, 85, 108
Kyater, 70, 85

Laird, Thomas, 125
Lam Rim, 126
Lam Rim Chen Mo, 43
Lamdre, 19-20, 65-66, 71-72, 81, 103,
112-14
Lamrim Yeshe Nyingpo, 88
leapover, 76, 136 n29, 149 n135
Lhase Damzin Drak, 86
lhündrub. See spontaneous presence
lineage, *passim*
    eight practice lineages, 21, 65-66,
    71-77, 80, 120-21, 126-27
    long (*ring brgyud*), 41, 57, 60, 75, 82,
    89, 137 n41
    short (*nye brgyud*), 41, 57-58, 60, 75
Ling Rinpoche, 124
Lobsang Chökyi Gyaltsen. See Panchen
Lama
logic, 4, 13, 94, 98-99
logical consequence (*prasaṅga*), 97
Longchenpa, 29, 40-42, 50, 59, 64-65, 68,
138 n54, 147 n108, 148 n111
Longchen Nyingthig. See Heart Essence of
the Great Expanse
Losel Tenkyong, 16
luminosity (*prabhasvara*), 32, 98

Machig Lapdrön, 72-73, 139 n62
Madhyamaka, 14-15, 30-33, 45, 52, 64,
66-68, 94, 106, 121, 147 n110,

154 n2
Great-, 31-33, 135 n21, 148 n111,
  154 n217
Prāsaṅgika-, 15-16, 33, 66, 97-98
Svātantrika-, 33, 68
Sutra-, 67
Tantra-, 67
Madhyamakālaṃkāra, 97
Madhyamakāvatāra, 101, 154 n2
Mahāmudrā, 14-15, 19-22, 28-31, 33-43,
  45, 52, 66, 69, 73-76, 133 n14, 136
  n27, n29, 137 n30, n37, 138 n54, 139
  n60, n62, 147 n108, 149 n135
Chöd, 73
Essence, 34-35, 37, 136 n24
Amulet Box, 75, 83, 149 n133
Sūtra, 34, 37, 136 n24, n25
Tantra, 34-35, 37, 67
Mahāmudrā: Ocean of Certainty, 74
mahāpaṇḍita, 25, 51, 94
mahāsiddha, 20, 38, 83
Mahāyoga, 19, 37, 75, 134 n24
Maitrīpa, 19-20, 136 n27
Mañjuśrī, 63, 95, 105
Mañjuśrīmitra, 36
mantra, 4, 8, 34, 38, 43, 65, 67, 69, 76, 92,
  105, 147 n110, 153 n188
Marpa, 9, 13, 19, 21, 144 n56
Martin, Dan, 59
Meditation's Ambrosia of Immortality, 80,
  150 n144
Milarepa, 9, 13, 19-20, 34-35, 41, 43, 113,
  135 n17
Milarepa, 108
Mindröling monastery, 78-79, 87, 140 n5,
  n10

Mind-only school. *See Cittamātra*
Mingyur Dorje, 39, 65
Minyak Kunzang Sonam, 92
Mipham Rinpoche, 4, 66, 90, 92, 94-100,
  102, 105, 109, 119, 121, 142 n33,
  148 n111, 153 n205, 154 n209, n217,
  n218, 155 n19
Mongol, 11-12, 18, 118, 132 n12, 140 n5,
  n10
Müchen Sangye Rinchen, 66
Murub Tsenpo, 86

Nāgārjuna, 31-33, 59, 68-69, 97-98
Nālandā monastery, 91, 120
Nālandā tradition, 120
Namkhai Norbu, 104
Nangchen, 85-86, 106, 108
Naropa, 19-21, 136 n27
nature of mind, 34-38, 42, 45, 69-70, 86,
  91, 108, 121, 136 n24, n29, 137 n38
negation, 17, 31-32, 66, 68-69, 94, 97,
  135 n17
Nepal, 4, 5, 8, 10, 47, 52, 104, 107, 109, 116
New schools (*gsar ma*), 7, 9-10, 20, 34,
  40, 45, 55, 70, 121, 126
New traditions, 10, 42, 55, 73, 96-97, 106,
  121
New Treasures (*gter gsar*), 84, 88, 108, 128
Ngari, 48, 152 n179. *See also West Tibet*
Ngawang Lobsang Gyatso, 119
Ngawang Zangpo, 87, 89, 111-12, 133 n18
  145 n78, 156 n36
Ngedon Tenpa Rabgye. *See Dazang Tulku*
ngöndro. *See Preliminary practices*
Niguma, 21-22, 63, 75, 83, 149 n133
non-distraction (*yengs med*), 43

non-duality, 97-98. *See also duality*
non-meditation, 35, 37, 69, 136 n28
non-sectarian, xi, 1-5, 16, 22, 40, 44-45, 47, 50, 64, 71-72, 79, 116, 118-19, 122, 124-26
Norbu Döndrup, 76, 110, 156 n36
North America, 106, 110-11, 116
Nyarong, 53, 95, 142 n30, n34
Nyingma, 3, 7, 10-16, 19, 27-29, 37, 39-45, 49-52, 55-59, 62, 65-66, 71-72, 75-76, 78, 80-82, 84, 88-90, 94, 96-97, 100, 103-5, 112, 118-19, 122-26, 127, 132 n9, n13, 137 n41, 140 n5, n10, 141 n14, n22, 144 n49, n62, 147 n108, 151 n165, 153 n201, n204
Nyingma School of Tibetan Buddhism, 30
Nyingma'i Gyübum, 51, 141 n18
nyingthig. *See heart essence*
Nyingthig Yabzhi, 42
Nyoshul Khenpo, 84, 103, 138 n53

Oddiyana, 57, 74, 143 n39
Old school. *See Nyingma*
Old tradition, 10, 13, 19-20, 25, 126
oṃ maṇi padme huṃ, 4, 43, 92
ontology, 94
ordinary mind (*tha mal gyi shes pa*), 43
Orgyen Jikme Chökyi Wangpo. *See Patrul Rinpoche*
Orgyen Rinchenpal, 74
Orgyen Tendzin Norbu, 101, 106
Orgyen Tobgyal, 87, 151 n162

Pabongka Rinpoche, 124
Pacification (*zhi byed*), 44, 65, 72, 121, 139 n62
Padmasambhava, 8, 10, 19, 28, 41-43, 50, 56-58, 60-61, 63, 70-71, 74-76, 84, 86, 123, 132 n2, n9, 138 n54, 143 n39, 151 n154
Palge Samten Phüntsok, 90
Palpung monastery, 49, 51-53, 61-62, 70, 85, 87, 102, 106-7, 109-10, 145 n77, n78, 156 n36
Palyül tradition, 39
monastery, 39, 87, 140 n6
Panchen Lama, 44
Lobsang Chökyi Gyaltsen (4th), 44-45
Sixth Panchen Lama, 122
paṇḍita, 14, 120
Patrul Rinpoche, 4, 36, 43-44, 50, 70, 80-81, 90-97, 99, 100-2, 106, 141 n17, 153 n188, n190, n196, 155 n19
Pema Lingpa, 65
Pema Nyinje Wangpo. *See Tai Situ*
Pema Tseyi Nyingthig, 106
Pema Wangchok Gyalpo, 77, 109
Pemajungne, 56
Perfection of Wisdom (*Prajñāpāramitā*) *Sūtras*, 32, 41, 58-59, 72, 76, 97
Phadampa Sangye, 72, 139 n62
pointing out (*ngo sprod*), 35-36, 108, 136 n24
Prajñāpāramitā Sūtras. *See Perfection of Wisdom*
Prajñāraśmi. *See Sherab Özer*
Prāsaṅgika. *See Madhyamaka*
preliminary practices, 4, 37, 74, 76, 91, 113, 153 n188
primordial purity (*ka dag*), 35-36, 69
primordial wisdom (*jñāna*), 67, 69, 148

Index

n114
protector. *See Dharma protector*
pure awareness (*rig pa*), xii, 35-37, 121
pure vision (*dag snang*), 21, 57, 77, 82, 88

Queen of Derge
    Chöying Zangmo (19th cent.), 53, 142 n29
    Tsewang Lhamo (18th cent.), 50-51, 90, 138 n53, 141 n12, n14, 150 n148

Rabsel Dawa. *See Dilgo Khyentse*
rainbow body, 76, 83
rangdröl. See self-liberation
Rangjung Dorje. *See Karmapa*
Rangjung Rigpai Dorje. *See Karmapa*
Rangjung Kunkhyab. *See Kalu Rinpoche*
rangtong. See emptiness
Rechungpa, 9
Retreat Manual, 71, 74
Ricard, Matthieu, 43, 107
Richardson, Hugh, 115
Rigdzin Gödem, 65
rigpa. See pure awareness
Rimé, passim
Rinchen Lingpa, 65
Rongzom Chökyi Zangpo, 25-28
Royal Genealogy of Sde dge, 49-50

Sakya, 3, 5, 7, 9, 13, 15, 19-20, 27-28, 34, 40, 45, 48-51, 66-67, 71, 78, 80-81, 84, 87, 90, 93-94, 100, 102-3, 105, 112, 114-15, 119, 123, 125-27, 132 n13, 140 n4, 141 n14, 142 n25, 155 n7
Śākya Chokden, 48, 64, 67

Sakya Paṇḍita Kunga Gyaltsen, 11, 13, 15, 20, 28, 98, 102, 114, 133 n14
Sakya Trizin, 115
Śākyamuni, 23, 25, 57, 119
Samten Gyatso, 107-8
Samye monastery, 7-8
saṅgha, 13, 51, 117, 153 n201
Sanskrit, xi-xii, 15, 49, 52, 61-63, 95, 99, 114, 127, 137 n34, 142 n25, 145 n77, 154 n209
Śāntarakṣita, 7-8, 19, 33, 97, 120
Saraha, 38, 137 n37, 139 n62
Saraswatī, 102
Sarma. *See New schools*
śāstra, 38, 94, 120
self-liberation (*rang grol*), 36, 136 n30
Sera monastery, 16, 43, 45, 68
seven transmissions, 59, 82, 84, 88
Seven Treasuries, 42
Shabkar Tsogdruk Rangdröl, 43-44
Shardza Tashi Gyeltsen, 142 n36, 143 n48, 155 n12
Shechen monastery, 13, 50, 61, 70, 87, 95, 105, 107, 140 n6
Shechen Kongtrul. *See Jamgön Kongtrul*
Shechen Rabjam, 107
shedra, 94-95, 102-3
Shenga. *See Khenpo Shenga*
Shenpen Chökyi Nangwa. *See Khenpo Shenga*
shentong. See emptiness
Sherab Özer, 80, 150 n146
Sherburne, Richard, 115
Shigatse, 18
Shije. *See Pacification*
Shukden. *See Dorje Shukden*

Six Branch Yoga, 72-73
Six Yogas of Naropa, 19, 29, 35
Six Yogas of Niguma, 21, 63, 75-76, 83, 110
skilful means (*upāya*), 23-25, 37, 45, 49, 134 n5
Smith, E. Gene, 44, 50-52, 61, 68, 99, 101, 112, 115, 139 n59, 142 n25, n31, 147 n100, 153 n196
Sogyal Rinpoche, 104, 119, 155 n19, 156 n21
Sonada, 110-11
Southern Tibet, 9, 18, 56, 123. *See also* Tsang
Sparham, Gareth, 18
spontaneous presence (*lhun grub*), 35-36
Śrī Siṃha Shedra, 92-93, 102
Stearns, Cyrus, 52, 83, 115-16, 133 n20, 140 n3, 147 n108
Stein, R. A., 54
Sukhasiddhi, 21-22, 75
Svātantrika. *See Madhyamaka*

Tai Situ, 49, 51-52, 62, 109, 140 n7
    Chökyi Jungne (8th), 51-52, 95, 142 n25, 145 n78
    Pema Nyinje Wangpo (9th), 53, 62, 65, 79, 85
    Pema Wangchok Gyalpo (11th), 76-77, 109-10
tantra, tantric, 8-10, 13-15, 19-20, 25, 28, 34-35, 37-38, 40-41, 51, 55, 59, 65, 67-69, 72-73, 78, 82-83, 85, 88-89, 91, 94, 96-97, 109, 113, 121, 126, 134 n24, 136 n24, n27, n30, 137 n37, 141 n14, 146 n80
Tāranātha, 17-18, 21, 52, 64, 67-68, 74, 110, 134 n23, 140 n4, 148 n112
Tarthang Tulku, 104
Tashi Chöpel, 60, 77, 109, 149 n139, n140
Tashi Peljor. *See Dilgo Khyentse*
terma, 3-4, 30, 39, 41-42, 44, 50, 55-60, 65, 70-71, 75, 78, 81-90, 92, 103-4, 106-8, 122, 127-28, 132 n9, 137 n41, 138 n47, n52, 143 n40, n45, 144 n56, n62, 149 n140, 150 n153, 151 n154
    Bon, 56, 65, 89, 143 n40, n45
    earth, 42, 57, 82, 84-85, 87-88, 151 n165
    mind, 42, 57-59, 82, 86, 88, 151 n165
    recollected, 82-83, 88
    re-concealed, 82-83, 151 n154
    rediscovered, 82, 88
Terrone, Antonio, 51
tertön, xi, 3, 30, 39, 41, 55-57, 62, 65, 70, 77-78, 80-89, 108, 119, 143 n45, 144 n49, 148 n118, 150 n151, 151 n164, 152 n179, 155 n12
Tertön Sogyal Lerab Lingpa, 83, 104, 119, 155 n19
Thangtong Gyalpo, 48, 65, 75, 82-83, 139 n3
Tharlam monastery, 113-14, 116
Thekchok Dorje. *See Karmapa*
Thirteen great texts, 96, 101, 154 n2
thögel. See leapover
Thrangu monastery, 87
Three Sections of Dzogchen, 87-88
three series (*sde*), 84, 87
Three Vajras, 66, 72, 74-76, 126
three-year retreat, 5, 22, 40, 43, 62, 71-74, 76, 107, 109-12, 121, 138 n46,

Index

145 n78
Thubten Gyatso. *See Dalai Lama*
Traleg Kyabgon Rinpoche, xi-xii, 137 n30, n37
tranquillity, calm state (*śamatha*), 37, 137 n36
transformation, 8, 35, 73, 76, 136 n30
transmission, 9, 14, 18-19, 21, 27, 35, 41-42, 52, 55-57, 59-60, 63-65, 71, 73-79, 81-84, 87-88, 90, 95, 98, 100-1, 103, 105, 106, 108-11, 113, 128-29, 132 n9, 138 n47, 140 n3, 143 n47, 147 n97, 155 n12
treasure. *See terma*
treasure revealer. *See tertön*
Treasuries. See Five Treasuries
trekchö. See breakthrough
Trijang Rinpoche, 122, 124
Trisong Detsen, 7, 55, 58, 81, 86, 120
Tsādra Rinchen Drak, 62, 87, 109-10, 146 n80
Tsang, 18, 47, 110, 133 n16, 152 n179
Tsele Natsok Rangdröl, 29, 37, 135 n14, 138 n54
Tsering Döndrup. *See Jamyang Khyentse*
Tsewang Dorje Rigdzin, 49-50
Tsewang Lhamo. *See Queen of Derge*
Tsewang Norbu, 90
Tsikey Chokling, 108-9
Tsongkhapa, 9, 12, 15, 17, 27-28, 30-33, 43, 67, 98, 120, 126, 133 n20, 139 n60
tulku, 5, 50, 61-63, 90, 105, 108-9, 113, 128, 131 n4, 155 n11
Tulku Urgyen, 5, 98, 104, 107-9, 128
tummo. See inner fire

turnings (of the Wheel of Dharma), 32-34
Ü, 47, 152 n179. *See also Central Tibet*
Uncommon Treasury. See Five Treasuries
United States, 5, 112, 114-15

Vairocana, 19, 58, 63, 86, 150 n145
Vajra Yoga, 65, 72, 73-76
Vajrakīlaya, 20
Vajrayāna, 8, 64, 85, 136 n24
Vajrayoginī, 74
van Schaik, Sam, 42, 49, 78, 129, 137 n35
Vikramaśīla, 120
Vimalamitra, 19, 30, 83, 138 n47
Virūpa, 9, 20

West Tibet, 8, 21, 47, 55, 75, 89, 118, 152 n179
wisdom, 59, 63, 67, 69, 72-73, 92, 95, 96, 148 n114, 153 n196
Wish-Fulfilling Jewel of the Oral Tradition, 45
Words of My Perfect Teacher, 4, 91, 106
Wylie, Turrell, xi, 115

Yarlung, 58
Yellow Book, 122-23
Yeshe Tsogyal, 41, 58, 75
Yogācara, 32-33, 68-69
yogi, 9, 13, 27-29, 40, 43, 45, 48, 50-51, 60, 72, 83, 110, 114, 138 n52
yogic, 8, 29, 43, 136 n24
Yongey Mingyur Dorje, 108

Zhang zhung snyan rgyud, 56
Zhang-zhung, 55-56, 143 n39, n43

THE NINETEENTH CENTURY Rimé (non-sectarian) movement, which was centred in East Tibet, has played a major role in shaping modern Tibetan Buddhism. This book, based on a series of talks given at the 2010 Buddhist Summer School at the Maitripa Centre in Healesville, provides an overview of the movement, the major figures within it, its background context and why it has exerted such an enduring influence. The central figures in the Rimé movement were Jamyang Khyentse Wangpo (1820-1892), Jamgön Kongtrul (1813-1899), Chokgyur Lingpa (1829-1870), Patrul Rinpoche (1808-1887) and Mipham Gyatso (1846-1912). They opposed the solidification and political rivalries of the various lineages and schools while encouraging the study and practice of them all. The Rimé movement also played an important role in reviving marginalised traditions and saving others on the point of extinction. The vast body of visionary and treasure teachings (*terma*) were also collected, clarified, arranged and made accessible to those with a serious desire to practice them. The majority of Tibetan lamas teaching in the West, including His Holiness the Fourteenth Dalai Lama, have been influenced by the Rimé movement, and a number of important present-day lineages are directly connected to it. An appreciation of this movement is therefore invaluable for understanding Tibetan Buddhism as it is currently practised.

PETER OLDMEADOW is retired Head of the Department of Indian Subcontinental Studies in the Faculty of Arts at the University of Sydney where he taught Sanskrit language and Indian and Buddhist Philosophy. He has a long-standing interest in Buddhist theory and practice which he has pursued both through the study of the classical languages of India and Tibet and personally through contact with living traditions of Buddhism in Australia and Asia. He also has an interest in comparative philosophy and religion and in how the wisdom traditions of the world can help answer the fundamental questions of modern humanity.